ARTHUR *and* LILLY

The Girl and the Holocaust Survivor

LILLY MAIER

English Translation
Dominique Rotermund

TITLETOWN
PUBLISHING

For information, or to order additional copies, please contact:

TitleTown Publishing, LLC
P.O. Box 12093 Green Bay, WI 54307-12093
920.737.8051 | titletownpublishing.com

Publisher: Tracy C. Ertl
Editor: Lori A. Preuss

Publisher's Cataloging-in-Publication
(Provided by Cassidy Cataloguing Services, Inc.).

Names:	Maier, Lilly, 1992- author.	Rotermund, Dominique, translator.
Title:	Arthur and Lilly : the girl and the Holocaust survivor / Lilly Maier ; English translation by Dominique Rotermund.
Other titles:	Arthur und Lilly. English
Description:	Green Bay, WI : TitleTown Publishing, [2023]	First published in German as "Arthur und Lilly" by Heyne (Munich, 2018).	Includes bibliographical references and index.
Identifiers:	ISBN: 978-1955047302 (trade paper)	978-1-955047-59-3 (ebook)
Subjects:	LCSH: Kern, Arthur, 1928-2015.	Jews--Austria--Vienna--Biography.	Kindertransports (Rescue operations)--France.	Œuvre de secours aux enfants (France)	Kindertransports (Rescue operations)--United States.	Holocaust, Jewish (1939-1945)	Engineers--United States--Biography.	Holocaust survivors--California--Los Angeles--Biography.	Maier, Lilly, 1992-	BISAC: HISTORY / Modern / 20th Century / Holocaust.	HISTORY / Wars & Conflicts / World War II / General.	HISTORY / Jewish.
Classification:	LCC: DS135.A93 K4613 2023	DDC: 940.53/18092--dc23
Original title:	Arthur & Lilly. Das Mädchen und der Holocaust-Überlebende. Zwei Leben, eine Geschichte by Lilly Maier © 2018 by Heyne Verlag, a division of Penguin Random House Verlagsgruppe GmbH, München, Germany.

For Frieda and Hermann Kernberg,
Who possessed the strength, love and foresight
To send their son into the unknown
 – and without whom I would never have met Arthur

The Book Club Discussion Guide for this book
is available at titletownpublishing.com

TABLE OF CONTENTS

PROLOGUE

I am writing this book almost fifteen years after my first meeting with Trudie and Arthur Kern. Every so often I like to think back to that warm day in March, with birds singing outside, the buds on the trees the first harbingers of spring. At the time, none of us realized how deeply this meeting would affect all of our lives – or how a single apartment in Vienna would unite our families forever.

Years later, Arthur called our first meeting "one of the highlights" of his life. Referring to the famous nostalgic expression, he said, "Sometimes you can't go home again. But," he added with a big smile on his face, "I did. And it was magnificent."

* * *

The *Gussenbauergasse* in Vienna, Austria, is a small, sleepy street, located in the *Alsergrund*, the ninth district of the city. The street ("*gasse*" means street in the Austrian-German dialect) was named after a surgeon, Carl Gussenbauer, and is situated a few minutes' walk from the *Donaukanal* (Danube Canal) or the *Palais Liechtenstein* (Liechtenstein Palace), one of the many grand buildings lending Vienna its imperial charm. There are only six buildings on *Gussenbauergasse*, five of which were built around the turn of the century, while the last one, the *Sigmund-Freud-Hof* (Sigmund-Freud-House) – a big public housing block – was added in the 1920s. From the outside, the corner house on *Gussenbauergasse 1* is by far the most magnificent, its facade adorned with stone carvings. As is customary in old Viennese buildings, the second floor is typically called a mezzanine, and the five-story building thus only has four official floors, a fact that enabled the builders around 1900 to pay fewer taxes. The house has seen better days, but the turn-of-the-century apartments still flaunt their high windows, spacious rooms, and stucco-decorated ceilings.

From 1999 to 2011, throughout my entire school years, my mother and I lived in the mezzanine apartment on *Gussenbauergasse 1*. At first, our home was just an ordinary apartment, but it all changed on March 30, 2003, the day Arthur and Trudie Kern came to visit us.

This is the house Arthur grew up in, on *Gussenbauergasse* 1. Sixty years later, Lilly and her mother moved into the same apartment.

* * *

March 30,2003 was a Sunday, one of the first warm days of the spring. Every corner of our apartment sparkled and shone, even my own bedroom which I had painstakingly managed to turn into a prime example of orderliness, far from the chaos my eleven-year-old self usually created. All my books stood perfectly lined up on my shelf, my stuffed animals sat in a row on top of my bunk bed and the freshly washed red linen curtains gave off a subtle smell of detergent. My mother and I had just stepped into the kitchen to get *Marmorkuchen*, or marble cake, a typical Viennese vanilla-chocolate cake, when the doorbell rang: Trudie and Arthur Kern stood at the door.

Arthur looked like a typical 75-year-old American man, half bald with a white crown of hair cropped short. He wore navy blue trousers, glasses with big round lenses, and a grey-striped polo shirt that brought out his California tan. Even though he had just got off a transcontinental flight, the retired rocket engineer did not look tired or jet-lagged, his eyes shining as he strode through our apartment, right after we had welcomed him inside. "*Das war das Klavierzimmer!*" he exclaimed enthusiastically as he stepped into my room. "This used to be the piano room!"

Indeed, my bedroom had once been a piano room, back in the 1930s. As a small boy, Arthur Kern had grown up in the same Viennese apartment on *Gussenbauergasse 1* my mother and I moved to decades later. Now, over sixty years later, he returned to the place for the first time.

For Arthur, visiting his old apartment was a trip down memory lane, a reminder of a happy childhood on another continent and in another time. A time he still went by another name: Oswald Kernberg.

* * *

Little Oswald, or "Ossi," as he was nicknamed by his family, lived on *Gussenbauergasse 1* together with his older brother Fritz, his parents Frieda and Hermann Kernberg, and a nanny. (Their surname, Kernberg, is a typical Jewish name that loosely translates to "core-mountain.") The Kernbergs lived the good life of a Jewish middle-class family in Vienna in the interwar years. Hermann Kernberg owned and ran a knitting factory where his wife Frieda also worked. The family traveled a lot – to go skiing on the Semmering near Vienna, to Marienbad, a popular spa town in the Czech Republic, or to Italy for the summer holidays. Yet all this changed abruptly with Austria's annexation to Nazi Germany in 1938 (the so-called *Anschluss*). Only the youngest member of the family, Ossi, would survive the Holocaust.

In 1941, Frieda and Hermann were deported to Opole, Poland, together with their oldest son, Fritz. Two years earlier, Ossi's parents had managed to send him to safety and freedom on a so-called *Kindertransport*, or children's transport. The ten-year-old boy was sent to France alone, where he lived in various children's homes together with other Jewish refugee children. The homes were financed by French aristocrats like the Rothschilds and run by Ernst Papanek, an exiled Austrian teacher and educator.

When the German army invaded most of France, the children were hastily evacuated to the still unoccupied south. But they were not safe there either. With the greatest effort and difficulty, international aid organizations were finally able to save Oswald and 250 other children on a second *Kindertransport* to America. In 1941, the boy traveled from Portugal to New York on board one of the last ships that still managed to leave Europe.

Shortly after his arrival in New York, Ossi received a letter from his family, congratulating him on his 13th birthday as well as on his bar mitzvah: "And now my sweet golden *Burli* [young boy], please receive my innermost congratulations and blessings on this most important and solemn day," Hermann Kernberg wrote his son from a Polish ghetto. "May your luck shine as bright as the stars in heaven and may we soon be granted the joy to hold you in our arms and be able to brighten your life as we have always strived to do."

This letter was the last time Oswald ever heard from his family.

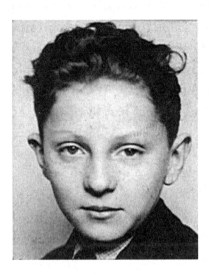

This picture was taken especially for Oswald's *Kindertransport* application.

* * *

More than 60 years later, Arthur Kern, by then no longer called Oswald, told us his family story as we continued our tour of the apartment. He meticulously wrote down every little detail in a small notebook, his descriptions bringing his childhood's surroundings to life. Back in the 1930s, my bedroom had been the piano room, my mother's office the dining room, our living room had been Frieda's and Hermann's bedroom, and the adjoining small bedroom, where my mother now slept, used to be the brothers' room. The storage room on the left side of the kitchen had accommodated the nanny, and Ossi had often used the long corridors, typical of old Viennese apartments, as bike lanes, but only when his mother was not around.

When we came back to my room, the notes of *Für Elise*, Beethoven's famous piano piece he had composed in Vienna in the early 19ᵗʰ century, suddenly echoed throughout our apartment. More than 60 years after the Kernberg family was violently forced to leave their apartment, the sound of a piano once again filled the "*Klavierzimmer*," the piano room. The music came from a music box shaped like a small black piano with gold ornaments. Tiny chubby baroque angels, with white wings and huge smiles painted on their pink faces, moved to the melody. When the music stopped and the angels stood still, one simply had to turn the crank three or four times and the music box would start playing again. Trudie and Arthur had brought it as a present for me, a reminder of the piano that had once stood in my room.

We went to the living room to have some of the marble cake my mother had served and as we sat at our dining table, Arthur told us his story, the three-hour talk a funny mixture of German and English. I had only started regular English classes the year before and Trudie, despite having grown up in Vienna just like her husband, had forgotten most of her German after half a century in the United States. "*Sprich Deutsch*," Arthur would remind his wife over and over again. "Speak German." He still spoke German fluently enough, even though he smilingly admitted possessing only the vocabulary of a ten-year-old – his age when he had been forced to leave Vienna.

That day in March 2003 had actually been Arthur's second attempt to visit his old apartment. During his first visit to Vienna in the 1970s, he could not even get inside the building. When decades later he had planned another trip to Vienna, he had asked a Viennese couple he had befriended on a cruise in Turkey, for their help. In the fall of 2002, Brigitte and Fritz Kodras showed up at our door unannounced, to explain their friend's request. My mother immediately invited Trudie and Arthur to visit us. We knew how important and emotional a visit to his old apartment would be for Arthur and it did not occur to my mother to deny him such a request. But we also knew the previous tenants of the apartment we were living in had all been murdered by the Nazis, except for the youngest son. How does one deal with such knowledge?

As chance would have it, *A Letter To The Stars*, a nationwide history project for high school students was launched at that same time and my mother signed me up for it. Austria has a long history of refusing to admit complicity in the Holocaust, insisting they were the first victim of the Nazis. *A Letter To The Stars* was the first large-scale school project dealing with Austria's long-repressed Nazi past, initiated considerably later than similar projects in Germany. The project aimed to provide more personal access to contemporary history, all the while preserving the memory of the Holocaust. With the help of teachers, librarians, and archivists, thousands of students began researching the biographies of Austrian Holocaust victims – people with whom they shared the same first name, who had attended the same school, or who had lived in the same apartment, as in my case. To this day, 50,000 students have taken part in the project. In a moving memorial ceremony in 2003, we released 80,000 white balloons into the sky over Vienna, one for each Austrian man and woman murdered during the Holocaust. Clouds of white balloons rose into the sky, drifting away with the wind, so numerous the airspace around Vienna was blocked for half an hour.

For *A Letter To The Stars*, I researched the biography of Frieda Kernberg, Arthur's mother. Arthur had told me about his family during his stay in Vienna. He had also brought a few documents so that I could find out more about Frieda. If for no other reason than that, our meeting was much more than a brief get-together over coffee and cake. Dealing intensively with the subject of the Holocaust actually helped us, my mother and me, to handle the knowledge of our predecessors' fate. As it turned out, my mom need not have worried about the emotional impact of the visit at all. Far from bringing sadness or unresolved bad feelings into our home, Arthur and Trudie came to us with an open heart, peacefulness, and a huge serving of

Jewish humor. To this day, I have never met a person more at peace with himself and his past than this cheerful 75-year-old Holocaust survivor.

At the end of Trudie's and Arthur's visit, my mother took a picture of us. It shows me sitting between the two of them, each with an arm wrapped around my shoulders. Trudie wears a comfortable paisley t-shirt in different shades of blue and I wear a white blouse. I look pale and quite small compared to the two tall and tanned Californians. All three of us are smiling.

When my mother took this picture, Arthur and Trudie had been with us for almost three hours. That photograph could have been the end of our story. But it was not. It really was only the beginning of a modern-day fairy tale.

Lilly Maier's first meeting with Arthur and Trudie
Kern in Vienna, on March 30, 2003.

* * *

In the weeks after Arthur's visit, I wrote a short biography about his mother, Frieda, which was later published in an *A Letter To The Stars*-anthology. The fact that Arthur and I had lived in the same apartment also aroused the interest of several newspapers. One of them, the Viennese daily *Kurier*, printed an article with a picture of me holding a sepia photo of Frieda. Immediately after the article was published, Valerie Bartos, an 83-year-old lady called the *Kurier*, asking for my family's contact details. Newspapers do not usually give out personal information of people they write about, but Mrs. Bartos just would not take no for an answer and kept calling the paper for days on end until they finally came to a compromise and gave my mother her phone number, so we could call her ourselves. When we did, we found out Valerie Bartos had been keeping a parcel for Arthur Kern for over 60 years!

Shortly before he was deported to Poland in 1941, Hermann Kernberg had gathered important family and company papers in an envelope and entrusted them to a friend in Vienna for safekeeping. In the retrospectively utopian hope he and his family would be able to return from the Polish ghetto, these documents would have helped the Kernbergs to a fresh start in Vienna.

Hermann had given the envelope – which contained passports, pictures, business documents, insurance policies as well as a tiny mezuzah, a rolled-up parchment inscribed with biblical passages and inserted in a small decorative case observant Jews attach to the doorposts of their homes – to a man named Otto Kürth. But being himself a "Half-Jew," as the Nazis called him, and scared to keep the documents, Kürth had passed them on to his cousin Valerie Bartos. Afraid the Gestapo might come and look for it, Valerie Bartos hid the envelope, fastening it to the underside of a wooden chest of drawers, where it remained for several decades. In the spring of 2003, Mrs. Bartos recognized Frieda's photograph in the newspaper and after managing to contact my family, she was finally able to return the documents to their rightful owner.

Arthur was ten and a half years old when he had to part with his parents and his brother forever. At 75, more than 60 years later, he received a last parcel from them – a memento from a long-lost past.

* * *

But Arthur's was not the only life that was changed by this parcel. I am a historian and a journalist. I inherited my love for words from my parents, but it was my chance encounter with Arthur and his unique life story as an eleven-year-old girl, that made me want to study history. I feel incredibly grateful to him for choosing to share his story with me. Thanks to *A Letter To The Stars*, I went on to meet many more wonderful and inspiring Holocaust survivors. I started researching the long-term effects of the *Kindertransport* and became a museum docent at the Dachau Concentration Camp Memorial Site. I started giving talks about the Holocaust. And now I am writing this book.

Our meeting not only instilled a passion for history in me, but it also gave me something much more precious: a third "pair of grand-parents." I don't recall exactly when, but at some point in the last decade, Arthur and Trudie began calling me their "Austrian grand-daughter." On my countless visits to the Kerns, the entire family clan would always welcome me with open arms. They too became my American family.

Arthur once told me that at some point in his life he had delib-erately decided to make peace with his terrible past – for his own and also for his family's sake. "You have to defeat the hatred in your heart," he told me. Since then, Arthur has visited Austria many times and spoken about his experience in front of several Austrian high school classes.

* * *

Arthur passed away in the summer of 2015 after a period of illness. Until then, I had had the opportunity to extensively interview him about his life. Shortly before his death, I began to research his biography and the background of his unique rescue on an academic level. Children are the survival and the future of a people. The Nazis turned that thought around and tried to prevent the next Jewish generation from growing up. Six million Jews were murdered during the Holocaust, at least a quarter of them – 1.5 million were children. Only 100,000 children survived.

The *Kindertransports* stand out in Holocaust research as one of the few positive events in a time of horror and atrocities. Arthur's life story serves as an example to tell the story of the French *Kindertransports*. Many of the former *Kindertransport*-children became very successful after the end of the Second World War, some of them even winning Nobel prizes or becoming billionaires. To this day, these particular Holocaust survivors remain a very close-knit group, largely thanks to the annual garden parties Arthur and Trudie used to hold for the former refugee children.

I spoke with all of Arthur's family members and many of his friends when researching for this book. People who knew him as a child in pre-war Vienna, a rowdy refugee boy in French orphanages, a young student in New York, a rocket engineer, or as a pensioner in Los Angeles. For months, I scoured archives in Vienna, Paris, New York, Washington, D.C., and Los Angeles, analyzing thousands of letters and documents and interviewing many historians to try and reconstruct Arthur's biography, along with the life stories of the other Jewish child refugees saved by the French *Kindertransport*.

Next fall I will once again fly to California to celebrate Thanksgiving with Trudie and her large family. And upon my return home, a miniature piano flanked by chubby baroque angels will be waiting for me on my bookshelf, as always.

PART 1 – VIENNA

PART I — VIENNA

1. "WE HAD A GREAT LIFE!"

"*In dem Lande der Chinesen, Chinesen, Bin ich zwar noch nie gewesen, gewesen,*" Arthur sings in a firm voice. "In the land of the Chinese, the Chinese, I have never been, never been." – "*Erstens hatt' ich keine Zeit, keine Zeit, zweitens ist der Weg zu weit, zu weit,*" he continued. "First, there was no time, no time, and second, it was too far away, far away."

Gathered around him, his large American family does not understand the words, but they swing along to the music anyway, joining in the chorus with great enthusiasm: "*Boom-killy-vitsky, Yan Kon Kooly Yan Kann Kow!*"

I first hear the *Kern Family Song* in November 2013, when I visit Arthur and his family in California, for Thanksgiving. Due to a very rare shift in the Jewish calendar (which has leap months instead of leap days), that year Thanksgiving also happens to be the second night of Hanukkah, the festival of lights. And thus in order to celebrate "Thanksgivukkah" properly, tiny turkeys wearing yarmulkes on top of their bobbing heads have been scattered all over the table, their plumes adorned with a miniature Star of David.

Except for Arthur and Trudie, I am the only person in the room who actually understands the lyrics of the German song. I am also the only one who knows Grandpa Kern did not come up with that song by himself; it is in fact an old German nursery rhyme. Arthur transcribed the words phonetically, so the rest of the family may sing along.

It is the first time I get to see all the Kern generations in one place, even though I have known Arthur and Trudie for more than a decade. Just like the two of them, I too have learned bizarre children's songs about China as a pupil, my own version involving three Chinese men who roam the land with their contrabass.

Arthur's story began in Vienna. Even after decades in America, the city on the Danube is still very present in the life of his family, in many small details such as Trudie's thick German accent or the *Kern Family Song.* For Arthur's children and grandchildren, the song with the nonsensical chorus is but a quirky family tradition – to him though, it is a reminder of his long-lost carefree childhood.

* * *

Frieda and Hermann Kernberg in Vienna.

Oswald "Ossi" Kernberg was born on October 19, 1928, in Vienna. His father, Samuel Hersch "Hermann" Kernberg, was born in Stanisławów, an originally Polish city situated in today's western Ukraine, on October 11, 1894, and his mother, Frieda Goldfeld, in Romania, on December 26, 1897. Both parents had moved to Vienna in the early 1900s, attracted to the multiethnic city like so many of their contemporaries. They had met there and got married in 1925. Frieda was 28 years old and Hermann was 31. It was his second marriage: despite his young age, he was already a widower. Nine months later, their first son, Fritz, was born, and Oswald followed three years later.

Merely twenty years before Oswald's birth, Vienna had still been a city of grandeur and pomp, the capital of the Austro-Hungarian Empire – the second-largest European country at the time. Yet after the end of the First World War and the collapse of the Habsburg monarchy, the multiethnic Empire broke into pieces, with no fewer than seven independent countries emerging from the rubble.

Oswald Kernberg with his older brother Fritz, around 1929.

Before the First World War, Vienna had had a little over two million inhabitants, a fitting number for the capital of an empire that was home to more than 50 million people. After 1918, Vienna still had about two million inhabitants — in a country whose population had shrunk to only 6.5 million citizens.[1] Vienna had become the *Wasserschädel* or "water head" of Austria.

After 1919, Austria became a federal republic with universal suffrage. From then on, "Red Vienna" was a Social-Democratic island within a Christian Conservative country.[2] During the "Roaring Twenties," Vienna was – just like Berlin – a vibrant combination of the new democratic ideas and a lingering royal charm, which found its ultimate expression in the famous *Kaffeehauskultur* (coffee house culture). Great writers and literary figures, artists, and politicians gathered and worked in the coffee houses, surrounded by billowing clouds of cigarette smoke, liveried waiters, homemade pastries, and piano music.

"We would sit there for hours on end every day and nothing escaped us," Stefan Zweig wrote in *Die Welt von Gestern* (World of Yesterday), describing the Viennese *Kaffeehaus* institution at the time of the monarchy and in the 1920s.[3] Just like Zweig, many of the regular guests were Jewish, like Arthur Schnitzler and Franz Werfel, for instance.

Another prominent Viennese Jew, Sigmund Freud, saw patients within walking distance from the Kernberg's apartment. To reach Freud's practice from *Gussenbauergasse 1*, one merely had to cross a small square, walk past the Franz-Josef train station, and up the *Porzellangasse*, or "Porcelain Street." As a child, Oswald often played on these streets with his cousin Otto – who decades later would follow in the footsteps of the Viennese psychoanalyst, becoming well-known as the "modern-day Sigmund Freud" of America.

mal, a form of epilepsy more commonly known today as absence seizures, often appearing during adolescence. Fritz would suffer sudden attacks that would leave him staring into space, motionless and utterly unresponsive. Specialists today speak of "brief lapses in consciousness." The attacks lasted around ten or twenty seconds, before subsiding on their own. Fritz also had learning difficulties, a common side-effect of *petit mal*. When Oswald started fourth grade, his brother, although three years older, attended the same class as him.

Decades later, Arthur told me he had been very close to his brother. But his cousin Otto Kernberg remembered that the three of them would never play together whenever he visited. Fritz "was bigger, he was older, and in addition to that, he wasn't really sociable," Dr. Kernberg told me. As a child, Fritz had seemed to him distant and withdrawn. "I always had the feeling there's something wrong with him. And my parents conveyed the feeling that there was something wrong with him, but nobody talked with me directly. And I never talked about him with Ossi," the 88-year-old recalled.

Unlike his strict mother in charge of his education, Oswald loved his father Hermann, ever the outgoing, good-natured joker who always carried candies in his pocket. The neighborhood children were also very fond of Hermann Kernberg, who, just like his son Ossi, liked to play tricks on his family. He always carried a silver pen in his vest pocket, his neat and round penmanship rivaling that of any elementary school teacher. Hermann spent most of his days working, often only returning to the apartment in the evening. "At night, sometimes, my father used to smoke," Arthur Kern remembered decades later. "And I used to love lying in bed between my parents in the evening when they went to bed, and he would smoke a cigarette and it was dark, and I saw the glow of the cigarettes. And it's something that's stuck with me, which we really enjoyed."

Hermann put on *tefillin* every morning for his weekday prayer, the pair of black leather boxes containing parchment rolls inscribed with Torah verses observant Jews tie to their head and left arm with leather straps. Although he would pray every day, Hermann did not keep Shabbat: the Kernberg's factory was open on Saturdays. It is difficult to evaluate just how religious the family was – Oswald and his brother Fritz had a private tutor for religious instruction, but the family mainly went to temple during the High Holy Days.

Yechaskell
Goldfeld with Ossi

Oswald with his grandfather, Yechaskel Goldfeld.

* * *

In the 1920s, about 200,000 Jews lived in Vienna – roughly ten percent of the city's population – making it one of the largest Jewish communities in Europe.[4] Many of them – like Oswald's parents – had come to Vienna from the eastern parts of the multicultural Habsburg Empire, significantly shaping Jewish life in the capital.

While a liberal reform movement had swept across German synagogues since the 1820s, all attempts to liberalize religious service in

Vienna had failed because of the large presence of Hungarian Jews in the city.[5] "All they succeeded in doing was getting the aesthetic qualities of the liberal movements," explains historian Marsha Rozenblit, professor at the University of Maryland and author of *The Jews of Vienna, 1867-1914: Assimilation and Identity*, when I speak to her in the fall of 2016. These aesthetic qualities included sermons in German, a choir as well as more elaborate decorations inside the synagogues. But it did not come to any liturgical reform. "They were modern, but not liberal," Rozenblit says, comparing Jewish life in interwar Vienna to today's "modern orthodox Judaism," widespread in America. Women still sat in the balcony, separated from men, and the traditional prayers were not altered. Another feature of Jewish Vienna was the fact that all Jews – no matter which religious movement they belonged to – were part of one and the same congregation, the *Israelitische Kultusgemeinde Wien* (IKG), or Vienna Israelite Community.

* * *

Laughing, Oswald, Fritz, and their cousin Gina dashed across a large green meadow, past the goldfish pond, and on towards the fruit trees, where they readily proceeded to pick berries from bushes. The large estate was part of the *Goldfeld & Co* knitting factory, owned and run by Gina's father, Sigmund, in *Heidenreichstein*, Lower Austria. Just like almost every summer, Oswald and his family spent a few weeks in the refreshingly cool *Waldviertel* (Forest District) that year too. "I loved it in *Heidenreichstein!*" remembered Arthur Kern, decades later. "We went swimming all the time." And so it was that day as well: having strengthened themselves with berries, the children strolled to a nearby lake, where they swam and raced each other all afternoon. As was typical for the time, they wore striped bathing suits with short sleeves. Oswald enjoyed these weeks with his mother's family in Lower Austria – despite the fact his cousin Gina, who was nine years older, called him *Putzilein* (a diminutive term of endearment) and treated him like some kind of life-size doll she could dress and style however she pleased. Oswald was also very fond of his aunt Erna, even though he considered her just as old-fashioned as his own mother.

The Kernberg family was close-knit and most of their social life happened within the family circle, which was common for the time. Frieda Kernberg had three brothers and one sister, who all lived in Vienna with their families, while Hermann had four brothers back in Poland and one in Vienna. Three couples and their children stood at the heart of the lively and buoyant family life: Hermann's brother Leo and his wife Paula (Otto's parents); Frieda's sister Erna, her husband Sigmund and their daughter Gina, as well as Frieda's brother Israel, his wife Dora and their daughter Detta. Oswald and Otto were the "babies of the family," Detta and Gina being respectively four and nine years older.

In Vienna, Oswald saw his cousin Otto almost every week. Since his mother Frieda was, as mentioned before, a terrible cook, everybody was always very happy to eat at Otto's place; his mother Paula, on the other hand, was a very talented cook. Her baking was particularly appreciated, even more so since she had taken a special course in traditional Austrian baking and had learned to make much-beloved cakes and other typical Viennese *Mehlspeisen*, flour-based sweet dishes often eaten as an entrée, and not as a dessert. Oswald called Paula his *moderne Tante*, his "modern aunt," especially in comparison with his own mother. Paula and her husband Leo were more interested in Viennese cultural life than Oswald's parents and would often take their son Otto to concerts.

Going to the movies was a big adventure for Oswald and Otto. They usually went to the *Phönix-Kino* on the *Lerchenfelder Straße*, one of the most luxurious cinemas at the time – complete with balconies and loges – that had opened in 1913 and could accommodate up to 600 visitors. Otto lived close by and the boys would go to his place afterward to play with Otto's tin soldiers or his hand-painted model railroad designed by the Swabian toy company, *Märklin*.

Oswald's maternal grandparents lived in *Leopoldstadt*, the second Viennese district. In the early 1920s, about forty percent of the population in *Leopoldstadt* was Jewish, which earned the district the nickname *"Mazzeinsel"* (Matzo Island).

Oswald's paternal grandparents lived in Poland: the boy never met his grandfather and only saw his father's mother once for a week, when she visited from Poland. She was initially supposed to stay with Otto's parents, but Otto was even more mischievous and misbehaved than Oswald himself, so she fled to her son Hermann instead. "My father put the fear of God in me," Arthur Kern still recalled, more than seventy-five years later. "He said, 'You better behave and not be like Otto!'"

The Kernbergs liked to travel. They took day trips to the *Kahlenberg*, a mountain in the Viennese Woods or the *Semmering* in Lower Austria, went skiing and ice skating in the wintertime, and spent their summers in *Heidenreichstein*. Frieda and her sister Erna also regularly traveled to *Marienbad*, a spa town with healing springs, now part of the Czech Republic.

In 1935, shortly before Oswald's seventh birthday, his parents sent him, together with Fritz, to a vacation camp in Grado, Italy, where the brothers spent the entire summer. It was the first time Oswald was away from home for an extended period of time, and he greatly enjoyed it. "I suddenly discovered a new-found freedom, away from what I thought were the dictatorial instructions/demands of my parents," he wrote in a short story, eight decades later. Everything just seemed better to him during these holidays: the food was tastier, sharing a room with other boys was more fun than sleeping at home, and the whistle of a passing train he could hear every night fascinated him to no end. "It gave me a wonderful and peaceful feeling which I still enjoy to this day," he wrote.

Ever since his sixth birthday, Oswald attended elementary school on *D'Orsaygasse*, about 10 minutes walk away from his home. Today the building houses a music school.

Twenty-seven fourth graders scurried around their benches to hang up their coats and woolly hats on the hooks fastened to the wooden paneling on the back wall, below drawings of landscapes and farmhouses. The official class photo for the year 1937/1938 was due that day and the boys hurried back to take their seats, three boys sharing one wooden bench. Most of the pupils had their hands folded on the table in front of them for the picture. The class photo was a serious business: one child alone smiled at the camera, all the others – the bespectacled teacher, Weissenböck, included – looked ahead sternly. It is not hard to spot Ossi in that picture: he is the only one standing, so he would be better seen from his seat in the second last row. He too appears unsmiling, his head slightly tilted.

Oswald was an excellent pupil who only ever got A's and B's. His favorite class was gym. Some of the boys in Oswald's class had Jewish names, yet most of his school friends were not Jewish. The children's religion was irrelevant when it came to playing and learning. The only time it really became apparent was during religious instruction, which the Jewish children did not attend, as they took private classes at home.

After the class photo, Oswald visited his father at the family factory. The ten-year-old was very proud to be allowed to take two different streetcars to get to the 19th district all by himself. At the time, Vienna already had the *Elektrische*, electric street cars rather than those pulled by horses. The Kernbergs' knitting factory was located on *Hardtgasse 32* in *Döbling*, a district north of *Alsergrund*, where the family lived. Although the factory was owned and run by Oswald's father, Hermann, the company was named Goldfeld & Kernberg, listing Oswald's mother's maiden name first. Frieda's father, Chaskel Goldfeld, was the founder of the factory he later ran together with his son-in-law. Chaskel died shortly before his eightieth birthday in 1931, and from then on, Hermann remained the sole owner.[6]

In the same way, the ownership of the factory in *Heidenreichstein* was kept within the family. Two of Frieda's brothers had founded it in 1922 and their brother-in-law, Sigmund, who had married into the family, now ran it.

As Arthur recalled, Hermann Kernberg's factory employed seventy people in Vienna, which made it a fairly large business – especially since it was located within the city. Vienna was not an industrial city and many of the factories were situated in the countryside. Oswald's mother, Frieda, often worked in the factory and the family thus employed live-in nannies to help take care of the boys and to cook, much to everyone's delight. Three or four of those *Kindermädchen* (literally "children's girls") succeeded one another during Oswald's childhood. His favorite was a girl called Agnes. Many years later, Arthur still remembered with great sorrow the day Agnes suddenly stopped coming.

* * *

From March 1938 on, Christian women under 45, like Agnes, were no longer allowed to work for Jews, as one of the many Nazi laws swiftly enacted after the *Anschluss*, the annexation of Austria to Hitler's Germany.[7]

Austria itself had a long history of anti-Semitism. In fact, in the early 20th century, Austrian Jews often experienced more prejudice in their daily lives than Jews in Germany. "Anti-Semitism was always part of the political culture," Professor Rozenblit explains. Yet it only ever happened on a personal or professional level, as the "Austrian government never passed any laws against the Jews. They were no pogroms as there were in other places, there was no violence," she goes on to point out. Life in Vienna might not have been perfect for Jews, but they still were certainly much better off than in Poland, Hungary, or Romania – or Germany, after Hitler's rise to power in 1933.

The *Anschluss* changed all that overnight. On the morning of March 12, 1938, the German *Wehrmacht* marched into Austria – without firing a single shot. Hitler himself entered his country of birth in the afternoon, reaching Vienna on March 15, where a cheering crowd of around 200,000 people welcomed him at the *Heldenplatz*, the Square of Heroes, in the city center.[8] Anti-Jewish

laws that had taken five or six years to be enacted in Germany immediately became a reality in Austria.[9] Yet to the Jews in Vienna, the
enthusiasm and excitement displayed by their fellow citizens at the
Nazi's arrival, as well as the countless acts of violence against them
that swiftly followed came as an even greater shock.[10] "The neighbors
next door dragged them out of their houses, plundered their homes,
and chased them through the streets," Christof Habres writes in his
book, *Jüdisches Wien (Jewish Vienna)*, describing the events.[11]

Oswald's peaceful life was literally shattered to pieces. "Suddenly the
kids who were not Jewish were not allowed to play with me anymore,"
Arthur told me. "So, I couldn't play soccer anymore. And suddenly,
rather than being friends, they used to chase us." His cousin Otto had
to watch on as a mob forced his mother to scrub the pavement.

When Oswald walked down the street, he now saw many signs reading *"Juden und Hunde Zutritt verboten"* – "No entry for Jews or dogs."
Parks, coffee houses, or his beloved movie theater – from now on, he
could no longer go to any of these places; it had become illegal.

Class photograph of 1937/1938. Oswald is standing on the
right side of the picture, in the second last row.

Ten-year-old Oswald was allowed to finish the two remaining school months, but Jewish children now had to sit at the back of the room, previously reserved for the less gifted students, which struck him as a great injustice. He passed the test to attend a *Gymnasium*, a more advanced version of high school, but none of the high schools in Vienna would accept Jewish children anymore. Instead, he was forced to go to a hastily opened and not very good Jewish school, quite far away from where he lived. Hitler Youth members often waylaid the Jewish children outside the school, regularly beating up Oswald and his friends, even though the boy's blond hair and grey eyes often spared him even worse consequences in his daily life. Afraid to go shopping, Oswald's parents would therefore send their son to the stores, who could easily pass for an "Aryan" child.

Ten-year-old Oswald never discussed these changes with his cousin Otto. "Our relationship became more distant because we were more imprisoned in our daily life," Dr. Otto Kernberg recalled, decades later. It also became more difficult for the boys to visit each other as regularly as before. "So, we both had to deal separately… and we didn't have – as children – full awareness of that experience, either. It just seemed like a change in the weather. We took it as 'this is the way the world was,'" he said.

Until the one night, even children realized nothing was normal anymore. The night of November 9-10 went down in history books as the so-called *Kristallnacht*, the "Night of Broken Glass," or November Pogroms. The Nazis used the murder of a German diplomat by a Jew as an excuse to unleash an unprecedented orgy of violence. Beginning on the evening of November 9, 1938, thousands of Jewish businesses were destroyed, over 1,000 synagogues and prayer houses were set on fire, and hundreds of Jews were murdered. While Nazi propaganda spoke of a spontaneous reaction of the people, the whole pogrom was in fact long prepared in secret. On the morning of November 10, tens of thousands of Jewish men were arrested and deported to concentration camps.

During the night, Oswald and Otto's fathers managed to hide in the family factory on *Hardtgasse*. But Uncle Sigmund from *Heidenreichstein* was arrested by the Nazis – along with about 7,800 Austrian Jews – and sent to Buchenwald concentration camp shortly after.[12]

That was the beginning of the end for the Kernbergs in Vienna.

* * *

Almost exactly 75 years later, the Kerns finish the last verse of the *Kern Family Song* and go on singing another round of the gibberish chorus, *"Boom-killy-vitsky, Yan Kon Kooly Yan Kann Kow!"* Then it is time for the festive Thanksgiving dinner.

Next to the obligatory turkey and other typical dishes such as a pumpkin pie and sweet potato mash, we are also served *rugelach*, a Jewish pastry filled with nuts and chocolate. After most of the family has left, Arthur and his oldest son Aaron light the candles and recite traditional prayers to mark the second night of Hanukkah.

The next day, I meet with Arthur in a festively decorated hotel lobby, for one of our extended interviews. We are comfortably seated in yellow lounge chairs, while next to us and half listening to our conversation, Trudie plays Sudoku on her iPad. Recalling his time in Vienna, Arthur says to me, "I really had a particularly nice childhood until I was ten years old."

"We had a great life," he adds after a short pause.

2. GETTING THE CHILDREN OUT

Hermann Kernberg was an optimistic man – at least according to his son's and nephew's recollection. "At first, my parents thought it would blow over," Arthur recalls. "I'm sure my parents would have left Vienna if they had known what would happen."

Otto Kernberg confirmed his uncle Hermann's and his aunt Frieda's unrealistic and excessively optimistic attitude: "They were worried and affected in their daily life, but at the same time, I think, they shared the illusion that this was a transitional situation," he told me when we met in New York. (Otto's father himself shared the same conviction; it was his mother, Paula, who recognized the danger quite early on and urged them to emigrate.)

* * *

"Goood mooorning! Coffee?" two men with an Israeli accent call to the policemen posted at the far end of the *Seitenstettengasse*, sheltered from the rain in a house entrance. A young officer gratefully accepts the offer and follows the men inside the kosher Alef-Alef-Restaurant, right next to the Jewish community center. His female colleague chooses to stay outside, reminding him of the upcoming change of shift. The *Seitenstettengasse* is a street situated in Vienna's Old City, not far from the *Stephansdom* (St. Stephen's Cathedral). When looking down from the top of the steep street, all the buildings on the right side belong to the Jewish community while the left side is a long stretch of bars. From the outside, one does not immediately identify the *Stadttempel* (City Prayer House) as a synagogue. The building is located right in the middle of the street, with a Hebrew inscription engraved over its wooden entrance: "Enter His gates with thanksgiving and His courts with praise!" The obligatory safety measures all around Vienna's *Hauptsynagoge* (main synagogue) are barely visible at first glance: the safety gates are pushed against the walls of the building, the metal detectors concealed inside, and to make out the figures of the two policemen standing in the rain, one has to take a close look at the place.

The *Seitenstettentempel* is the only synagogue in Vienna that wasn't burned down by raging mobs during the November Pogroms in 1938, as it stood too close to other houses and people feared the fire would spread. Today, the archive of the *Israelitische Kultusgemeinde Wien* (Vienna Israelite Community, short IKG) is located right next to the synagogue, which is where I meet Susanne Uslu-Pauer in September 2017.

The chief archivist is sitting in a fully renovated office, its walls lined with metal shelves. Merely an ancient wooden index card drawer reminds us of the century-old history of the Vienna IKG. Founded in 1816, the archive is the only Jewish community archive that survived the NS-era in one of the territories occupied by the Nazis. Yet for decades after the end of the Second World War, it remained closed until over 500,000 documents dating from the NS-era, and until then believed to be lost, were found in 2000, inside an old, forgotten house belonging to the IKG. Since 2009, the IKG Archive is once again an independent structure, where Uslu-Pauer and her colleagues attempt to handle over 10.7 million documents.

The over 50,000 emigration request forms, filled out by Viennese Jews, constitute one of the IKG's most significant archive collections. "The IKG was closed after the *Anschluss* in March 1938 and reopened in May. It was then forced to organize the emigration and later the deportation of the Jewish population," Uslu-Pauer explains to me. This "new" IKG was however under the control of the infamous SS-*Obersturmbannführer*, Adolf Eichmann, who systematically furthered the forced emigration of the Jewish population. Jews living in Austria could register at the Emigration Department of the IKG and fill out an emigration request form, the IKG supporting them insofar as possible in obtaining specific documents and financial aid.

The registration itself was voluntary, yet most of the community members applied for it. "Exactly 50,000 filled out request forms have been conserved, on which about 97,000 persons in total are recorded," Uslu-Pauer tells me. "That means about half of the Jewish population in Vienna applied for emigration. But many of them also managed to emigrate via the Palestine Office, the Youth Aliyah organization, and the emigration aid organizations for non-Mosaic Jews."

Generally filled out by the head of the family, the emigration request forms would contain information on the family's professional and financial background, the languages spoken by its members, as well as the presence of relatives abroad, who might help provide a visa. The form also asked to specify which family member was supposed to emigrate first, as well as the location the family wanted to emigrate to – a question Uslu-Pauer considers as "catastrophic," as no one actually *wanted* to emigrate, people only being forced to by the circumstances.

* * *

On June 3, 1938, Hermann Kernberg filled out the three pages of the form inside the IKG's office on *Seitenstettengasse*, specifying "America or Australia or overseas" as his choice of emigration country.[1] In his careful and round handwriting, he indicated his wish to "begin anew [abroad] and start to work," writing, "My line of work in the fashion industry will always be favored anywhere." He mentioned "independent knitwear manufacturer" as his profession, adding he could also "work as a chauffeur." Regarding the question of whether he had some relatives living abroad, he wrote down the name of a cousin in Mexico. Hermann also registered Frieda, Fritz, and Oswald, stating he would prefer if they "could all emigrate together."

On June 10, 1938, exactly one week later, he filled out the same form again – yet giving slightly different answers. When asked about his professional training and expectations, he wrote down "dish-washing and similar jobs" next to "chauffeur." As for his choice of emigration country, he appeared to be no longer particular, noting the family wanted a country that "offered livelihood opportunities." When asked about his plans for the future, he added that he was willing to take just "any job." Yet the major difference with the first form was in the list of the family's relatives abroad: instead of just one single cousin, he mentioned the names of six more, in Mexico, New York, and Palestine.

According to the IKG chief archivist Uslu-Pauer, the fact Oswald's father filled out a second form shows quite plainly that he had heard that people's chances of success were improved if they declared more manual skills, as well as a longer list of relatives. "Many people had realized by then that they had to write down as much information as possible," Uslu-Pauer said to me.

Not all of the 200,000 Jews in Vienna registered at the IKG. Hermann Kernberg obviously gave the idea of leaving the country some thought, yet just how serious his emigration plans were at the time remains unclear. The IKG does not hold any other documents concerning the Kernberg family, unlike many other applicants, which points to the fact that Oswald's father did not submit any fur-ther requests after filling out the two emigration forms. For a long time afterward, nothing hints at the family having actively sought to emigrate.

And yet, after the *Anschluss*, Hermann traveled abroad on several occasions – but he returned home each time. His passport bears witness to the fact: in July 1938, he applied for a visa for Switzerland and traveled to Zurich, officially for "professional" reasons, according to what is stated in the document. There he entrusted the financial advisor F. Reiss with part of his money, also leaving a few valuables with a distant relative, Leon Tempelhof, among which a golden watch, Frieda's wedding ring, eight silver coins, a silver cigarette case, a few items of clothing and shoes.

Even after the November Pogroms that completely shattered the lives of the Jews in Vienna, the attitude of Oswald's parents did not seem to shift significantly, at least at first. Uncle Sigmund was arrested during *Kristallnacht* and incarcerated in a concentration camp, and some of Frieda's relatives, expelled from their apartments, moved in with the Kernbergs on *Gussenbauergasse*. Yet it would be several months before Oswald's parents decided to emigrate. Two events occurring in February 1939 probably played a significant part in that decision.

First, the Nazis seized Hermann Kernberg's family factory. On February 7, 1939, they appointed a certain Dr. Josef Tomasi as temporary administrator and trustee for the Goldfeld & Kernberg company, as I discover in the files of the Vienna Trade Office.[2] A law issued only a few weeks after the *Anschluss*, enabling the Reich Governor of the "*Ostmark*" (Eastern March) to appoint temporary administrators or monitoring persons to run Austrian businesses "in order to safeguard important public assets" provided the legal basis for such an action.[3] Oswald's father would continue to work at the knitwear factory, but he could no longer make any decisions and received preposterously low wages.

Only one day later, on February 8, Oswald's uncle Sigmund was released from Buchenwald concentration camp, his discharge papers stating that the "prisoner in protective custody, the Jew Shulim

Lieblich" is "released and sent back to Vienna … by order of the secret state police."[4]

"I remember my uncle Sigmund, who came from Buchenwald, came to our house and told my father 'You gotta get out. You gotta leave. Just leave the factory, leave everything, just get out of here.'" Arthur told me years later.

Hermann and Frieda listened to their brother-in-law's advice. But by the spring of 1939, almost no country was willing to welcome adult refugees anymore. Besides, any emigration attempt came with a great deal of bureaucracy and months of waiting, which is why Fritz and Oswald were supposed to be saved first. "My parents recognized that leaving Austria would take time and like some other parents, they tried to send their children out of harm's way," Arthur reflected much later.

Oswald's application for the *Kindertransport*.

* * *

"Kernberg!" a weary voice called into the crowded waiting room. Taking his two sons Oswald and Fritz by the arm, Hermann weaved his way through the throng of waiting families to the office bearing the sign "Child Emigration." He had heard from acquaintances that the IKG *Fürsorgezentrale* (IKG Care Center) organized so-called *Kindertransports* (children's transports), sending children to safe foreign countries, without their parents. As difficult as the idea of parting with his sons must have been for him, here he was, waiting to register them for a *Kindertransports*. On Oswald's file, an IKG member of staff wrote: "The father is jobless and the family had to sell all its possessions to survive."[5]

It is no longer possible to determine exactly when Hermann Kernberg registered his sons at the Child Emigration Office. Neither do we know whether he only registered them in general or specifically asked for them to be sent to France. What is clear though, is that Fritz and Oswald both appear on a list of "urgent cases [to be sent] to France," established by the IKG probably sometime at the end of February or early March 1939.[6] There are 109 names on that list, kept in the archives of the IKG. The children named on it were between six and fifteen years old, nearly two-thirds of them boys.

Just like so many things in a time of complex emigration and immigration regulations and strict visa issuing, the organization of the *Kindertransport* involved a great deal of bureaucracy: Hermann Kernberg left the IKG building on *Seitenstettengasse*, carrying a stack of forms. The *Comité Israélite pour les Enfants venant d'Allemagne et d'Europe Centrale* (Israelite Committee for children from Germany and Central Europe, in short *Comité*), in charge of the *Kindertransports* on the French side, asked for seven signed parental authorization forms, five medical certificates and three passport pictures.[7]

On February 22, 1939, Hermann Kernberg signed a sworn statement for Oswald, transferring "all rights and authority regarding [Oswald's] health and moral interests" to the *Comité* (and other affiliated organizations) until his son's eighteenth birthday. This authorization could only be annulled when Hermann would be able to prove he had a permanent address in the country of his choice, as well as life circumstances allowing him to take care of the child himself. In yet another form, Oswald's parents had to agree they would not try to use their child (who by then would be living in France) as a pretext to apply for a French visa themselves.

One week later, on March 1, 1939, Oswald passed a medical examination. In order to be allowed to immigrate to France, the children had to be in perfect health and demonstrate normal behavior. Chief medical officer of health, Dr. Claudio Schmidt, acting as the medical examiner for the French Consulate, issued the medical certificates, certifying that Oswald was "in perfect condition, both physically and morally."[8]

* * *

Hermann returned once more to the office with his sons, so more certificates could be issued. "What grade are you in?" the clerk asked ten-year-old Oswald.

"I'm in fourth grade."

"What about you?" the man asked, turning to Oswald's brother.

"I'm in fourth grade too," replied Fritz, who was three years older.

Later, Arthur would not be able to remember in which office that conversation had taken place. Yet decades later, he did recall all the more clearly his father's attempts to cover up his son's answer. Distract the clerk's attention from the boy's words. Somehow put them into perspective. Unsuccessfully. Although both Kernberg boys were considered "urgent cases" and candidates for a swift immigration to France, in the end, "healthy" Oswald alone was allowed to get on the *Kindertransport*. Fritz had to stay behind.

Almost his entire adult life, Arthur told himself, and others, Fritz had to stay behind because of his age – he had been thirteen at the time – ignoring the real reason.

In 1995, during an interview with Steven Spielberg's *Shoah Foundation* which conducts interviews with Holocaust survivors throughout the world, Arthur said: "The organization would only take children up to the age of 13. Once you were 13, you were just too old. So consequently, my brother didn't get out."⁹ The first time I interviewed Arthur – I was eleven at the time and writing a short biography of his family – he also told me the same thing. "Fritz wasn't accepted… as only children under thirteen years of age could be part of the transports," I thus wrote in my text.¹⁰

And yet, almost 40 children aged thirteen or above were chosen for a *Kindertransport* to France, as a look at the final transportation lists shows. Even adult Arthur was aware of that contradiction: "Inexplicably, other 13-year-olds did get on the final list," he noted in an autobiographical text he wrote for his family in 2006.

As it is, Fritz's epilepsy and the learning difficulties related to his condition were probably the reason why he was not accepted. As already mentioned, the children had to be in perfect health. The French *Comité* also sent the IKG several letters, demanding it should "select children possessing a fairly normal level of education." This strict selection occurred in light of a specific background: as many children as possible had to be saved over the long term. All organizations involved hoped the French government would allow further transports and insisted the refugee children arriving in France must make as good an impression as possible. Oswald and Fritz were not the only siblings that were separated for that reason.

It was only two years before his death that Arthur acknowledged for the first time, during one of our interviews, why his brother had not been able to go to France with him. It was not because Fritz had been *too old*, but because he had been ill. In the end, his epilepsy and learning difficulties had condemned him to death. "That's probably why they didn't take him," Arthur said pensively.

3. LEAVING VIENNA

Und der Pfiff des fernen Zuges
jetzt in meinem Ohr noch gellt.
Was ist los? Nichts.
Ein paar Juden fahren in die weite Welt.

I can still hear, ringing in my ear, the shrill whistle
Of the train in the distance.
What is happening? Nothing.
A few Jews leaving on a journey.

These are the final verses of Walter Lindenbaum's poem "Juden am Bahnhof" –"Jews at the train station,"[1] recited in a clear voice by well-known Austrian actor Cornelius Obonya. It is March 14, 2008, and the poem is part of the solemn unveiling ceremony of the statue *Für das Kind* (For the Child), in the ticket hall of Vienna's *Westbahnhof* (West Station). London-based sculptress Flor Kent has created a brass memorial to the *Kindertransport*, showing a small Jewish boy, wearing a hooded sweater and a kippa, sitting on an old-fashioned suitcase, his eyes staring sadly into the distance. The inscription on the marble base of the statue simply reads: "Who saves one life saves the world entire." This sentence – or a slightly altered version of it – is known worldwide since the movie *Schindler's List* and is one of the most frequently cited passages from the Talmud, one of the most important text collections of Judaism.

Nine-year-old Sam Morris, a great-grandson of Sarah Schreiber, who was sent on a *Kindertransport* from Vienna's *Westbahnhof* to England when she was sixteen, sat for the artist. "If all this hadn't happened seventy years ago, I would never have been born," Sam declares during the ceremony with a heavy English accent and in a slightly oversized suit.

The statue was created on the initiative of Mili Segal, who lives in Vienna and has been supporting memorial projects for years. "Leaving a significant memento at the *Westbahnhof* to remember the children by really mattered to me," Segal tells me later. "Lots of people will probably pass by without noticing the statue; it's important that those who stop in front of it should know about [the *Kindertransport*]. And most importantly: the children survived!"

Similar statues by Flor Kent or Frank Meisler have been erected in Berlin, Prague, and Gdańsk, as well as in Liverpool Street Station in London, all of them dedicated to the British children's transports. Yet almost no one knows that – exactly 69 years to the day before the unveiling of the statue in Vienna – one *Kindertransport* also left Vienna's *Westbahnhof* for France.

* * *

After Oswald's registration at the Child's Emigration office in mid-February 1939, everything went very fast. In the first week of March, the Jewish community applied for passports for one hundred children, who were thus ready to leave.[2] The same emigration regulations applied to children and adult refugees alike: each child was allowed one suitcase, one piece of hand luggage, and ten *Reichsmark*.

Any valuables were confiscated.³ Because her son could only take so little with him, Frieda packed all his best clothes in his suitcase, so that he would make a good impression upon his arrival in France. She also added Oswald's beloved book on Greek and Roman mythology, but his many toys had to stay at home. Frieda and Hermann told their son time and again that they would only be separated for a short while and that the whole family would soon emigrate to the United States.

The night before he was due to leave, Oswald sneaked into the dining room and carefully opened the door of the big cabinet where his parents kept the photo albums they had so often leafed through together. Opening one of them, Oswald began to remove a few pictures: Hermann Kernberg wearing a suit and a broad-brimmed hat, a pocket square and a silver pen in his breast pocket; Frieda in a dark dress, a huge smile on her face; Fritz, his necktie slightly undone, glancing upwards. Little Ossi, as a grouchy toddler, sitting on his grandfather's lap; his grandmother in her darkened apartment in the city's second district. Frieda and her two sons in a photo studio; the whole family by the lake in *Heidenreichstein*; portraits of his favorite uncles and aunts. Very carefully, Oswald took the black and white and sepia-toned pictures and put them in his suitcase. "I wanted to have them with me," Arthur explained to me later. "And I'm glad I took them. These pictures are the only reminders that I have of my parents."

Today the pictures have once again found their way inside a photo album that Arthur's wife, Trudie, lovingly put together. Thanks to these photographs, I was able to get my own impression of Arthur's family and childhood, which I would otherwise have known about only through his memories. Simply because little Oswald secretly took the pictures and kept them with him throughout the long war years.

* * *

March 14, 1939. Time to say goodbye. It could no longer be postponed. Frieda, Hermann, and Fritz hugged and kissed Oswald on the platform of the *Westbahnhof.* Frieda cried. Shortly after eleven o'clock in the evening, the little boy stepped on the express train to Paris, managing to secure a seat by the window. The hand of the clock moved forward, minute after minute. At 11:25 pm the train pulled out of the station with a loud screech. Oswald waved to his father, who ran along the accelerating train. The ten-year-old boy saw the silver pen Hermann always carried in his pocket drop to the ground as he ran on. Hermann stopped to pick it up, but before he could even straighten up, the train was gone. It was the last time Oswald saw his father.

Along with Oswald, 49 underage children traveled in the same carriage, among them a few siblings; yet most of the children set out on their journey to an uncertain freedom alone. Trude Frankl, a Viennese educator who worked with the IKG, was the only adult supervising the group of children. She had to promise to return to Nazi Germany to be allowed to escort the children. That condition applied to all *Kindertransports*: if one of the accompanying adults had failed to return, the transports would have been stopped at once.[4]

The journey lasted almost an entire day. The French *Comité Israélite* took charge of the young travelers in Karlsruhe, who then resumed their train ride to Paris via Strasbourg.

Oswald's brother Fritz was not allowed on the *Kindertransport.*
He remained in Vienna with his parents.

* * *

Oswald was ten years old when he was forced to leave his home, his family, the soccer games at the *Spittelauer Platz* (Spittelauer Square), and the evenings spent in his parent's bed – forever. Ten years old. Almost the same age I was when I met him decades later – by then he had already become Arthur Kern.

When I tell people I was eleven when I met Arthur and began writing his family biography as part of a history project, they often act surprised by my young age. How can an eleven-year-old girl be interested in *such* a story? This always makes me wonder: how could a ten-year-old boy live through *such* a thing?

When asked about it, Arthur assured me that leaving had not been difficult for him at the time. "I remember some kids were crying and so, but I was not particularly unhappy," he declared in 1995, during an interview with the *Shoah Foundation*. After all his parents had promised the whole family would soon emigrate to America. His journey to France was no more than a temporary situation in his eyes, as well as an exciting adventure. He also felt very relieved to be able to get away from the *Hitlerjugend* (Hitler Youth) and avoid getting beaten up. "You know, you think that when you are ten years old, you don't know much what is going on. You don't really recognize the extent like an adult would, but believe me, I knew what was going on. I knew the dangers that had occurred," he told the interviewer.

Yet the fact Arthur secretly stole several family pictures contradicts his claim his departure did not disturb him. Along with a parting letter he wrote just before leaving and which he would regret for the rest of his life.

"I specifically remember [writing] things like… Today I am ten years old and I must leave my parents' house," Arthur told me, his voice clear and steady, during one of our conversations. The letter had not necessarily been intended for his parents – Oswald wrote it more or less for himself – but he nevertheless left it in his room. Relatives told him much later that his mother suffered a breakdown when she found the note. "I felt guilty about having done something stupid like that, but I still wondered, why do I have to leave?" Arthur recalled.

According to the IKG's reports, at the time of Oswald's departure, only 90,000 Jews remained in Vienna – almost half of the entire Jewish population had thus already emigrated by then. Frieda, Hermann, and their eldest son Fritz were among those who stayed behind, trapped in increasingly threatening circumstances.

On Wednesday, March 15, 1939, at 7:35 p.m., Oswald arrived in Paris.

PART 2 – FRANCE

4. THE *KINDERTRANSPORT*

Melissa Hacker opens the *2015 Kindertransport Association Conference* in Detroit with a warm "Welcome, *Kinder.*" The American deliberately uses the German word for "children," not the English one. Whether they meet in Vienna, London, Israel, or New York, the Holocaust survivors who were saved on a *Kindertransport* still call themselves *Kinder*, saying for instance "I am a *Kind*" or, as mentioned before, "Welcome, *Kinder.*"

About a hundred members of the *Kindertransport Association* (KTA) listen to the welcome address of their president, sitting at round tables in the Charlevoix ballroom of the Westin hotel. The KTA is a North-American organization for Holocaust survivors who owe their rescue from Nazi Germany to a *Kindertransport*. Created in the early 1990s, it offers the survivors, but also their children and grandchildren, a forum where they can connect and learn more about their family history. In 2015, the theme of the KTA Conference reads *Generations Together: Our Legacy and the Future*. The following three days are mainly dedicated to the ideational legacy of Holocaust survivors, whose number dwindles with every year. One glance across the room shows how relevant that theme is: where at previous conferences the *Kinder* used to make up more than half of the audience, today they barely represent a fifth of the participants. Even the fourth generation attends the conference this time: a few three- and four-year-old slalom through the fabric-covered chairs in the ballroom, much to the 70 and 80 years old *Kinder*'s delight. The whole weekend feels more like some big family reunion than a conference. People know each other – and even when this is not the case, it still seems to them as if they do, because of everyone's shared *Kindertransport* experience. The warm and easy atmosphere also spreads to the outsiders, a small group of historians, invited, just like me, to present their research.

Lilly Maier during a lecture at *Deutsches Haus* in New York.

A lot has changed since Arthur told me for the first time about the *Kindertransport*, twelve years ago. In the fall of 2015, I am 23 years old and I have been studying history for the past four years. For my bachelor dissertation, *Ein Leben nach dem Kindertransport* (A life after the *Kindertransport*), I have conducted interviews with twelve other *Kinder* apart from Arthur, some of them also attending the conference in Detroit. My dissertation, questioning the influence of their rescue through a *Kindertransport* on the *Kinder*'s adult life, has been distinguished by the University of Munich. In Detroit, I take part in a panel discussion and give a lecture on the history and remembrance of the *Kindertransports*. Given the large number of the *Kinder*'s descendants attending the conference, I am asked to explain in detail the historical development of the *Kindertransports*. As it turns out, there's a lot of uncertainty about the background and context of their rescue, even among those concerned at the time. And absolutely no one has ever heard about the *Kindertransports* to France.

* * *

Roused to action by the November Pogroms, international organizations began to prepare for the *Kindertransports* in the fall of 1938. In the 1930s, the economic situation worldwide was very dire and the unemployment rate was extremely high. Host countries were therefore more inclined to issue visas for unaccompanied minors rather than for adults or families. Children and teenagers were not considered a threat to the labor market and they also aroused people's pity, which made it easier for governments to enforce aid and relief programs in the eyes of the public. Until the beginning of the war in September 1939, almost 15,000 children were thus rescued from Germany, Austria, Czechoslovakia, and Poland, the vast majority of them Jewish.[1] The fact the Nazis would allow the *Kindertransport* in the first place, sometimes even supporting their organization, is quite astonishing: they ensured, for instance, the swift delivery of passports. A circular, sent on December 31, 1938, by the *Reichsführer SS* and chief of police, Heinrich Himmler, speaks to the fact: "In order to promote and encourage the emigration of Jewish children and teenagers, I request that the passport authorities should be instructed without delay to issue identity cards and passports for the persons in question as fast as possible."[2] (At that time, the Nazis wanted to expel all the Jews from Germany. It would be some time before the "Final Solution," that is the extermination of the Jewish people, would be decided.)

Because of a global entry permit, the *Kindertransports* sent to Great Britain were successful. The British government was the only country to issue an unlimited number of visas for unaccompanied children under 17, as long as somebody could guarantee their education and leave a 50-pound guarantee sum for the children's future further emigration. The Jewish organization *Movement for the Care of Children from Germany* (later called *Refugee Children's Movement*, RCM) committed to both. Refugee children arriving in England would be placed in foster care whenever that was possible, so they would fit into the British way of life and attract as little attention as possible. More often than not, they were placed in Christian families. Around 4,000 minors were also sent to exile schools and supervised hostels.[3]

The first transport reached England on December 2, 1938, barely four weeks after the November Pogroms. In the frantic early days of the *Kindertransports*, the most urgent step was to rescue the most vulnerable among the children: orphans, stateless children who were at risk of being expelled from Germany at any moment, children whose parents had been arrested or expelled, and most of all older boys, threatened with deportation to a concentration camp. This explains why until March 1939, mostly adolescent boys were sent to England. After that date, only children for whom a foster family had already been found were accepted as candidates for a *Kindertransport*. British families could choose a suitable child from a card index, often favoring girls between seven and ten years old. Finding a family for boys over twelve was quite difficult and the latter would only rarely be part of the later transports.[4]

About 10,000 children from Central Europe could thus be brought to England until September 1939. Israeli historian Judith Tydor-Baumel-Schwartz describes this as probably the largest rescue operation that took place during the Holocaust.[5]

The Child Emigration office of the IKG in Vienna worked relentlessly to organize and prepare the *Kindertransports*. "The IKG was able to send away over 2,840 children until the beginning of the war," says IKG's chief archivist, Uslu-Pauer. 43 transports left Vienna for a safe country abroad – England, Holland, France, Sweden, Belgium, America, and Switzerland.[6]

Yet the IKG was not the only Viennese institution organizing *Kindertransports*. 1,400 children and teenagers were able to leave the country via the Palestine Office in Vienna. The Quakers too arranged *Kindertransports* for "non-Aryan Christians," thus saving 882 children. Furthermore, after the beginning of the war, six more transports to the USA took place.[7] Even though it is not possible to establish with any certainty exactly how many children were able to leave Austria on a *Kindertransport* due to incomplete and fragmentary records, we still know they numbered more than 5,000.

IKG's welfare department was run by Rosa Rachel Schwarz, who was rumored to "have an excellent memory" and "know almost all the [Jewish] children in Vienna."[8] In April 1940, Rosa Schwarz wrote a short text about "the Jewish community's social work in Vienna under Hitler," reflecting on "the unbelievable amount of detail work" necessary to organize a *Kindertransport*: "Out of the chaos of request forms, I suggested the names of those among the children whose emigration was the most urgent due to their health, moral or material circumstances. Then we had the children tested and examined by a doctor, we provided passports for them and checked the luggage they were allowed to take along with them."[9]

Lilly Reichenfeld, who run the *Jugendfürsorge* (Youth Welfare Center), and Franzi Löw, worked together with Rosa Schwarz to arrange and organize the *Kindertransports* from Vienna. Franzi Löw, who was 23 years old at that time, had to conduct interviews with the children and their families and write reports about them. Decades later, Löw explained in an interview how she would always try to highlight each child individually: "I once asked a four-year-old during a test: 'Why do you have teeth?' and the child answered 'To brush them' – 'What do you have ears for?' – 'To listen' – 'And why do you have your *Mutti* (Mom)?' The child opened his eyes wide, glanced at his mother, and said: 'I have *Mutti* to love.' This I chose to write in the child's report, to show its reaction."[10]

As the fate of Oswald's brother Fritz shows, selecting the children for the transports – especially the later *Kindertransports* – was submitted to very strict conditions. "The children couldn't have any kind of problem; they had to be healthy, smart, and adaptable," historian Gerda Hofreiter outlines in her book *Allein in die Fremde (You must go alone).*[11] These strict rules applied to all *Kindertransports*, following the requirements set by the host countries.

Sick and disabled children, or those with learning disabilities or behavioral problems, could not be part of the transports. The British *Refugee Children's Movement* also rejected children with treatable diseases such as mild asthma, diabetes or even squinting. This would lead to repeated conflicts with the IKG in Vienna that tried to downplay the children's condition or attempted to nominate physically ill children for a *Kindertransport.*[12]

As mentioned before, the reason for these strict regulations lay in the hope entertained by the organizations involved that they would be able to save even more children, if those who had already been welcomed in host countries were able to make a good impression. From today's perspective, historian Claudia Curio condemns the organizations' rigorous selection: "Given our subsequent knowledge about the Holocaust, the realization more children could possibly have been saved with a bolder, less deliberative approach is hard to bear. If people had known that the war would soon put an end to all *Kindertransports* anyway, the fear to see the action interrupted … would have been pointless."[13]

* * *

The *Refugee Children's Movement* was the only aid organization in England responsible for the rescue and care of the refugee children.

The situation was quite different in France, where half a dozen organizations were involved in the *Kindertransport*. The places from where Oswald's rescue to France was planned are all within walking distance of the center of Paris – back then, just like today, surrounded by impressive palaces, romantic cafés, and luxury shops. That is where I set out on my journey, in September 2017, searching for traces of the past.

The *Hôtel de Saint-Florentin* is located right in front of the famous *Place de la Concorde* and the *Tuileries* Garden leading to the Louvre. In 1838, the Jewish banker Baron James de Rothschild, who is said to have been the richest man in France or even the world, bought the magnificent neoclassical palace, built in 1767. In a newspaper article, Heinrich Heine wrote in the middle of the nineteenth century, he called the *Hôtel* "the Versailles of absolute plutocracy," praising the palace's tasteful furnishings.[14] A hundred years later, Baroness Germaine de Rothschild lived in the palace. Baroness Germaine – who, in keeping with the times, would only be referred to in letters by her husband's name, as Baroness Edouard de Rothschild – was a well-known philanthropist and used her power and influence to stand up for the refugee children from Germany and Austria. After the end of the war, the Rothschilds sold the landmark *Hôtel de Saint-Florentin* to the US government, which in turn organized the Marshall Plan from there. Today the palace belongs to the American Embassy in Paris.

My quest next leads me to the *rue du Mont Thabor*, a quiet little street merely a stone's throw away, named after a mountain in the French Alps. At the beginning of the war, *38 rue du Mont Thabor* was home to the office of the *Comité Israélite pour les Enfants venant d'Allemagne et d'Europe Centrale* (Jewish Committee for the Children from Germany and Central Europe). Baroness Germaine de Rothschild founded the *Comité* in 1939, to provide more effective help for children like Oswald. Today a new building has replaced the old one, and a jewelry store and a Vietnamese restaurant share the ground floor.

Leaving the *rue du Mont Thabor*, I walk towards the *Champs-Élysées* enjoying the mild Parisian autumn. Large parts of the great avenue are closed to traffic due to an open-air concert and as I stroll along in the middle of the boulevard towards the *Arc de Triomphe*, I suddenly feel as if I have traveled back in time to the last century. I buy a *crêpe* at a small stand and sit down on a bench to watch the hustle and bustle of midtown Paris. Although it is Sunday, all the shops lining the magnificent shopping mile are open and a great number of tourists crowd the sidewalk between Louis Vuitton and Disney Store. A lavishly renovated corner house stands at the northwest end of the *Champs-Élysées*, at number 92 of the boulevard. The brick-colored building houses three stores: a Spanish fashion store chain, an eyewear shop, and a British fashion label. Thomas Jefferson lived for some time at this address before he became President of the United States, as I can gather from the inscription on a marble memorial plaque. Yet, much more importantly in my eyes, the building used to host the office of the aid organization that would have the greatest impact on Oswald's life: the Œuvre de Secours aux Enfants (OSE, Children's Aid Organization). OSE was created in 1912 in St Petersburg by Jewish doctors and soon developed branches in over thirty countries. In 1933, the organization's headquarters were transferred from Berlin to Paris, its teams working to help and support Jewish children. After the 1938 November Pogroms, OSE began to make arrangements ahead of the arrival of refugee children from Germany and Austria.

* * *

The number of unaccompanied minors traveling on a *Kindertransport* to France is comparatively small: only about 200 children under fifteen arrived in Paris on February and March 1939, on two different transports, the children from Vienna making up for a little more than half of them, the IKG having sent 103 children.[15] The other children came from Berlin, Frankfurt, and Mainz. Personal contacts between the IKG in Vienna and committed individuals in Paris, who jumped into action months before the November Pogroms, probably account for the large percentage of children from Vienna.

Actually, this concerned a small group of girls from the Merores Jewish orphanage. Mid-July 1938, a certain Madame Nathalie Louriée contacted the Baroness Germaine de Rothschild, who agreed to accommodate eight to ten girls in the Parisian Rothschild orphanage and place about twenty older girls in French families.[16] The Baroness put the director of the old-established *Fondation de Rothschild* in charge of the whole matter, whilst also being involved herself.

At first, everything went very fast. In the second half of July alone, 25 letters were exchanged between Louriée, the IKG, the Merores orphanage, and the Rothschilds and on July 15, 1938, a definitive positive reply was received concerning eight girls. On July 18, 1938, the director of the Jewish orphanage in Vienna sent the *Fondation* a list of names, expressing his hope for "a positive progress of such an eminently philanthropic action."

By the end of July, Madame Louriée received a letter from Vienna, requesting that "*Knaben*" (boys) should be helped too, as it was much more difficult for them to find places within families. On July 28, the *Fondation* confirmed the selection of eight girls for the Rothschild orphanage, promising to take good care of the children. Shortly after though, the whole matter began to falter and it was not before December 26 – five months after the positive reply – that six girls traveled from Vienna to Paris, two of the eight candidates having already emigrated elsewhere because of the long delay.

Unconnected to these events, several French committees began to organize *Kindertransports* on a larger scale, after the November Pogrom. Once again IKG was informed about it through private contacts. In early December, 1938, Pauline Beer, the daughter of Viennese commercial councilor Landsberger, wrote from Paris about the expected sending of 500 Jewish "boys from six to twelve" to France. Upon inquiry at the office of the American Jewish Joint Distribution Committee (Joint), an American Jewish aid organization, the IKG learned that the Jewish organization Œuvre de Secours aux Enfants was behind the expected action.[17] Baroness Germaine de Rothschild herself also planned to organize a *Kindertransport*, as she told the IKG in December 1938, in a letter written in German: "Please allow me to bring to your attention that I have founded a Jewish committee in France for the children coming from Germany and Eastern Europe." Finally, the IKG also read about a third action of this kind on the part of the *Bureau Central d'Accueil aux Enfants* (Central Office for the Admission of Children) in a newspaper article. To put some order in these coinciding efforts, the director of the IKG turned to the Baroness Germaine de Rothschild, asking her whether she could help the organizations reach "an agreement… experience showing that any independent action on the part of different bodies pursuing parallel goals usually isn't effective."

Whether this letter turned out to be decisive or not remains unknown, but in any case, the French State decided it would exclusively negotiate the issuing of visas with the Rothschild Foundation. From then on, the *Comité Israélite pour les Enfants venant d'Allemagne et d'Europe Centrale* (in short *Comité*), newly founded by the Baroness Germaine de Rothschild, was the sole interlocutor, committing to "ensuring the livelihood and education, as well as the professional education of the children under its care for years to come." This also put an end to Madame Louriée's work – from January 1939 on, there are no more letters from her in the files.

On February 13, 1939, the IKG received confirmation from the *Comité* that the French government had approved the delivery of 200 group visas for children under 15. A hundred of these were given to Vienna, 50 to Berlin, 40 to Mainz, and 10 to Frankfurt. Because of the high proportion of Viennese children, the IKG was asked to establish two separate transport lists, each stating the names of 50 children. The *Comité* instructed to only select children who would stay in France over a longer time, a crucial difference to the British *Kindertransport*, where all visas issued were considered transit visas given the children's eventual further emigration.

Exactly one month to the day after the French agreement, the Kernbergs took Oswald to the *Westbahnhof* – at least their youngest son would soon be safe!

The second transport left Vienna on March 22,[18] this time with 53 children on board instead of 50 as expected. The IKG usually applied for more visas than initially foreseen, in case some children would take ill or their parents changed their minds at the last minute, as was the case for six children on the first transport, but this did not happen at all on the second. Still, France granted the additional three children entry into its territory.

After two successful transports, the Rothschilds attempted to have 800 more child visas issued. However, with the imminent threat of war, the French government did not allow further *Kindertransports*, only now and then issuing the occasional visa for children with relatives in the country.

About 100 further children "from migrant families already living in France under the most dire circumstances" were additionally taken on by the *Comité,* as educator Trude Frankl wrote in a report for the IKG. Many of these children had initially immigrated to France illegally, and the *Comité* retroactively obtained residence permits for them.

* * *

I conclude my one-hour lecture at the *Kindertransport Conference* in Detroit quoting Viennese-born Anita Weisbord, who was rescued by a *Kindertransport*: "I truly believe my mother gave birth to me twice: once when I was born and when she had the strength and foresight to send me out on the *Kindertransport*."

On the following day, we are to visit the *Holocaust Memorial Center* in Farmington Hills, where a *Kindertransport* Memory Quilt is exhibited. The colorful patchwork blanket was carefully sewn and stitched by former *Kinder* – the embroidered Quilt squares show the parting with parents, trains, boats, and suitcases, as reminders of their rescue. Taking a very close look at the different squares, one could get the impression that only girls were rescued on a *Kindertransport*. This, however, is not historically accurate and is merely due to an obvious lack of enthusiasm for quilting on the part of the male *Kinder*.

At the close of the conference, the participants are invited to attend the play, *The Pianist of Willesden Lane*, at the Detroit Jewish community center theater. In the one-woman show, concert pianist and actress Mona Golabek recounts her mother's *Kindertransport* story.[19]

Golabek sits at a Steinway grand piano, wearing an elegant black dress, her loose blond hair falling on her face. "When I was a little girl and my mother taught me how to play the piano, she would always tell me about a mysterious journey she once took," Golabek begins, playing a slow tune.

The music becomes louder and faster as she goes on talking about the November Pogroms and her grandparents' decision to send one of their daughters to England. "I will always pay tribute to my mother with music," Golabek says as she plays a piece by Bach.

At the end of the show, Mona Golabek tells the spectators that several *Kinder* are sitting in the audience. "Could you please stand?" she asks them. It is a very moving moment indeed when a dozen seventy and eighty-year-old Holocaust survivors get to their feet to thunderous applause. Many people have tears in their eyes. So do I. Ralph Samuel, a former Dresdner, holds onto my shoulder as he stands next to me, staring into the large auditorium, while people continue to applaud.

When writing a biography, it is very important to stay true to the historical course of events. One should not link every childhood experience to the adult the child became and neither should we reinterpret experience and remembrance in a certain way just because we know the end of the story. Still, it is nice to recall from time to time how the story ends: be it during a Thanksgiving dinner with Arthur and his family or in a theater hall somewhere in America, where a crowd of total strangers applauds the *Kinder* who managed against all odds to survive the Holocaust.

5. ARRIVAL IN PARIS

After about twenty hours' journey, the refugee children reached the *Gare de l'Est* (East Station) in Paris, at 7:35 pm on March 15, 1939. After sitting for such a long time, Oswald's body felt stiff and he had a good stretch before getting off the train and stepping into the spacious station hall. Boys and girls had to stand in two rows next to the platform so their chaperones could count them – only after they had made sure their protégés were all present and accounted for did they lead them to a bus already waiting for them. Oswald did not get to see much of Paris on that March night, as they drove through the dark city, lit up here and there by the flare of a street lamp. After a thirty-minute ride, they finally reached the *Hôpital Rothschild*, on the *rue de Santerre*, merely a few minutes walk from the *Place de la Nation*. After having built the first Israelite Hospital in Paris in 1852, the Rothschilds opened a second one on the *rue de Santerre*. The building was renovated several times over the years and today it is a modern glass and metal hospital construction. In the lobby, an elaborately designed photo wall calls to mind the eventful story of the hospital; during the German Occupation in Paris, the Nazis had turned the building into a prison.

The young refugees spent their first night in France in the Jewish hospital. They were submitted to a medical examination and a health card was created for each child.[1] Arthur would remember later that the children were also given a laxative "to clean us out," as he put it. "And the bathrooms were a mess after that."

Fortunately, the children did not stay for long at the hospital and after only three days, were divided into several groups and placed under the care of different aid organizations, OSE, and the Rothschilds each taking one group.

* * *

In 1939, the Œuvre de Secours aux Enfants (Children's Aid Organization, OSE) was well located on the prestigious Avenue des Champs-Élysées. Nothing like today, since OSE's headquarters are now situated on a derelict street in the immigration area of Belleville, in Eastern Paris. I visit the place in September 2017. From the outside, the grey, unremarkable building only stands out because of its barred windows and security gate at the entrance. Once inside though, OSE's headquarters turn out to be a lively place of communication, its walls lined with elaborately designed exhibition boards recounting the eventful past of the Jewish children's aid organization. Some pictures show laughing children, and teenagers during sports, advertising posters in Yiddish, as well as a huge portrait of Albert Einstein, OSE's long-standing president of honor. The building is named after Georges and Lili Garel, two former OSE members, who succeeded in the 1940s in hiding 2,000 Jewish children via an underground rescue network.

Today OSE employs over 750 people, conducting programs for young people with behavioral problems, people with disabilities, elderly people suffering from dementia, and Holocaust survivors. Unlike in the past, many OSE employees are not Jewish. Katy Hazan and Dominique Rotermund explain to me the exhibition boards were set up so the employees could draw inspiration from OSE's history.

Hazan is OSE's historian, leading the organization's archive department for the past fifteen years, and the author of many books about the association. I had already been in contact with her even before my visit to Paris.[2] Her colleague Rotermund mainly sees to the various requests addressed to OSE by Holocaust survivors who were saved by the Jewish organization. She has a German mother, which makes my conversation with them a funny mishmash of German, French, and English. Hazan serves tea, adjusts her big, black glasses and elegant, patterned silk scarf, and starts telling me about the beginnings of the organization: "In 1912, in the declining Tsarist Empire, Jewish doctors in St. Petersburg founded the 'Society for the Health of the Jewish People,' in abbreviated form OZE. From the start, OZE was a medico-social aid organization." Not only did these doctors provide medical care, but they also built on prevention and hygiene campaigns. Between 1914 and 1917, OZE ran among others 125 kindergartens, taking care of 120,000 Jewish children in Russia.

"During the First World War, the organization worked with refugees and later with the victims of pogroms in Russia," Hazan continues. In 1922, the organization was shut down by the Bolsheviks and spread to other East European countries. The *World Union OSE*, a federalized association of individual country groups, was created in Berlin, in August 1923. The acronym OSE, still valid to this day, comes from the Latin version of its original name, *Organisatio Sanitaris Ebraica*. Albert Einstein became *Union OSE's* first honorary president, a position he kept until his death. Lazare Gurvic, a Lithuanian lawyer, was appointed general secretary. Soon OSE branches opened in over thirty countries, from Scandinavia to Australia. OSE activists built public baths and Jewish sports facilities, distributed baby milk, and provided professional training for doctors. On the eve of the war, OSE ran 505 medical facilities worldwide.[3]

With the Nazi rise to power in 1933, *Union OSE* left Berlin, transferring its headquarters to Paris. The French branch of OSE called *Œuvre de Secours aux Enfants* (Children's Aid Organization), was created that same year. The initials of the name matched those of the parent organization, so it was possible to keep the abbreviated form, OSE.[4]

At first, the association focused mainly on providing medical care and support to poor Jews, the organization also provided assistance for doctors.[5] In 1934, OSE opened a daycare center in Montmorency, on the outskirts of Paris, for the children of Jewish refugees from Poland and the Soviet Union. For a few weeks, each group comprised of 30 preschool-aged children was taught the basics of personal hygiene. By 1939, 1,200 children had been welcomed into the facility.[6]

Things would probably have continued that way, "but history forced OSE to change its course," Hazan explains. After the November Pogroms in 1938, a great number of German and Austrian refugee children began streaming into the daycare center and OSE realized much older children needed care too. Before the *Kindertransports* even started in March 1939, OSE already took care of Jewish children from Germany, some of them having entered the French territory illegally, as historian Claudia Göbetzberger retraced: "The children were brought to France with the help of French men and women, who had been sent to Germany or Austria as tourists, to collect one or two Jewish children and bring them back with them, pretending to be their parents."[7]

After France had officially granted the *Kindertransports*, OSE first took care of children under 11, while the older ones were accommodated in the Rothschild home of *La Guette*.[8] As of January 1939, OSE opened four new homes in Montmorency and its surroundings: *Villa Helvetia, Villa La Chesnaie, Les Tourelles,* and *La Petite Colonie.* OSE appointed the Viennese Ernst Papanek – an extraordinarily progressive pedagogue in exile – director of its homes.

The care of the children, and most importantly the purchase of the homes, was funded to a great extent by one woman: Baroness Yvonne de Gunzbourg. The wife of a Russian aristocrat in exile, she donated 40,000 francs to OSE in early 1939 for the rental of *Villa*

Helvetia. But her generosity did not stop there. One month later, she donated another 40,000 francs and by the end of 1940, Yvonne de Gunzbourg had become the very busy president of OSE's fundraising committee, having herself donated over a million francs.[9]

* * *

I contact Yvonne and Pierre de Gunzbourg's grandson in London. "Giving was a major part of their life, so I am not surprised they supported OSE," Peter Halban tells me. Halban, who runs a small publishing house in London together with his wife, is very impressed by his grandparents' generosity. "I am immensely proud and fascinated by their philanthropic life," he declares with a strong British accent. "They realized that far back on both sides of their families, they came to be very well off. Especially in Russia, and later in France. And in connection with that, they felt a huge social responsibility."

The Gunzbourgs (originally Günzburgs) were a dynasty of Russian Jewish merchants. In the middle of the 19th century, they represented the interests of the Grand Duke of Hessen in St. Petersburg, which earned them a high title of nobility in 1871, making them one of the few Jewish families to ever have been ennobled.

After the Russian Revolution, the family fled to France, where many years later, Yvonne de Gunzbourg would learn about OSE. Peter Halban had not known about this aspect of his family's history until recently. It was only in 2016, after having received inquiries from various historians, that he learned about the active part his grandparents had played in the rescue of Jewish refugee children.

"On the one hand, I am surprised they never talked about OSE, on the other hand, it fits their character. To do something quietly, without discussing it too much," Halban says. "For example, they used to rent houses on the border to help out refugees from Germany. But all very quietly."

From 1939 on, Yvonne de Gunzbourg and her husband Pierre supported Oswald and the other Jewish refugee children. With the more than one million Francs they donated, OSE bought eleven chateaux and turned them into children's homes.

At that time, many French aristocrats were glad to get rid of their chateaux, for which they paid exorbitantly high taxes. Pierre de Gunzbourg's reaction demonstrates this quite clearly when he jokingly complained to home director Ernst Papanek that he had now become France's "Chateaux-King." According to Papanek's recollection, every now and then the Baron would ask: "What am I going to do with all those castles you're getting my wife to buy? When the war is over, the children will all return to Germany and I will be stuck with them... The taxes alone will make a poor man of me. Nothing can save me from fate now except a return to the Age of Chivalry."[10]

* * *

Before moving into one of the newly opened OSE homes, Oswald spent three weeks in *Château Maubuisson*, in Saint-Ouen-l'Aumône, a medieval abbey near Paris.[11] Today the abbey accommodates vulnerable young people in social housing, funded by a Rothschild trust; it thus seems very likely indeed that *Maubuisson* should have belonged to the Rothschild family in the late 1930s too.[12]

A few days after his arrival in *Maubuisson*, Oswald received a first letter from his parents, forwarded to him by the Rothschild hospital: "My dearest *Burli*! I thank you for your card from Paris and [we] are very happy to have heard from you and that you are fine and doing well," Hermann Kernberg wrote. "I will enclose a stamp in each of my letters, my dearest *Burli*, and *Papa* asks to write quite often," he went on. Frieda reminded her son to eat a lot so he would stay in good health and Oswald's brother Fritz sent "kisses and best wishes." At the end of the letter, Hermann repeated his promise the separation of the family was only temporary: "We hope to God to be able to leave too very soon and then we'll bring you over to us quickly."

Otto too sent his cousin Oswald a postcard that reflects the increasingly worsening situation of the Jews in Nazi Vienna: "I envy you for having already made it out," the ten-year-old wrote.

As an adult, Arthur would later barely remember his time in *Maubuisson*, quite unlike Erich Grünebaum, who would become his best friend in France. In his unpublished autobiography *The Loneliest Boy*, Grünebaum – today Eric Greene – describes the medieval abbey: "It had beautiful park-like grounds that we children were free to roam."[13]

Greene also recorded his first encounter with Oswald: "We were grouped by age in the sleeping dormitories at Maubuisson…. It was here that we formed lifelong friendships. I formed a particularly lasting friendship with a boy from Vienna by the name of Oswald Kernberg who was only three months younger than I and had similar likes and dislikes."

6. VILLA HELVETIA

Paris, April 1939: Spring was in the air, and the branches of the trees were covered with tiny buds. At the same time, Hitler secretly planned the attack on Poland. In Germany and Austria, the situation for Jews became increasingly precarious – and now, some of them felt the added concern for their children. The Jewish Community of Vienna sent out panicked messages to the French aid organizations: The parents had not heard from their children in weeks! In retrospect, the reason for the interrupted communication seems quite moving: Oswald and the other children had written so many letters to parents and relatives that the budget of the aid organizations was completely overstrained.

The Rothschild Committee tried to find a cost-effective solution: "To remedy this problem, … we decided… to centralize the mail going to Germany … and send it to you twice a week per express parcel."[1]

The children missed their parents. Most of them had never been separated from their families for such a long time. Especially the younger children suffered from a situation they did not quite grasp. Many of them did not understand why they had to leave home and feared they had been sent away by their parents as a punishment. The feeling of being lost was even amplified by the unstable circumstances in the first few weeks since their departure: first the twenty-hour train ride, then three days in a hospital, and then a good three weeks in a monastery – the young refugees could not come to rest.

"My dear, sweet *Putzilein*," cousin Gina wrote to Oswald, trying to console him: "Don't get upset and don't cry because we are not with you. With God's help, we will see each other soon."

The encouraging letter reached Oswald in *Château Maubuisson*. Then, it was time for yet another move.

* * *

"Two newly remodeled country houses surrounded by a magnificent park on a hill near Paris have become home to 130 young immigrants," Trude Frankl wrote in a letter to the Viennese Jewish Community in April 1939.[2] The educator was in Paris at the time, having once again accompanied a children's transport. "Furnished in accordance with *Montessori* principles," she went on, "these 'children's houses,' with all their small colorful furniture and funny children's scenes painted on the walls, are a delightful sight. For the time being, the children have not been given any specific duties, only learning French and doing a lot of crafts and gardening, and appear to be immensely happy." Frankl's almost euphoric report paints a completely different picture than the previous descriptions of the first few weeks in France. What had happened?

Oswald and over a hundred other children had moved and now lived in the *Villa Helvetia* on *rue de Valmy*, in Montmorency, a residential suburb 12.5 miles from Paris. Formerly a resort hotel for wealthy Swiss, *Villa Helvetia* had not been ready when the young refugees arrived, which is why they had not been able to move in at once.

Whenever the weather allowed it, the OSE liked
to teach the young refugees outdoors.

When Ernst Papanek first took up his position as director of the OSE children's homes at the beginning of 1939, there were only a few months left to convert the newly acquired and quite run-down *Villa Helvetia* into a child-friendly home. Floors were torn out and walls installed to create smaller rooms, dozens of bathrooms were built, and colorful, child-sized furniture was made. Like Ernst Papanek himself, most of the 100 or so craftsmen were Social Democrats or communists from Austria and Poland who had fled to France, most of them working without work permits. The local prefect turned a blind eye to the illegal work, because the influential Gunzbourg and Rothschild families supported the home and because it was meant to house needy children.[3]

When the renovation was finally completed, Ernst Papanek welcomed the first group of children at the nearby train station in Enghien-les-Bains and accompanied them to their new home. The hard work had paid off: "I was very, very impressed," Arthur later recalled. "They had set up little tables for children. They were our size and we could eat and play there. And it was all colorful. The tables were blue and red and yellow. It immediately made us feel like we were in a nice place. And as it turned out: it really was a nice place to be!"[4]

A large, curved staircase led up to the entrance of the three-story *Villa Helvetia*. The villa had been built before 1900 and appeared inviting and almost homely with its gable roofs and numerous verandas and balconies. On the floor above the spacious wooden veranda was a winter garden with large windows and tastefully carved wooden decorations. From the window on the third floor, you could catch a glimpse of the Eiffel Tower's light flashing in the distance. Japonism, which especially in France served as inspiration for Impressionism and Art Nouveau, was very dominant in the noble villa. Exotic birds and Japanese temples, fishing boats, and lilies peeped out between mountains, lakes, and bamboo plants, the idyllic pictures radiating a cheerful kind of peace – until the *Villa's* peaceful times were over in the spring of 1939.

From now on, children's laughter replaced contemplative silence. In a photo album sent to OSE supporters and donors as an annual report in 1940, none of the pictures allow a clear view of the veranda, since it was always crowded by dozens of children doing gymnastics on its railing, peeling potatoes sitting on its stairs or rehearsing for parties and events in front of the entrance door.

The *Villa Helvetia* was surrounded by a large park, including a few palm trees. This huge garden in particular left a strong impression on the refugee children upon their arrival. "May Jewish children go into the garden?" they asked Ernst Papanek in astonishment.[5] In the light of the children's experiences, the question seemed justified: In the National Socialist *Reich* Jews were strictly forbidden from accessing public parks.

Refugee children peeling potatoes.

The wonderful and freely accessible park, the colorful children's chairs and the spacious veranda all made Oswald feel very welcome at *Villa Helvetia*. Even more important to him though, was the fact he was now among peers: "It was all German and Austrian kids. And they had all been sent away by their parents," he told me later.

* * *

"Dear *Mama*," Oswald wrote and put down the pen. Lost in thought, he tucked a reddish lock of hair behind his ear, then gave up with a sigh and began to paint a picture. A good dozen boys and girls sat around him at a long table the adults had carried into the garden. Everyone was staring at their drawing blocks with concentrated faces. It was the beginning of May and Mother's Day was coming up soon. After the mail tragedy, OSE made sure all children would send Mother's Day poems home on time.

Oswald struggled badly, but the result apparently went down well. The Kernbergs received his letter two weeks later and promptly replied: "And now my sweet, sweet boy, I thank you from the bottom of my heart that you were so sweet to draw such a nice picture for your dearest loving mother for Mother's Day and that you added such a beautiful poem. We were deeply moved by your kind attention," Hermann Kernberg wrote to his son. To reaffirm their delight over Oswald's letter, the family sent him a big package of chocolate.

In the beginning, there were no real lessons at *Villa Helvetia*, but the teachers played and crafted a lot with the children. Photos show a wide range of leisure activities: the young refugees pushing each other around in wheelbarrows, playing dodge ball or tug-of-war with over 30 participants. When the weather got warm enough, a teacher regularly hosed down the children, who kept running through the water jet in their bathing suits, squealing. There was a sandpit for the little ones, which they loved as much as the aquarium in their playroom.

Montmorency: a group of girls performing the "dance of the flowers in bloom."

According to OSE reports, their protégés were all in good health, the association managing to avoid epidemics and childhood diseases, common in children's homes. After their arrival, many children gained up to twenty pounds, roughly the level of malnutrition they had suffered from before coming to France.

Today, when looking at the many photographs that have been preserved from the days of the children's home at *Villa Helvetia*, the first thing I notice is the children's neat clothing. Quite unlike how you would picture refugee children! The boys wore knee-high socks and tweed jackets, sometimes also sailor suits or lederhosen, and the girls wore bows in their hair, almost all of them sporting the same pageboy hairstyle. Even the three- and four-year-old kindergarten children always appeared primly coiffed and dressed up. As much as this might have been in line with the zeitgeist, it also showed the great importance OSE attached to personal hygiene and proper appearance. However, the clothes and shoes the children had brought with them were often in very poor condition – once again the Baroness de Gunzbourg helped out with a generous donation.[6]

A thrilling chess game in *Villa Helvetia*.

* * *

Nowadays, two dozen police cars stand in a concrete parking lot where the children once used to play catch in the garden. Since 1976, *Villa Helvetia* has been home to the Montmorency police station. In the fall of 2017, I meet Major Julien Trotet there, the chief communications officer for the police in Val-d'Oise, the greater Paris area. Due to the terrorist attacks of recent years, the state of emergency is still in force in France, which is why it is not possible to visit a police station without prior permission. I thus had to file a formal request with the Ministry of the Interior. After four weeks of waiting, I was finally informed I could come and visit.

The formerly magnificent *Villa Helvetia* is now in a terribly desolate state, the paint on the walls peeling off both outside and inside, one window smashed and broken chairs piling up in the conference room. The *Commissariat* (police station) is the only house in the villa-lined neighborhood that has not been extensively renovated. Five years ago, many of the police tasks were handed over to the police headquarters in the neighboring town, and the number of employees was reduced, leaving a lot of unused office space.

"Are you all dressed?" Major Trotet calls out through the closed door in a loud voice before leading me into the changing rooms in the basement, which used to be a wine cellar, serving as an air raid shelter during the war. A broad-shouldered man is tying his combat boots, another pulls his bulletproof vest over his bare torso. Movie posters, group photos of policemen in riot gear and pictures of scantily clad women hang on the lockers.

Unbothered by our entry, the men give me a warm welcome. Lots of polite greetings echo across the room and I find myself shaking a multitude of hands. The major too is greeted personally by each officer. Politeness seems to be the top priority here: During shift change half an hour later, each police officer says goodbye to every one of his colleagues with a handshake, and the female officers and secretaries get two kisses on the cheek, as is customary in France.

For over an hour and a half, I explore every corner of the police station with Trotet – from the basement to the attic, from the archive to the toilets. The major – or "majoor" (as in "door") as his colleagues call him in melodic French –, a slim, young-looking man in his forties, wears a short-sleeved light blue shirt with a small French flag on the breast pocket. Apart from him, none of the officers here speak English – although they try to amidst great laughter. Three patrolmen desperately try to offer me something to drink, but the only sentence they manage in English is "What else?" – George Clooney's famous reply from the Nespresso ad – their own way to ask me if I want to have a coffee.

Today, the Villa Helvetia houses Montmorency's
police station. Lilly Maier visited there in 2017.

Two of the secretaries have historic postcards hanging next to their desks, showing the *Villa Helvetia* as a Swiss resort hotel. The two have been working in the police station for 40 years and are the only employees who know the building once housed an orphanage. Yet they believed the home had accommodated real orphans. When I tell them that it was actually Jewish refugee children who used to live here alone, because the French government banned their parents from entering the country, they look at me, baffled. Most of the police officers stationed here are completely unaware of the history of their police station. They all listen carefully to Major Trotet as he translates my explanations and leaf with interest through the photos I have brought with me.

Of all OSE homes, *Villa Helvetia* is the one with the most surviving photographs. Together we compare the black and white pictures with the current building. Today, the open wooden veranda – the heart of the old *Helvetia* – lies hidden behind an outer wall, Wanted posters and photos of missing young people hang on the Japanese-painted tiles. In the adjoining room, Major Trotet taps the walls to find out which ones are still original and which have been added later. "If walls could talk, they would have a lot to tell," he says with a thoughtful look.

The visit leaves a strong impression on me too: After months of researching in archives and books, the building feels surprisingly alive to me. As I look through the window towards the park where the children hosted a big circus in 1939, I can almost hear their voices and laughter. In my mind's eye, I see Oswald and his comrades dance around in their colorful costumes.

* * *

"One, two, jump!" a loud voice boomed over the great meadow, still slightly damp with dew. The children always started the morning with rhythmic gymnastics, jumping jacks, and running. One boy did gymnastics in lederhosen, the rest wore short sports pants and undershirts. Then it was time for breakfast, which Ernst Papanek always started with a *"Bon appétit, mes enfants,"* ("Enjoy your food, my children"). Boys and girls in turn had table duty; even the three and four-year-olds took part, carrying bread from table to table. The children were also encouraged to assume responsibility in the home in other ways: they had to make their beds themselves, clean their shoes and tidy up their classrooms, the youngest wielding brooms twice as high as themselves. Visitors frequently reported on the good table manners and general pleasant nature of the OSE charges – no small matter what with such a large group of young people.[7]

The fact the teachers reminded the children of home made their new life at *Villa Helvetia* easier. "Almost all of the teachers were refugees from Germany or Austria," Arthur explained to me. In her report to the Viennese Jewish Community, Trude Frankl too had observed that the charges were particularly pleased by the fact the young teachers were "all from Vienna."[8] However, some of the children complained about having first had to learn a new language upon their arrival in France: Viennese.

Jause (snack), *Schlagobers* (whipped cream), *Servus* (hello), *Faschiertes* (minced meat), *Mäderl* (girl) – albeit German, were still foreign words for the young refuges from Berlin, Mainz, or Frankfurt. Very soon though, the director Ernst Papanek familiarized them with his broad Viennese dialect.

In the memories of the now adult children, Papanek is over-whelmingly described positively; he was the most popular adult in Montmorency. One fact, in particular, is emphasized again and again, namely that the teacher would show such sincere respect for each and every child. "Papanek had the incredible ability to relate to each child," Ernst Valfer told me in the summer of 2016. "As if it were a special child that he personally knew." A retired psychologist, Valfer was fourteen years old when he came to Montmorency and thus has a better recollection of many details than Arthur. "Papanek was just an incredible and a very lovable man," Valfer continued. "But with a strong determination to do what he needed to do."

In photographs, Papanek's smile and bright eyes behind his big, round glasses are striking. Despite being in his mid-thirties and thus still relatively young, he was already half bald and usually wore a suit, shirt, and tie to work. His formal appearance stood in stark contrast with his socialist manners: Papanek allowed the children to address him casually and call him by his first name, just one of many signs of his extremely progressive and anti-authoritarian style that shaped the spirit of *Villa Helvetia*. Arthur liked Papanek for his open nature: "Papanek was always very direct and kept us informed about all current events – whether good or bad. All the children loved him."

7. ERNST PAPANEK: MORE THAN JUST A TEACHER

Ernst Papanek was born in Vienna in 1900 into a Jewish middle-class family. Very early, he demonstrated a keen enthusiasm for the Social Democratic movement and gradually turned away from Judaism. He began to study medicine, before interrupting his studies and training to become a teacher at the *Pädagogisches Institut* (Pedagogical Institute) in Vienna instead.[1] From the very start, the charismatic young man connected his work with children to his political activities: "In his eyes, pedagogy and politics merged seamlessly together," sociologist Hanna Papanek claims in a text about her father-in-law. Ernst Papanek's educational work was the "extension of his political conviction that it is possible to change the world through education and democracy."[2]

In 1925, he married Dr. Helene "Lene" Golstern, a doctor from a wealthy Jewish family, whose father owned and ran the renowned Fango-sanatorium in Vienna. Lene too was a Social Democrat and as little religious as her husband. The couple raised their children as atheists.

In 1932, Ernst Papanek, serving at the time as the chairman of the *Wiener Sozialistische Jugend* (Viennese Socialist Youth), was elected into the city council. He kept that office until the February Uprising in 1934, when Austria was shaken by a civil war ending with hundreds of dead, after the Social Democrats' revolt against the authoritarian regime of Chancellor Dollfuss. After the violent repression of the uprising, Papanek and the other leaders of the Austrian Social Democratic party had to flee to what was then Czechoslovakia – right in time too, as shortly afterward the fascist Corporate State issued a death sentence against Papanek.[3]

The OSE's home director, Ernst Papanek, with his wife Lene, in Montmorency.

In Brno, Papanek joined the international office of the Austrian Social Democrats. His wife Lene had not left with him, as it was believed at first that the exiled politicians would soon be allowed to return to Austria. Furthermore, she provided for the livelihood of the family in Vienna, all the while financially supporting her husband in exile. She did visit Papanek during the summer holidays with their two sons, Gustav and Georg.[4]

Shortly before Nazi Germany annexed Austria in the spring of 1938, the exiled leaders of the Austrian Social Democratic Party relocated from Brno to Paris. Papanek – now reunited with his family – was able to enter the country thanks to a personal visa delivered by the French Prime Minister Léon Blum, a socialist himself.[5]

The family planned to immigrate to America. For a few months, in order to earn money for the passage, Papanek took over the management of a holiday camp for children of socialist refugees in La Baule, on the Atlantic coast. Once back in Paris, arrangements ahead of the journey were in full swing, the ship passage was paid for, the suitcases packed – until in the end it all turned out very differently. Three weeks before their scheduled departure, Papanek was contacted by one of his wife's relatives, who worked for OSE and offered him a position as general director of the OSE children's homes. Despite his wife's vehement and anxious protestations, Papanek, then 38 years old, accepted the job. "I… had the queasy feeling that this was not a very good time for a man who had done so much talking about standing up to Hitler to be running off to America," Papanek wrote in his autobiography.[6] Initially, he had only meant to work for OSE for six months, but the war changed everything. In the fall of 1939, Papanek let his visa for America expire, so he would not have to leave Oswald and the other refugee children.[7]

* * *

"My father was a great optimist," Gustav "Gus" Papanek tells me in the winter of 2017. "And he had tremendous faith in the goodness of human beings."

"I thought that occasionally he was too optimistic," Gus' wife Hanna adds. "But I didn't think any less of him for that."

As a thirteen-year-old, Gus (who back then was still called Gustl) lived together with the other refugee children – and separated from his parents – in one of OSE's homes in Montmorency. Just like the other children, he addressed his father in the socialist way, calling him Ernst. Today the professor of economics lives in Massachusetts, in the USA, with his wife Hanna. They have known each other since their youth: Hanna's parents were German Social Democrats, who had fled their country and lived in exile in Paris, just like the Papanek family, and had sent their daughter Hanna to the home in Montmorency. Hanna Papanek, an anthropologist, has written several essays and books about her father-in-law Ernst, following a distinctive approach she calls "participative history," namely the historical reappraisal of events one has experienced oneself – much in the manner of a sociologist conducting a field study. Yet during my interview with the Papaneks, it is mostly Gus who gives a quite vivid account of his father.

"He was also very courageous and totally dedicated to pursuing what he thought was the right course," Gus recalls. "He spent all his life trying to improve things for humanity. And he was quite willing to make all sorts of sacrifices to do that and take all sorts of risks." Ernst Papanek drew his strength from his optimism and his unshakable faith in democratic socialism. "He always believed that ultimately the forces of truth and justice and righteousness would triumph," his son declares.

Papanek tried to exemplify and convey this view of the world to the Jewish refugee children. "His main aim was that we felt that our situation was not hopeless," Gus explains to me. "That we were not helpless and that we were not inferior beings as we had been told by the Nazis. I think that was his principle aim, to create an environment in which the children felt safe and secure. And that even though their parents were not there in most cases, in the end, things would come out alright."

Ernst Papanek would often remind the young refugees not to lose hope, as his son recalls. "Even when the German army was at the gates of Paris, he always said, 'Ultimately we will win.'"

Even after the end of the war, Ernst Papanek pursued his work as a pedagogue in America, working mostly with youths with behavioral problems. Yet he saw his work in France as his "most significant" and considered the time he spent in the country as the most important period in his life.

* * *

Three hundred and four children arrived in the OSE homes in Montmorency in 1939, 21 among them in such a weak state they were immediately sent to Arcachon for a cure. 283 children thus lived under the care of Ernst Papanek and his team, most of them Jewish, along with a small group of children of persecuted Austrian Social Democrats.[8]

To accommodate and provide education and care for the children, OSE rented and bought other chateaux throughout France, Ernst Papanek running the four homes in and around Montmorency: *Villa Helvetia, La Petite Colonie* for preschool-aged children, *Les Tourelles* (the turrets) for the older, non-religious children and *Villa La Chesnaie* in Eaubonne for the religious children. After a brief stay in *Villa Helvetia*, Oswald was sent to Eaubonne, which put an end to his constant moving, at least for the time being, as he would spend a little over a year in *Villa La Chesnaie*.

Today researchers consider community life in homes and exile schools as a much better type of accommodation for unaccompanied minors. Living within foster families, as in the case of the British *Kindertransports* for instance, often proved a quite traumatic experience, because the children were subjected to a new environment completely on their own. On the contrary, thanks to the company of their comrades in misfortune, the children experienced "less individual helplessness and isolation," psychotherapist Anna Wexberg-Kubesch explains.[9]

The four OSE homes in Montmorency must be considered an especially successful example in this regard, being far more than just a safe home for the refugee children. Within just a few months, Ernst Papanek managed to build an impressive educational system, which would be deemed progressive even today. In that connection, OSE archivist Katy Hazan speaks of the "innovative education methods" Papanek brought to OSE. Papanek himself confidently called his undertaking the "most massive experiment in progressive education ever attempted – saturation treatment twenty-four hours a day."[10]

Young teenagers compete during a sports event.

* * *

As an adult, Arthur would often tell me: "Apart from the fact many of us were homesick, life in the homes was really nice. Almost like in a holiday camp."

Yet young Oswald's character had noticeably changed in France. In hindsight, all his former friends describe him as a serious and quiet child – nothing like the little rascal he had been in Vienna, pulling out hair from horses' manes and dropping water balloons on passers-by. The cause for this change in behavior was probably not only due to his new circumstances but mostly to what Oswald himself experienced after the Austrian *Anschluss* to Nazi Germany.

"Deeply traumatized by what happened in their home countries, the children first had to get reaccustomed to the normal life of a child," Claudia Göbetzberger writes.[11] From the very start, Ernst Papanek devoted a lot of thought to the psychological problems of his protégés. Most children experienced fear and mistrust towards others, as well as feelings of guilt, being themselves in safety when their families were not. After years of Nazi persecution, they had also often developed a feeling of inferiority, with some children feeling ashamed of being Jewish, especially those who would have liked to join the Hitler Youth like their friends had. Papanek speaks in this regard of a *"Massenneurose"* (mass neurosis) – in his view, the community life provided by the OSE homes was exactly what the children needed to treat that.[12]

Papanek based his approach on Alfred Adler's individual psychology. A renowned psychotherapist and Social Democrat, Adler ran the Viennese institute where Papanek trained as a teacher. According to Adler, people can only thrive under favorable circumstances, living in a group provided such circumstances. In later writings, Papanek himself frequently emphasized the "supporting function of community feeling" especially in the case of traumatized children.[13]

Papanek felt his most important mission was to make the children happy again. In his autobiography *Out of the Fire*, he recounts how, after years of living under Nazi rule, many of them had to be taught again how to play: "They just stood around waiting to be told what to do. They didn't ask any questions. They didn't even wander around aimlessly... We were going to have to show them how to play. We were going to have to teach them how to be children."[14]

Helping the children understand they bore no responsibility for all that had happened to them was equally important in the eyes of the pedagogue. Group singing, sport, celebrations, and festivities, as well as a lot of different recreational activities all served the purpose of creating a feeling of community and helping the children relearn social patterns. Papanek and his colleagues also attempted to help the children work on their traumatic experiences within playgroups.[15]

Papanek's optimistic spirit was also reflected in his educational work. As mentioned previously, he told the children time and again that Hitler would not win the war. This did not mean he ignored the world outside the homes, quite on the contrary: Papanek always informed his protégés in great detail about world events, never concealing the danger the children's parents were in. He would also always clearly insist on the fact that "the past of the Jewish refugee children must not be repressed, but on the contrary must be used to build their personality," sociologist Gabriele Rühl-Nawabi says, describing his work.[16]

Life within the homes was supposed to prepare the children for their future life. In an essay he wrote in 1940, Papanek says: "We had tried to morally educate the refugee children in the Montmorency homes, so they would become conscious and upright persons, bravely willing to take charge of their own lives, and able to do so because they were not educated to become charity cases, but daring and knowing young people, who have learned to work."[17]

The school that he opened in *Les Tourelles* played a significant part in Papanek's educational concept. One easily forgets the fact most of the children had not been to a proper school in a long time! For some of the children coming from Germany, it was years since they had last been at school. At first, Jewish pupils had been relegated to the back rows before being expelled from schools altogether. Hastily opened and desperately overcrowded Jewish schools had not been able to offer an appropriate replacement. The educators in Montmorency thus resorted to many tricks to gradually reaccustom the children to classes and turn the learning process into an adventure. Classes often took place outdoors for instance, as a great deal of pictures document: six school benches had promptly been carried outside in the great garden, the children listening closely to a teacher in a dotted dress reading to them from a book. Very often the children were not even aware of the fact they were having classes, because Papanek and his team would hide the fact behind exciting debates or practical games.

Ernst Papanek's wife Lene was his most important ally at all times. Despite her initial protestations against her husband's appointment as director, Lene Papanek became a committed OSE member herself, working as a doctor in the Montmorency homes. Besides her medical work, she also assumed many organizational duties, at times even standing in for her husband as director. Hanna Papanek describes her as having been, in Montmorency, "inseparable from her husband. Most letters from the home children mention 'Ernst and Lene' as if it were but one name, not two."[18]

Besides Alfred Adler, Ernst Papanek's educational work was greatly influenced by Otto Glöckel and his Austrian School Reform that Papanek himself witnessed as a young teacher in the interwar period. Glöckel, who had been president of the city's School Board in Vienna from 1922 to 1934, promoted the so-called "work school" (at odds with the previously in force monarchic "cram school") that would leave the students plenty of individual room. Characteristic features of the reform, many of which Papanek put into practice in Montmorency, included mixed classes for boys and girls, lively and child-friendly lessons, plenty of excursions, the election of class and school presidents, as well as a general "democratization of school life."[19]

Glöckel meant to push open the classroom doors and allow the children to come into contact with "real life." With this in mind, Papanek planned frequent excursions for his OSE protégés, who visited the workshop of sculptor Nahum Aronson several times, for instance. Papanek's worst fear was to see the homes turn into some kind of ghetto and the field trips were a good way to counteract this.

An excursion to Paris, planned weeks in advance, was a highlight of the year 1939. The OSE's board members came in person to collect the children and drive them to Paris, 12.5 miles away, in fifty elegant black cars. The children crammed into the backseats, chatting excitedly and wearing their best clothes for the day in the big city. The visit to the Eiffel Tower was of course, an obligatory stop, the young refugees managing to stand still on the stairs just long enough to have a souvenir picture taken. At the end of the day, they returned to their home, exhausted but full of beautiful new impressions. "You could sense the growing feeling that we were finally becoming part of Paris and therefore of France," Ernst Papanek recalled.[20]

The Jewish refugee children on a daytrip to Paris in the spring of 1939.

Because of the constant influx of new protégés, setting up regular classes such as language or science lessons proved quite difficult at first. Instead, the children were divided according to their age into three different discussion groups to talk about current issues that included elements from various school subjects. Papanek was especially anxious to incorporate knowledge about world events into the children's education. The sensational sinking of the American submarine USS Squalus, in the spring of 1939, was thus extensively discussed in Montmorency. Papanek and the children calculated the amount of oxygen left inside the submarine, marked the distance between the boat and Montmorency on a huge world map, and discussed the innovative techniques used to rescue the men on board – the children hence incidentally learning basic mathematical and physical principles.[21]

With his deliberately anti-authoritarian educational method, Papanek would not hear of homework, grades, or any kind of physical punishment in the classroom.[22] Next to theoretical classes, it was very important to him to prepare the children for a successful life in a practical way, notwithstanding their uncertain future. In this regard, OSE's partnership with another Jewish organization proved quite beneficial. Founded in 1880 in Russia, ORT, an association promoting handicraft and agricultural work among Jews, campaigned worldwide for the practical training of Jewish youth, establishing workshops in all OSE homes to that end.[23] Learning a trade was supposed to enable the young refugees to provide for themselves and earn a living in the future. Much like an apprenticeship, the older boys were trained to become carpenters or cobblers, while the girls were given sewing classes. "These were all skills that were transferable to other countries," Gus Papanek explained to me. "You didn't have to have an education in the country to be able to fix shoes."

The young refugees received craft training in France, as cobblers for instance.

The workshops were well equipped: leather polish, cloths, hammers, an old pair of shoes for practice, and a youthful teacher in the middle of it all, instructing a group of three students each on the various tricks of the trade. In the carpentry workshop, groups of half a dozen youths each sawed, planed, and hammered at the workbench. Oswald was the youngest apprentice in the carpentry workshop, where he learned how to make furniture. The newly acquired handicrafts also helped furnish and maintain the villas the children lived in. "The carpentry shop was invaluable in a home which made much of its own furniture," Papanek stated in OSE's annual report.[24]

The younger children were given preliminary handicraft classes, such as knitting lessons for instance. Children were also taught cooking and each child was given his own garden bed to tend. The practical training provided within the ORT workshops made up most of the classes (20 hours a week, with 19 additional hours being dedicated to theoretical subjects such as languages, mathematics, or history.) At first, the classes were taught in German at *Les Tourelles*, later increasingly often in French. Some of the children would also attend the local French school.[25]

Giving up German was especially difficult for the older children, who felt the language connected them to their homeland. German was also the language the children would use when communicating with their parents and families. Once a week, the young refugees were encouraged to write to their parents, the educators regularly sending the latter reports about their children's well-being.

* * *

A lot of what we know today about the children's life in France we owe to Ernst Papanek's voluminous papers I find in the *New York Public Library*, in the heart of Manhattan.[26] From the outside, the most famous library in New York stands out with its temple-like columns and stone lions; inside over 55 million media are kept in no less imposing reading rooms, remindful of Hogwarts with their meter-long shelves, colorful ceiling frescos, and great, gleaming chandeliers.

A prestigious staircase leads to the *Brooke Russell Astor Reading Room*, specifically reserved for researchers. In the summer of 2016, this reading room becomes my second home. For weeks, I work my way through thousands of letters, newspaper articles, writings, and pictures from Ernst Papanek's long life. The midsummer heat outside is sweltering at 104°F, but because of the many old books, the temperature inside the room is kept so low I have to wrap three scarves around my neck as I sit working at my laptop.

A great deal of the letters were written on extremely thin and cheap paper, such as it was used during the war, tearing or disintegrating at the slightest touch, and I must wear white cloth gloves to handle the documents. I meticulously work my way through the 41 grey boxes, often finding some documents that have been misfiled or discovering a few of their pages stuck together. I would almost have missed, because of that, a quite remarkable trove indeed: a letter of thanks Oswald's parents sent to Ernst Papanek.

The letter, written in August 1939, is addressed to the "praiseworthy management of the home." In his very readable, rounded handwriting, Hermann Kernberg wrote: "My son, Oswald Kernberg, currently finds himself under your kind and attentive care and as a father, I feel the need to express my deepest thanks to you from the very bottom of my heart, on behalf of my family as well as in my own name. We shall never forget, as long as we live, the great kindness you showed in taking care of and protecting our dearest and most precious child. We pray to God our Lord every day for you, may his blessing reward you all for your good deed. Please allow us to express our deepest devotion to you and reiterate our most grateful thanks. With highest respect, Frieda and Hermann Kernberg."

This moving letter shows not only Hermann's gratitude for the rescue of his son but also that after over six months in France,

Oswald was doing very well, his parents no longer worrying over his well-being. There are a lot of such private letters in Papanek's papers, parents wanting to express their thanks for the good care he took of their children.

Papanek always referred to the parents – and not OSE – as his "clients," in the interests of whom he acted,[27] thus telling the children time and again their parents had sent them to France to protect them from National Socialism and not because they did not love them anymore. This prevented the children from "ending up caught in a loyalty conflict, as [the home management] did not cut them off from anyone at home and never questioned their parents' authority and love," historian Claudia Göbetzberger analyzes.[28]

* * *

Papanek's educational views began to show results already after a few weeks, the children feeling less and less homesick, as Trude Frankl wrote in a report to the IKG. What remained, though, was an "extreme worry over the well-being and emigration prospects of parents and siblings." Frankl also complained about an issue that put the children under a lot of pressure: "Unfortunately most of the children had been instructed by their parents to work towards their own immigration to France and having absolutely no means to do so, the children feel very bad about it. In the future, it should be made clear to the parents they only uselessly burden their children emotionally."[29]

Papanek relied on a way to help the children regain a sense of control over their own life that must be regarded as the most important educational element of his work in Montmorency: the introduction and implementation of a far-reaching co-administration of the home by the children themselves. The children's homes had their own constitution, meant to regulate the residents' coexistence regardless of their age. The preamble of that constitution reads as follows:

"The children and adults living in the OSE children's homes form a community that organizes life within the homes by means of a democratic joint management... The democratic rights and duties of our small community are the same as in any other larger one."[30]

The adults provided the first draft of the constitution, complemented by a set of house rules that would then be discussed, extended, and adjusted by the young refugees. In the final version of the constitution, all children from the age of eight years and up had active and passive voting rights, electing room representatives, group, house, sport, and celebration committees, an overall home council, as well as a disciplinary board including a court of appeal.[31] The children worked out proposals and suggestions within the different committees they would then submit to Papanek and the other educators.

In the children's homes' annual report, Papanek insisted on the fact that this collaboration between children and adults was by no means a game, but rather a matter of considerable educational significance. Involving the children in their own management was meant to restore their self-confidence and teach them about democratic structures at odds with the Nazi dictatorship. This moral character building was supposed to "form free and reliable men, able to fight all difficulties and not to be suppressed by any persecutions."[32]

The disciplinary board held a special significance for the children who had to justify their wrongdoings in front of their peers. Papanek was not in favor of punishments, rather considering that violence breeds violence. Moreover, in the case of the Jewish refugee children, he believed any punishment issued by adults would only awaken Nazi terror memories. Yet when justifying themselves to their peers, the children were forced to reflect on the consequences of their own actions on society – in Papanek's eyes a much more effective method.[33]

Important to him was also the fact that his concept of co-administration was not synonymous with self-administration. The children could always rely on the fact that the adults protected them and made the fundamental educational decisions.

At first, there was strong opposition to Papanek's reforms within OSE, with many wondering whether it was necessary to introduce an entirely new school system, especially in times of political unrest. What was more, this special kind of pedagogy required a lot of work and money, and many OSE members considered it far too progressive. But Papanek received a lot of support from the rich, liberal Jewish communities in Paris, led by Baroness Yvonne de Gunzbourg, who managed to stand up to the conservative and orthodox critics within OSE.[34]

* * *

For Ernst Papanek, the traditional conveying of knowledge was only ever a small part of his educational project. Creating a sense of community and communicating his optimistic attitude towards life, along with the democratic co-administration of the homes, the practical workshop classes, and even the various festivities and excursions were given a much higher priority in his pedagogy.

Many OSE students later became top of their class when attending French public schools, some of them even joining specialized schools, like Ernst Weil for instance, who was accepted at *Le Cordon Bleu* in Paris, one of the most famous cooking schools in the world and who would later become a well-known baker and TV cook in San Francisco.

If one measures Papanek's pedagogy by the later professional success of many of his protégés, as well as by the length and intensity of the friendships forged during their OSE years, one has to admit it proved very successful indeed. The pedagogue managed "not only to build a network of children's homes, that ensured the children's physical survival, but he also protected them from spiritual, cultural and social extermination," historian Slavka Pogranova asserts.[35]

The strong impact of Ernst Papanek's education methods on the lives of the children appears all the more impressive when bearing in mind the children only spent two years in France. And that is not all: Ernst Papanek was forced to leave "his" children after only one year.

8. *VILLA LA CHESNAIE* IN EAUBONNE

Mid-September 2017, I set off for Eaubonne to visit *Villa La Chesnaie*, a little more than three miles away from Montmorency. The *Journées Européennes du Patrimoine* (European Heritage Days) are held this weekend in France, an annual event during which private buildings are opened to the public. Unlike Montmorency, Eaubonne is not a villa area and the stately *Villa La Chesnaie* would immediately catch one's eye next to all the plain, new buildings, were it not entirely hidden from view behind a tall hedge. Even my taxi driver, who has been living in the neighborhood for years, has no clue a mansion is concealed behind the tall green bushes.

As I walk through the big wrought iron gate, I feel like I have just stepped into the children's book *The Secret Garden*: in the shade of great trees, tiny pale lilac flowers sprout from the leaf-covered ground and mossy stone tables and a single female statue stand on the lawn. The great oak trees after which the villa was named long ago (in French, the word *chesnaie* means "oak grove") have almost all disappeared, replaced by lime trees, cypresses, and maple trees. The gravel path leads from the gate to the backside of the mansion, in the front of which the wooded gardens give way to a well-tended park with mowed lawns, deck chairs, and wrought iron tables.

I let my eyes wander over the three-story *Villa La Chesnaie*, from the impressive, 13 feet high ground floor, sporting windows almost as high, to the converted attic under the roof. With its symmetrical design, the *Villa* looks simple, yet elegant. The mansion is flanked on either side by two wings, the *Grand Salon*, the most beautiful room in the *Villa*, lying in between. A dozen people are sitting in the sunlight-flooded *Salon* at the moment, listening to the words of Hervé Collet. The grizzled local historian reads from his book *Les belles heures du château de La Chesnaie à Eaubonne* ("The Beautiful Hours of Chateau La Chesnaie in Eaubonne") with a deep, sonorous voice. While Collet recounts the beginnings of the *Villa*, built in 1749, the mistress of the house, wearing an elegant flowered blazer, rearranges a few empty chairs. Silvery grey wood paneling with antique-looking stone friezes adorn the walls above the windows and doors, and glass candlesticks rest on the marble mantelpieces. A chandelier hangs solemnly from the ceiling. As shabby and run-down as *Villa Helvetia* appears to be today, *Villa La Chesnaie* on the other hand has lost nothing of its splendor and magnificence. Today, merely German names carved into the walls of the cellar point to the fact that Jewish children have lived here from 1939 to 1940.

* * *

A few months after *Villa Helvetia* was completed, OSE opened a home for orthodox children in *Villa La Chesnaie*. Opening a religious home had by no means been part of OSE's initial plan. The *Comité*, run by the Rothschilds, had even expressly requested no orthodox children should be sent to France – "out of purely technical and practical considerations," as taking care of these children appeared to be more complicated, according to what was stated in a letter sent to the IKG. However, despite the *Comité*'s direct orders, a representative of the German Jewish community failed to convey this wish to the Jewish community in Vienna, as I gather from a very heated letter exchange.[1] The reasons for this omission are not known, but the fact is the Viennese community was not the only one receiving this specific piece of information too late. The *Kindertransport* from Frankfurt, for instance, consisted almost exclusively of children from the Jewish Orthodox orphanage.[2] It is quite possible that Rabbi Marx from Frankfurt intentionally did not pass on that information to the representative of the IKG, so the emigration of the children from the orphanage would not be put at risk.

Forty Jewish orthodox refugee children thus arrived in France on a *Kindertransport*, causing "no little embarrassment" in Paris, as Trude Frankl noted in her report because kosher kitchens had now to be installed as quickly as possible.[3] OSE responded to these new, unexpected circumstances by opening *Villa La Chesnaie.*

After a short stay in *Villa Helvetia,* Oswald was sent to live with the orthodox children in May 1939, even though he came from a liberal family and had only received a very limited religious education. How did it come to this?

"So they asked me 'Are you religious?'" Arthur recalled. "And from what I remember, my father prayed in the morning, we went to the temple every once in a while, so I said, 'Yes.'"

OSE did not specifically ask Oswald's parents and the boy henceforth lived in a whole new environment, with daily prayers, regular synagogue attendance, and the constant wearing of a head covering.

Oswald was not the only liberally educated child, wrongly ending up in Eaubonne, far from it. His long-time friend Norbert Rosenblum, for instance, claimed to be orthodox, because he did not want to be separated from his relatives who had been accommodated in *Villa La Chesnaie*: "My sister was there and I had two cousins who were also there," Rosenblum told me during a conversation in Los Angeles, "The *Directrice* [French for female director] told me they had no room for me in Eaubonne and I started to cry that I'm very orthodox and wouldn't eat anything that wasn't kosher. So she said 'Okay, okay, you can stay there.'"

Fourteen-year-old Ernst Valfer was among the oldest children in Eaubonne and had been elected Home Speaker, which meant he knew all the other children personally. He believes that about thirty to fifty percent of the children in Eaubonne did not actually come from an orthodox family. The educators were aware of the fact, but if all the children from liberal families had been sent elsewhere, *Villa La Chesnaie* would have been left half empty, Valfer explained to me.

Regardless of their actual religious background, the children in *Villa La Chesnaie* now strictly followed Jewish laws and dietary rules. According to the children's recollections, life in *La Chesnaie* was not only orthodox but even ultra-orthodox. The children in Eaubonne had to pray three times a day, reciting the *Shaharit* morning prayers, *Mincha* in the afternoon, and *Maariv* in the evening. On Shabbat, the Jewish day of rest, beginning on Friday evening until Saturday evening, the children had to walk the 2.5 miles to the synagogue in Enghien-les-Bains, as they were not allowed to use public transportation on that day. "We couldn't play on Saturday, or touch a dog. There are so many rules if you're orthodox," Arthur recalled.

One recognized the boys as orthodox children at first glance: they usually wore a kippa or a French beret on their head, as well as a small prayer shawl under their clothes. Two orthodox communities in Paris ensured the children's religious education in Eaubonne, the other school subjects, along with the practical classes usually taking place in *Les Tourelles*. The children thus had frequent contact with their non-religious comrades.

It did not occur to the wrongly accommodated children to ask for their transfer into another home; having quickly made friends in Eaubonne, they did not want to leave. "Children want to adapt," Arthur commented dryly. "So I adapted to that lifestyle."

For many young refugees, *Villa La Chesnaie* became the first place in France they stayed at over a longer period and the children developed friendships that would last for decades. "We started to become a family. Instead of only friends, we became brothers and sisters," Arthur remembered decades later.

At first, the children stayed among themselves, the Austrians playing with the Austrians, and the Germans with the Germans. Very soon though, new groups began to form, according to the children's age. The dormitories were also divided according to age groups, with ten-year-old Oswald sleeping in Room D with five other ten-year-olds. Erich Grünebaum, who was also ten, was Oswald's best friend in Eaubonne. The two of them had met during Oswald's brief stay in *Maubuisson*. In his unpublished autobiography, Grünebaum, today Eric Greene, describes the two boys' funnily failed attempt to swear blood-brotherhood. "Oswald and I decided to pledge our friendship for all times. We found a piece of roofing slate and wanted to inscribe on it that we were lifelong buddies and then bury the slate in the fringe of the woods like a time capsule. Being in France, our adopted country, we of course wanted to make the inscription in French. The problem was that we did not know enough of that language to know the French word for friends. We asked one of the older boys who was only too happy to help us. He told us the inscription should read '*Erich et Oswald sont Ânes*.' Later we found out that the word for friends in French is really '*Amis*' and that '*Ânes*' means donkeys. What we had written on the advice of the practical jokester was that we were a couple of jackasses. The other boys in our group had a good laugh at our expense."

Stupid donkeys, as Oswald and Erich had been called, was by far not the only nickname the children in the homes came up with for each other. Almost all of them were given a nickname by their comrades, which incidentally makes it quite difficult today to identify the right persons. The nicknames were of course very seldom flattering, referring most of the time to the child's appearance or some other characteristic feature. Overweight children would thus be called *Kugerl* or *Dickerl* (round-as-a-ball or fatso), whereas a very tall boy would be nicknamed Jumbo. An unpopular child would be called Mussolini or Duce. One boy, the unfortunate owner of a pair of smelly feet was called Cheese. The children did not refrain from giving nicknames to adults: the two cooks, Käthe Hirsch and Käthe Bodek, swiftly became "fat Käthe" and "thin Käthe" to tell them apart. One French cook was called *Tröpfchen* (droplet), because she always had a runny nose.

Oswald's nickname was *Papakuss* (Daddy-Kiss), because of the many loving letters and parcels filled with treats he received from his father. The other children considered Oswald a truly spoiled Daddy's boy. Indeed the letters Hermann Kernberg sent his "dearest *Burli*" brimmed with love, more often than not ending with "most heartfelt embraces" and "warm kisses from your ever-loving daddy," In time, the German *Papakuss* was adjusted to sound more French and Oswald became *Papuss*.

* * *

"*Voilà*, this *Salon* was used as a prayer room by OSE," Marie-Caroline Soavina, the current owner of *Villa La Chesnaie* declares in a clear voice. After the lecture of local historian Hervé Collet, the audience and I are given an exclusive tour. The Soavina family finances the maintenance and preservation of the landmarked chateau thanks to wedding ceremonies and parties held in the *Grand Salon* and in the garden, among other things. Today we even get a glimpse of the mansion's private rooms, as we walk from the music room to the library, where several family photographs are displayed besides flowered fabric armchairs and lamps with hand-painted silk lampshades. Then the lady of the house leads us down a small stone staircase to the vaulted cellar, which has been entirely renovated a few years ago. The middle room however still offers an indication as to the *Chesnaie*'s past. "You will see names on the walls," Marie-Caroline

Soavina says, pointing to a few sections on the walls that have not been plastered over during renovation.

Fritz, Batch, Dudu, Mops, Beb, Sepp, Hans Martin, Tepper. Even though the names of the Eaubonne children have faded a little over the years, they are still perfectly legible. These names are the children's only legacy, the one remaining indication of their life in Eaubonne, their preservation a mere matter of chance.

"We discovered the names when we started renovating the cellar," Soavina explains, the visitors listening to her, spellbound. "Seeing these names on the walls of *La Chesnaie* really came as a surprise to us, because we knew nothing about the mansion's history. Some of the names, like Fritz, for instance, have a German ring to them."

Marie-Caroline and her husband Liv were ashamed of the German names in their cellar: the only explanation they could think of for their presence was to assume the villa had been used by the German army during the war and that German soldiers, possibly even Nazis, had immortalized themselves on the walls.

"But then, one day, a man suddenly appeared by our garden gate and when I asked him, who he was, he started crying. And then he told me what really happened at *La Chesnaie*," Marie-Caroline Soavina explains.

The man was Werner Dreyfuss, one of Oswald's old friends from his days in Eaubonne. In 2003, Werner, today an American citizen, paid an unannounced visit to *Villa La Chesnaie* and asked if he could have a look around his former home. Dreyfuss was overjoyed when he discovered the names of the children on the cellar walls and went on to explain their origin to the Soavinas. "That's how we learned about the whole story," Marie-Caroline concludes. "Then, when we began to renovate the cellar, we deliberately left the sections of the walls bearing the names untouched."

* * *

Every morning, Oswald and his friends would wake up to the loud ringing of a bell. Most of the time though, the children pulled their blankets over their heads and only got up when an educator came to shoo them out of bed. The children started their daily routine with gym and morning toilet, before gathering for the obligatory morning prayer. The young refugees would then attend classes. After lunch followed by afternoon prayer, they enjoyed one hour of free time before practical crafts teaching and their daily one-hour Hebrew class. Every day at six o'clock in the evening, the OSE protégés had to clean their shoes, before going to dinner and saying their evening prayers. Then they would have free time until half past eight.

The kitchen and the refectory were on the ground floor, the living room and salon of the former owner had been converted into class-rooms, while the adjoining music room served as a prayer room. A large spiral staircase led up to the two upper floors, the boys were accommodated in the left wing, the girls in the right. In the attic, a small door covered all over with paintings of shoes opened onto a little cobbler's workshop for the boys' practical teaching. The man-sion was surrounded by a large estate and OSE had established a sports field on the great lawn in front of the villa, where soccer games or so-called Olympic competitions between the various homes or against the Eaubonne youth would take place.

Oswald's French improved a great deal over time: the children sang French folk songs with their teachers and from time to time were even treated to a French film in Eaubonne's movie theater. A few older children, who were already fluent in French, did not attend class inside the home but were sent instead to the regular school in Eaubonne. Their attendance was not unproblematic though, as the orthodox children kept Shabbat and did not go to school on Saturdays. Some of the teachers would confront them every Monday morning anew, asking them why they had not come on the previous Saturday, which the children felt was unfair chicane.[4]

Oswald settled in well in Eaubonne, even though he often felt very homesick on Sundays. Sunday was visiting-day in the OSE homes and all the children who had relatives in France, or whose parents lived as refugees in Paris, would spend a few hours with their families. "I remember feeling very, very lonely because I never got any visitors," Arthur told me several decades later. "There were times when I wanted to cry because the other kids got visitors and I didn't."[5]

Ten-year-old Oswald received encouraging letters from his family, his parents professing, again and again, it was only a matter of time before they could all emigrate to America. His cousin Gina, who had been able to flee to England in the meantime, wrote to him quite regularly too: "My sweet, blond *Hascherl* (poor soul), your cousin Gina has not forgotten about you; even if you feel homesick from time to time, you must stay strong."

* * *

What the children did not know: a power struggle was raging behind the scenes over the correct management and guidance of *Villa La Chesnaie*, opposing Ernst Papanek and OSE's liberal supporters on the one hand, and religious OSE members and the Jewish orthodox community in Paris on the other hand, who categorically rejected certain aspects of Papanek's progressive educational methods. Particularly scandalized by the boys and girls co-education, the authoritative orthodox community would have loved to prevent any contact between the children. The fact boys and girls would live together under the same roof and attend the same classes was a huge thorn in the orthodox community's side. Ten-year-old Oswald once kissed seven-year-old Charlotte Bacharach on the cheek; incidents such as these were exactly what the community would have liked to avoid.

Ernst Papanek was frequently accused of not paying much heed to Judaism, some OSE members even going so far as to call him dismissively *Goi*, namely a gentile, a non-Jew. Yet Papanek showed great respect indeed for his protégés' faith. He was one of the first to recognize that the cohabitation between liberally educated and orthodox children would lead to problems and that opening a specific home for observant children would be a good solution. But that did not mean he was willing to alter his modern education program for all that. In the end, both parties agreed *Villa La Chesnaie* was to be a "home for orthodox children" and not an "orthodox home."[6] In plain English, this meant Papanek could make all the educational decisions, while the Parisian orthodox community was allowed to appoint a home manager, who would be in charge of daily matters as well as of the keeping of the religious rules. The compromise stood on shaky ground from the start and numerous problems arose over and over again, like the time when Lene Papanek gave aspirin to a girl who had taken ill during Passover, against the will of the orthodox *Directrice*.[7]

It is quite interesting to see, from today's perspective, how different Ernst Papanek felt towards the orthodox children: when describing the OSE homes, he always emphasized the specificity of *Villa La Chesnaie*. "Papanek grossly misrepresented the orthodox children in his autobiography," Arthur complained to me. In fact, when mentioning the orthodox children in *Out of the Fire*, Papanek sounds in parts like an explorer reporting about some exotic creatures he has just chanced upon – a fact which led more often than not to misunderstandings.

Papanek appeared quite surprised, for instance, by the outcome of a soccer game: "The orthodox had never played soccer in their lives before coming to Montmorency, and since we really had some good players on the other teams, everybody expected them to be the pushovers. To the astonishment of everyone, except perhaps the orthodox boys themselves, they got every break in every game and won the championship."[8]

However, Papanek had completely misinterpreted the sports

enthusiasm displayed by the Eaubonne children, who by all accounts kicked the ball every spare minute. "We played soccer. All day long, from morning to night," Norbert Rosenblum told me.

An event, which went down in OSE history as "the Eaubonne rebellion" had a far greater impact, though. Things were set in motion by Anna Feigenbaum Krakowski, the longest-serving home manager and a very controversial personality in the history of OSE homes. Her extensive theoretical knowledge of Judaism had earned her the admiration of rabbis and the orthodox OSE members. Her letters however also show that she actively attempted to undermine Papanek's education principles.[9] The scant source material does not allow us to form a definite opinion on that issue, yet there is much to suggest that Madame Krakowski considered it as her duty to proselytize to the less observant children. Most of the young refugees felt a strong dislike for Madame Krakowski because she was extremely strict and authoritarian. Oswald alone was an exception in this regard. He actually liked her, remembering her as a strict, yet fair woman.

But let us get back to the rebellion that occurred after a Rosh Hashanah celebration. The "rebels" were furious, because, unlike their non-orthodox friends, they had not been allowed to dance during the festival and had had to go back home earlier. Deciding to have a bit of midnight fun, a few overexcited boys dressed up as ghosts using bed linens and slipped into the girls' dormitory to scare them.

What appears today like a harmless enough prank caused a huge scandal in the orthodox home, as it violated the rule of gender separation. Madame Krakowski was beside herself with rage and demanded draconian punishments. According to Ernst Papanek, a few children had also rampaged through the home manager's bedroom: "Her door had been kicked in, her bed had been turned upside-down, her furniture had been smashed and her clothes had been ripped to pieces," he wrote in his autobiography.[10]

The only snag in the whole thing: the rebellion never took place, according to the former home children.

Ernst Valfer, who had taken part in the prank, assured me they had done nothing more than scare the girls. "Papanek made a much bigger deal out of it than it was," he told me, "It was not even started as a revolt... It was started because we wanted to have some fun." Arthur too did not recall a rebellion against the Directrice, Anna Feigenbaum Krakowski.

Whether a revolt occurred or not, the fact that boys dressed up as ghosts had entered the girls' dormitory caused great turmoil within OSE management. Madame Krakowski wanted to expel all the boys involved as a punishment, a suggestion Ernst Papanek found deeply shocking. Expelling the traumatized and persecuted refugees was absolutely out of the question for him. Instead, he revoked the democratic rights of the children involved, who could no longer take part in the home administration, a punishment he considered perfectly appropriate. This was by far not enough, though, in the eyes of Madame Krakowski and the orthodox members of OSE, who insisted on at least transferring the leader of the revolt to another home. Papanek is said to have threatened to quit if a single boy was forced to leave Eaubonne.[11]

The whole situation only returned to normal when several OSE board members came to Eaubonne in person and saw for themselves how crushed the children were by the removal of their democratic rights. "The whole incident proved to be an important step in the development of the OSE homes and casts light on Ernst Papanek's attitude regarding the children's freedom of opinion," Hanna Papanek assessed the incident decades later.[12] Madame Krakowski was allowed to remain in her position as home manager and did not change her behavior afterward, remaining as unpopular as ever among the children.

* * *

After the visit of *Villa La Chesnaie*, Marie-Caroline Soavina takes leave of the visitors and begins to prepare the *Grand Salon* for an upcoming wedding. I meet with her husband in the mansion's cozy and welcoming kitchen for a talk. Liv Soavina, a Frenchman of Malagasy origin, bought the "little *Chesnaie* chateau" as he calls it, in 1998. The successful engineer shows great interest in the mansion's history and enthusiastically tells me about the occasional visit of former OSE children or their descendants. "We are always very happy to welcome them," he says with a smile. He is just as much delighted by my visit, comparing me to Sherlock Holmes, as I put together Arthur's story from lots of small evidence and clues.

Everything Soavina knows about OSE and the Eaubonne home, he learned from the former home children, or else read about over the years. The former owners of the mansion, Jacques and Valentine Dupont, who rented the villa to OSE in 1939, never mentioned the villa's history later. The 51-year-old Soavina keeps apologizing for his inability to provide any specific information. "I'm afraid I can only offer very general information about OSE's boys and girls, nothing concerning single individuals," he declares. Not quite true, as it soon turns out.

"Oh, oh, here, here!" Soavina calls me, sitting at his laptop and browsing through his e-mail inbox, looking for messages from OSE children he has been in contact with over the years. Quite unexpectedly, he discovers an almost fifteen years old e-mail from Arthur. "Never deleting anything is a good thing," Soavina says, laughing.

"My name is Arthur Kern, formerly Oswald Kernberg," Arthur began his e-mail in November 2003. He had found out by chance that the Soavinas were trying to get in touch with people who had carved their names on the walls of their cellar. Arthur sent a translation of the names to help them identify the children: "Dudu is Herman Bacharach, he is deceased. Bep is Ernst Valfer, he lives in San Francisco," he explained in his e-mail. "These are the names of the older boys at *Chesnaie*. I was in the middle group."

I began writing this book two years after Arthur passed away and I deeply regret he is no longer here to see it. I can no longer call him in the middle of the night and tell him that I just discovered a letter his parents sent to Ernst Papanek. I cannot ask him who the people are, whose names are written on the cellar walls. He will never read this book.

And yet, Arthur manages time and again to help me in unexpected ways, be it via a fifteen-year-old e-mail I come across completely by surprise, in the cozy kitchen of a French mansion.

9. THE SUMMER OF 1939

While the young refugees settled in their new home, the Jews remaining in Germany strove to emigrate with growing desperation. The odyssey of the *St. Louis* achieved a sad notoriety in this context, with news of its journey dominating the world press in May and June 1939.[1] The Hapag luxury liner *St. Louis* left Hamburg harbor on May 13, heading for Havana, with 900 Jewish refugees on board. Despite a valid permission to land, the Cuban government unexpectedly denied entry to the passengers. When the American coast guards also prevented the *St. Louis* from docking at an American port, the Hapag ordered the captain to return to Germany. Aid organizations, especially the Joint, sent out calls for help all over the world to avoid the forced return of Jewish refugees to Nazi Germany. However, the situation seemed utterly hopeless, with fuel and drinking water becoming increasingly scarce and the passengers threatening to commit mass suicide. The German captain, Gustav Schröder, secretly planned to shipwreck in front of the British coastline to impose the rescue of his passengers on England.[2] Yet the negotiations initiated by the Joint succeeded at the last moment and the English, Belgian, Dutch, and French governments each consented to take in a quarter of the refugees. On June 17, 1939, after a 33-day odyssey, the *St. Louis* finally docked at the port of Antwerp.

At first, Ernst Papanek and the children followed the fate of the *St. Louis* during their classes on world current affairs: they retraced the route of the ship on an atlas and talked about the politics of socialist Cuba, gleaning a few English and Spanish words here and there.[3] Soon enough though, the children came to know the fate of the *St. Louis* passengers on a much more personal level.

So they would be granted entry into any of the four countries, the passengers had to be detained in internment camps. However, no one looked favorably upon the imprisonment of children. Ernst Papanek and OSE general secretary Lazare Gurvic, therefore, offered to take in a large number of *St. Louis* children as a solution.

There were 43 children among the 227 refugees who were granted entry into France. OSE took in 35 of them, the parents of the remaining eight children being unwilling to part with them at the time.[4] Papanek came to collect the children in person and took them to Montmorency. To make the parting with their parents easier for the *St. Louis* children, Oswald, and his friends had relinquished their chocolate rations, so Papanek could hand them out to the newcomers on the train. A big welcome party awaited them in Montmorency. The children had come up with a whole program including songs, plays, and concerts, the motto of the day – "Forget the past and follow us into a better future!" – written on a poster hanging above the staircase. The performance of the band from the *Petite Colonie* was the absolute highlight of the party: a gaggle of three- and four-year-olds, wearing checkered aprons, played music with drums, flutes, shakers, triangles, and a hi-hat. The welcome song was a bit out of tune, but the little musicians' enthusiasm more than made up for that minor shortcoming.

The newcomers were given a nickname right away – how could it have been otherwise? "We called them Cubans because they came from Cuba," Arthur told me. "They were all German or Austrian children, but we still called them Cubans."

Due to lack of space, the *St. Louis* children were first sent to *Villa Helvetia* and *La Chesnaie*, until the home of *Les Tourelles* was opened for them. Most of the newcomers came from wealthy, well-educated families, whose Jewish identity was very clear, but who nevertheless considered themselves German in the first place. The persecution they had experienced in Nazi Germany therefore came as a much greater shock to them than it had to the orthodox children, according to Ernst Papanek.[5] Still, the "Cubans" settled in quite fast in France and soon played an important part in the co-administration of the home. Hans Windmüller, for instance, was elected president of the Student Parliament by a large majority. Most of the newcomers were a little older than the other OSE children, as a child deplored in a 1939 letter: "We lost two [dodge ball games,] because the Cubans are as big and strong as ogres compared to us and they also play much better. They're very nice."[6]

* * *

Already in February 1939, Oswald's father Hermann had been forced to relinquish control over his factory to the Nazi *Gauleitung* (district leadership). On June 30, 1939, he was forced to sell the knitwear factory that had been in the family for two generations and the company was from then on "aryanized."

The Property Transactions Office informed Dr. Sepp Zedlacher, a Viennese business graduate, that "the sale and transfer, to you, of the Goldfeld & Kernberg company, located in the 19th district of Vienna, on Hardtgasse 32 has been… approved in accordance with art. I. § 1 of the decree of April 27, 1938." The purchase price set for the successful company was preposterously low – 4,000 *Reichsmark* – but Hermann Kernberg did not even receive that meager sum. The new owner did not have to pay a single Reichsmark to the Kernbergs, as a certified public accountant had found an alleged "deficit" and thus an over-indebtedness of the company.

"The closing of accounts of December 31, 1938 [showed] a loss of capital of approximately 10,000 Reichsmark," Zedlacher wrote in a letter addressed to the central office for Jewish emigration, in justification of the non-payment of the purchase price. "The Jewish Penance Tax of approximately 3,600 Reichsmark, as well as the income tax of approximately 1,100 Reichsmark, have been paid out of the company's assets. With German greetings!"

Oswald's parents seemed to have kept the loss of the factory from their youngest son, the letters they sent to him afterward were as optimistic and full of loving attention as ever.

* * *

"*Aux armes, citoyens. Formez vos bataillons. Marchons, marchons!*"

Hundreds of children were singing the "*Marseillaise*," the French national anthem, the song echoing across the lawn in front of *Villa Helvetia*. It was July 14, 1939, and OSE commemorated the French National Day with a great circus that attracted many visitors from the immediate surroundings as well as from Paris.[7] "We all dressed up for the circus," Arthur recalled, a broad smile on his face. The youngest home inhabitants shone, dressed up as 19th-century nobility, top hat and shawls included. The older children went as clowns, ladybugs, Chinese, dwarves, highway bandits, cowboys, a bubbly Mickey Mouse, and even a toadstool. Two kings wearing billowing capes and cardboard crowns were involved in a fierce sword fight and five young Indians posed, wearing extravagant feather headdresses.

There is no such thing as a circus without a circus tent: huge and white, bearing the inscription *Cirque Helvetia*, it had been set up in front of a tall tree, a few French flags fluttering in the wind at its top. Next to the tent on the left, a piano stood on the lawn, and one of the teachers accompanied the children during their performances.

At first, a few stumbling clowns led a massive pig inside the circus ring, four children concealed underneath the disguise (one child per leg). Afterward, the young refugees re-enacted their classes in a sketch, slipping into the roles of school supplies: there were cardboard copybooks and books, feet poking out below, a little head peeking out at the top. Four children wore elongated costumes on which the word *crayon* had been written, their pointed hats showing the color of the chalk they were mimicking. One boy made a particularly striking appearance, knock-kneed and wrapped in silver-colored paper to pose as a pair of scissors.

OSE organized a circus in 1939, on the occasion of the French National Day. For one of the sketches, the children dressed up as school supplies: notebooks, books, chalk sticks and even a pair of scissors.

Once again, the small children of the *Petite Colonie* were the highlight of the show, delighting their audience with their "blossoming flowers dance." About a dozen pre-school-aged girls in sleeveless camisoles and protruding tutus, a flower tucked behind their ear, held hands and danced, eyes directed upwards, moving in an opening and closing spiral that formed three circles symbolizing a flower. Afterward, there were jugglers, tightrope walkers, and lots and lots of sweets.

On another afternoon, Gus Papanek stood in the middle of armchairs placed in a circle, his arms raised up in the air, next to him was a nurse and a sick patient sitting on a chair and holding a pair of crutches: the older children had invited the audience to a theater performance in French of Moliere's play *Le Malade Imaginaire* (*The Imaginary Invalid*).

Ernst Papanek and the OSE children loved celebrating parties. Every birthday and every Jewish or French holiday was duly acknowledged and honored. Newly arrived children or children moving to another home, the smallest event was reason enough to perform a play, sing songs and enjoy a piece of cake. The frequent celebrations were part of Papanek's positive education strategy. "We loved celebrations so much," he explained in his autobiography. "When no country had an acceptable holiday coming up, we would put on a play or a circus of our own."[8]

Papanek strongly objected to the criticism of one visitor, who accused him of having turned the *Villa Helvetia* children's home into a Strauss Operetta, arguing that the traumatized children deserved to forget their worries: "They had come to us, strangers and afraid, and we had to make them happy again."[9] A June 1939 article in a Parisian German émigré newspaper demonstrated the success of this approach: "The summer party found [the children] in high spirits... which suggests it has indeed been possible to gradually free their souls from the horrors of the past."[10]

A very special celebration took place on August 20, 1939. Hundreds of OSE children organized a surprise party on the occasion of their director's birthday. One of the Eaubonne girls remembered the big day: "We welcomed him with a tremendous cheer. First he had to sit in a decorated armchair we then lifted up three times, all the while singing."[11]

A picture captured the happy event for eternity: Ernst Papanek stands, laughing, in front of the children, gathered in a semicircle, his hand stretched out towards the home speaker, Hans Windmüller, who presents him with a big cake. Papanek wears his usual suit, his clothes, and half-bald head making him look far older than his 39 years. Oswald stands in the second-to-last row, wearing a beret, just like the rest of the Eaubonne children.

There was cake, sweets, and lemonade for the occasion and then a few children recited a self-written poem in honor of Ernst Papanek.

In Montmorency ist es lustig, – What joy in Montmorency,
in Helvetia ist es schön, – What fun in Helvetia,
ja, da kann man viel erleben, – So many things to experience
ja, da kann man manches seh'n. – And just as many to see.

Hier ist Ernst der Herr Direktor – And looking after all of us,
und der sorgt fürs ganze Haus – Is our good director Ernst
und er denkt sich für die Kinder – Who always keeps for us children
immer etwas Nettes aus. – More than a few tricks up his sleeve.
Uns're Ärztin ist die Lene – His wife Lene is our doctor
und sie kennt sich sehr gut aus, – And quite a good one she is too,
hat die kleine Zehe Bauchweh – Hurting toe or aching tummy,
tupft sie gleich mit Jod darauf... – She treats it all with iodine...

Heute sind wir hier versammelt – We are all gathered here today
um zu feiern dieses Mal – To celebrate quite fittingly
unser Ernst hat heut Geburtstag – Our Ernst's birthday, hear oh hear!
gratuliert ihn zu dem Tag. – Let's all wish him a merry day.

Böses können wir nicht verraten – No complaint or grievance from us
Gutes nur hat er getan – The good man will ever hear,
darum lasst uns nicht mehr warten – Let's not wait a second longer
hochleben soll der brave Mann. – And cheer as one 'Long may he live!'[12]

The big surprise party for Ernst Papanek marked the end of the carefree period in French exile. Two weeks later, the Second World War broke out with the German invasion of Poland.

On the occasion of Ernst Papanek's 39th birthday, the
children planned a huge surprise party for him.

10. THE BEGINNING OF THE WAR

"Heave-ho!" Oswald threw a sandbag to his friend Erich Grünebaum before wiping away the sweat from his brow. Erich passed it on with another loud "Heave-ho!" A few minutes later, the two friends were replaced by older boys and sent to the front of the human chain to fill more bags with sand. A more appropriate task for ten-year-olds. The sandbags were then stacked in front of the ground-floor windows of *Villa La Chesnaie*, so they would not shatter in the event of an air raid. While the boys struggled with their heavy load, the girls glued paper sheets on the upper floors' many windowpanes, to obscure the entire house. Other girls sewed rubber bands onto washcloths that could be dipped into a sodium solution Lene Papanek had prepared in case of a gas attack to serve as makeshift gas masks.

On September 1, 1939, Adolf Hitler had declared in a speech at the Reichstag: "Since 5:45 am, we have been returning the fire!" The words heralded the attack on Poland and marked the beginning of the Second World War. On the previous day, German soldiers wearing Polish uniforms had faked an attack on a German broadcasting station in Upper Silesia, allowing Hitler to present the invasion of Poland as a defensive action. The fighting went down in history as a

"*Blitzkrieg*" (lightning war): within a few days, the German army had reached the Polish capital.[1]

Merely six months had passed since Oswald's arrival in France. The quiet and sheltered life of the Jewish refugee children ended abruptly. France and England had assured Poland of their support in the event of a German attack and they presented Hitler with an ultimatum, demanding the immediate withdrawal of his troops from Poland. The OSE homes in Montmorency and Eaubonne were only 12.5 miles away from the center of the capital and thus located right within the danger zone in case of air raids, the occurrence of which were expected even before France's official entry into the war.

On September 1, 1939, Ernst Papanek visited each of the four homes, arriving in Eaubonne last, as the children were getting ready for Shabbat, just like any other Friday. Papanek believed it was essential to be completely honest with the children and he informed them of the imminent war without any glossing over.

In order to comfort and reassure his frightened protégés, Papanek actively involved them in the preparation of their own defense. "There is always relief in the simple knowledge that you do not have to stand by helplessly and wait for your fate to overtake you, that it is possible to do something about it. And, I knew, an even deeper relief that comes with the physical act of doing it," he wrote on that subject at the end of the war.[2]

"Riiing, riiing!" The bright tone of the school bell echoed across the grounds and the children stopped working at once. Oswald took Erich's hand and the two boys ran toward the entrance of *La Chesnaie* until an educator exhorted them to calm down and they walked the rest of the way at a slower pace. All afternoon long, alarm tests had been conducted hourly, so the children could practice finding their way to the cellar from wherever they might just be – in the dormitories, the classrooms, or the garden.

Meanwhile, the wine cellar in *Villa La Chesnaie* was hastily converted into an air-raid shelter: the educators and a few older boys tipped over the shelves and laid mattresses on them. Then they carried down water, food supplies, and flashlights. "The home had a basement that was built like a fortress, with curved arches, and that's where we went," Arthur told me later.

The preparations lasted until late in the evening, and sure enough, on the very first night, the children were roused from their sleep by the alarm bell! A false alarm as it turned out. During this first air-raid warning, the children went to the shelter without difficulty and in an orderly fashion, behaving in an exemplary manner according to Ernst Papanek.[3] "We were organized in some sort of *buddy system*," Arthur recalled. "When the air raids occurred, the older children would be responsible for the younger ones, who would be responsible in turn for the still younger children. You made sure nobody would stay in the room when the air raids occurred."[4]

The children had been so busy with the preparations all day that they managed quite successfully to suppress their emotions. It was not before they found themselves unoccupied in the shelter, during their first air-raid alarm, that they began to feel nervous and scared. To distract the children, the educators sang the "*Marseillaise*" and other songs with them and told them stories.

In such troubled times, it was crucial to structure the children's days, which is why OSE made no alteration to their usual daily routine despite the war. The children would still get up at seven every morning, even when they had spent half the night in the cellar. To take away their feeling of helplessness, each child was assigned a special task during an air-raid alarm, be it only switching off the light. Two older boys were entrusted with a special responsibility in Eaubonne: as soon as the alarm sounded, they opened the Torah ark and carefully carried the precious Torah scrolls down to the cellar.

On September 3, 1939, two days after the attack on Poland, England and France officially declared war on the German Reich. At that time, 330,000 Jews were living in France, among which 140,000 foreigners, who had immigrated shortly before.[5]

The Jewish refugee children of OSE were faced with an emotional dilemma: as much as Ernst Papanek assured them that they were perfectly safe, the French and the English fighting for them against Hitler, it did nothing to allay their fears as to the fate of their families who had remained in Germany. "France had been the enemy against whom our fathers fought and now we were here and they were there. It became a very confusing time for us Jewish-German refugee children," Erich Grünebaum reflected in his autobiography.

The declaration of war put an immediate end to all *Kindertransports*. Hundreds of children, whose names were on the entry list to England, could no longer leave Germany. Yet on September 3, 1939, OSE took in one last larger group of children: the Robinsons.

The Robinson group was composed of children of German and Austrian socialist refugees, who had created a Social Democrat youth group in exile in France and had organized a holiday camp in the summer of 1939, in Le Plessis-Robinson, on the outskirts of Paris, hence the name Robinsons. Papanek's oldest son, Gustav, and his future wife Hanna were both members of the group. After France declared war on Germany, the Robinson children were taken straight from their summer camp to Montmorency by cab. "At exactly 5:00 pm, when the [German] ultimatum to Poland expired and the war began, we arrived there," the future Hanna Papanek wrote in her diary.[6]

The Robinsons were very different from the other OSE protégés: firstly, only half of them were Jewish – for the first time, children with no link whatsoever to Judaism arrived in an OSE home. Secondly, and even more strikingly, these youths' political consciousness was particularly pronounced. Indeed there could not have been more suitable residents for a home run by Ernst Papanek. Addressing adults as equals, progressive pedagogy, and gender equality – the Robinsons were already familiar with all this from home and from their youth groups.[7]

The Robinsons spent their first night in Montmorency, hiding in the air-raid shelter with their new comrades. In the first days of the war, air-raid warnings were a daily occurrence, all of them turning out to be false alarms, though. There were no actual air raids in 1939. After the initial excitement and the knowledge nothing bad happened, the children soon got accustomed to the nightly alarm, whiling away the time reading, playing bridge, or carving their names in the cellar walls of *Villa La Chesnaie.* Later, they would simply lie down to sleep, until they could return to their beds.[8]

Relatively soon, air-raid sirens stopped entirely. Germany and France were now stuck in what is called in German a *Sitzkrieg* (sitting war) or *drôle de guerre* in French (phoney war in English). Despite nationwide mobilization and the official state of war, no combat action was reported for nearly seven months.[9]

Even though there were no fights for the time being, still eleven OSE members were forced to leave the children's homes in September; the French nationals among them drafted into the army, and the emigrants arrested.[10] In France, German and Austrian men between 17 and 65 years old were detained as *étrangers indésirables* – "enemy aliens."[11] "Whether these men were Jewish or not was not taken into account," OSE historian Katy Hazan emphasized during our meeting in Paris. "Nor did it matter whether they were opponents of the National Socialists who had fled the country."

Ernst Papanek himself was sent for some time to one of these foreigner camps. "Ernst was very quickly gotten out of there by OSE," his son Gus told me. Lene Papanek ran the home during his absence, the student co-administration gaining an even greater importance than before. Especially the older children actively helped organize the home's daily life and their younger comrades' class schedules.

On October 6, 1939, after five weeks of war, Poland surrendered. Two weeks later, on October 19, Oswald celebrated his eleventh birthday in Eaubonne. Just like every OSE birthday child, he got a cake with candles at dinner and presents from his closest friends. However, he did not receive any birthday greetings from his parents.

Hermann and Frieda had not forgotten their beloved son, of course, but sending a letter proved simply impossible for them: postal service had been entirely interrupted between the warring parties since the beginning of the war. "Children turned into letters" was a common figure of speech among German Jewish families in the 1930s, letters being the only thing parents could cling to as a replacement for the children they had sent away.[12] Now even these letters stopped.

When Ernst Papanek announced the children's communication with their parents was interrupted for the time being, a deadly silence fell over the room. "A terrible, stony silence which I shall never forget," the educator remembered decades later. For many children, this ultimate separation from their families was much more difficult to bear than their fear of air raids.[13]

Yet Oswald was lucky in his misfortune. His parents managed to get in touch with their son through relatives and acquaintances abroad. In the early days of November 1939, he received a first postcard, sent from Italy by a certain Sabine Eimer, one of Frieda Kernberg's relatives. Mrs. Eimer was on her way to America and wrote to Oswald from Trieste: "Your parents came to see us in Vienna before we left the city, to say goodbye, and they asked us to send you their greetings and best wishes. They're both in good health, as is your brother, and anxious to leave Vienna as quickly as possible, so they can meet you in a neutral state and emigrate with you to America. Your d[ear] parents have not received any news from you since the beginning of the war and are therefore very worried. Your d[ear]est parents hope you are doing well and wish you will soon have the opportunity to join them."

Later on, a distant relative living in neutral Switzerland forwarded letters from and to Oswald and also helped a few of his friends in the same way. One of the few letters Oswald received in 1940 shows Hermann Kernberg's attempt to fulfill his role as a father and exercise an influence on his son's education, despite their long separation and the great distance between them: "Rather than writing better and more beautifully, I am afraid quite the opposite must be said of you sometimes! I do mean well, but please make it a habit of keeping everything neat and painstakingly clean. ... Writing a letter with a pencil is somewhat insulting. My dear, golden *Burli*, do not be upset by this clarification of your loving *Papa*, but make sure to use a fountain pen next time you write, so your letter will be all neat and nice."

The same letter also included one of Fritz's rare messages – Oswald's brother would usually sign the letter his parents sent, without adding any comment. "I'm glad you're doing well and are in good health," Fritz wrote Oswald. "I envy you your freedom and the fact you're able to talk freely with your friends. I wish you lots of luck."

"I didn't really understand, back then, what my brother had meant to say," Arthur confessed during one of our conversations in Los Angeles. "I couldn't imagine the kind of life he had, which was a lot worse than I had had before I left Vienna."

Oswald's childish ignorance also shows in the repeated requests he addressed to his parents, asking them to send toys or clothes to France, a fact Arthur came to regret bitterly as an adult: "In retrospect, I realized that's not the thing to have done. Because they were in dire straits themselves, and of course wanted to do everything for their child. But they thought possibly I was hurting, I was suffering – which was really not the case at the time."[14]

But then Frieda and Hermann always embellished their living conditions in their letters to their son, in a wish to sound positive. It is thus more than understandable that eleven-year-old Oswald would have misjudged his parents' situation.

* * *

"With everything Ernst Papanek was doing to distract the children from the war, do you recall being afraid?" I ask Ernst Valfer, the former home speaker in Eaubonne, in February 2017.

"We were both," the 92-year-old answers. "We were so afraid that we had fabulous defense mechanisms. We sang, we played, and we did sports. We were in grand denial. Otherwise, I don't think we could have managed."

Ernst Valfer, whose nickname Bep is written on the cellar wall in *Villa La Chesnaie*, later became a successful psychologist in California, which probably also accounts for the fact that he dealt quite extensively with his experience during the war.

"We functioned by not accepting, or not facing reality," he goes on to explain with clear, carefully considered sentences. "We knew about the German invasion of Poland. We followed the Finnish-Russian war. We knew, but we didn't let it *really* register."

The children's traumatic experiences from that time, added to the fear they would feel during the course of the war, obviously left scars on their souls.

"We all managed to deal with it in different ways," the Frankfurt-born man points out in our conversation. "I was still able to be a good student. Later I did my doctorate at the university and did a lot of research. It didn't impair that. What it impaired was some of my social abilities. I used to think of myself as a good person, but after some years of therapy – and being a psychologist myself – I know now that there were a lot of blocks and barriers in my free understanding of myself as well as of others." After a short pause, Ernst Valfer adds: "Maybe it would have been different if we had been older."

* * *

After the troubled weeks of September, life in Montmorency and Eaubonne resumed back to normal. "The war continued, but we still had a reasonably good life," Arthur told me. Food may not have tasted as good as before, but there was plenty of it, just like before. The children went to school in the morning and played soccer in the afternoon. In the spring of 1940, the homes hosted another sporting event and a circus, with chocolate and ice cream for all. In March, the children celebrated Purim together, the only Jewish festival on which orthodox Jews too are allowed to dress up in costumes.

Meanwhile, the German-French phoney war continued. "We heard rumors about parachuters," Arthur recalled, "*Fallschirmjäger*" coming down and about a fifth column, German spies." In this tense situation and for the first time since their flight from Nazi Germany, the Jewish children were confronted with racism and anti-Semitism. "The local people started to call us *sales boches* (dirty Germans) or *sales Juifs* (dirty Jews)," Arthur told an Eaubonne local newspaper in an interview in 2010.[15]

On May 10, 1940, the phoney war on the well-secured French-German border was suddenly over. The German army marched into the neutral states of Belgium, Luxemburg, and the Netherlands, so it could attack France from the north. Luxemburg fell in just one day, the Netherlands surrendered on May 15, 1940, and Belgium on May 28, 1940. On June 10, fascist Italy declared war on France and launched an offensive along the Alpine front.[16]

Once again, air-raid sirens sounded in Montmorency and Eaubonne and the children spent long nights in the cellar, the air strikes very real this time. Due to their proximity to Paris, the residents of the four OSE homes were in constant mortal danger; they could hear cannon fire in the distance and several buildings in their immediate vicinity were hit by bombs.

What with the numerous false alarms at the beginning of the war, the children were more or less prepared for the situation, still a morale-building singing evening was organized in *Les Tourelles*. As the German army inexorably got closer, the Jewish refugee children sang German classical pieces from Mozart and Schubert, concluding the evening with Beethoven's "Ode to Joy."[17]

To make sure all the children were together in case of emergency, OSE took its protégés out of the public schools, once again teaching them within the homes. Each child was given an emergency kit that was to be placed next to their bed, always at hand. It contained a pajama, a toothbrush, a comb, some chocolate, and a gas mask.[18]

On June 14, 1940, after only one month, the Germans marched into Paris without a fight. Prompting OSE's protégés to flee once again.

11. FLIGHT TO THE SOUTH

After the rain of the previous days, the sun shines warmly upon my face today. It is a beautiful Monday morning in September 2017 and I enjoy a nice breakfast in a *Pâtisserie* in the Marais, the Jewish district of Paris. As I dip my croissant in a cup of hot chocolate, I watch the hustle and bustle of the street around me – mothers dragging their children away from the cake counter, street artists singing for the tourists – and reflect on the past few days. Then I write a few postcards to Arthur's family: pictures of the Eiffel Tower for his three sons, a Henri de Toulouse-Lautrec print for his granddaughter Rachel, who works as a graphic designer, a view of Eaubonne for Arthur's widow, Trudie.

My search for traces in France is not yet completed: my next step is the *Mémorial de la Shoah* nearby, the central Holocaust memorial site in France. The *Mémorial* hosts several monuments, a research center, and a museum that opened in 2005. I am struck by the monument to the unknown Jewish martyr, an impressive stone cube outside the building, towering over the adjoining buildings. Beneath the monument, a crypt where ashes from Auschwitz and Treblinka concentration camps, and the Warsaw Ghetto, are kept, offers a symbolic grave to the six million Jews murdered during the Holocaust. An eternal flame, set in a star of David made of black marble, burns in the middle of the room, and on the back wall a quotation in Hebrew from Jeremiah's Book of Lamentations reads: "Behold and see if there be any sorrow like unto my sorrow, which is done unto me."

Before entering the museum, I pass by two more monuments. In the *Mémorial*'s courtyard, the *Mur des Noms*, the Wall of Names, made of white marble, bears the engraved names of the 76,000 Jews, including 11,000 children, who were deported from France during the Holocaust. Only 2,500 of them survived.

On the outside of the building, there is yet another memorial wall: the *Mur des Justes*, the Wall of the Righteous. To this day, the State of Israel has awarded the honorary title of "Righteous Among the Nations" to 28,217 people, who have saved Jews during the Holocaust.[1] The names of the over 4,000 French Righteous are carved in the black stone of the *Mur des Justes*, preserved for all eternity.

It is in vain however that I look for the names of Ernst Papanek, the Rothschild and Gunzbourg Baronesses, or OSE's general secretary Lazare Gurvic. It is considered a religious duty for observant Jews to help other Jews. Actions like those of Papanek and his colleagues are therefore not singled out and honored by the State of Israel, which considers them natural and takes them for granted. Inside the museum though, OSE is mentioned several times, for instance in a separate area dedicated to the children's homes and the rescue of Jewish children.

I have visited a great number of Holocaust museums over the years – since 2012, I even work in one, as a guide at the Dachau concentration camp memorial site – yet the *Mémorial de la Shoah* is one of the most impressive I have ever been to.

A Holocaust Museum or a concentration camp memorial site in Germany, the "perpetrator country," must face up to an altogether different kind of responsibility than the museums and memorials in occupied countries such as France. It is often much easier to remember foreign crimes than one's own. The *Mémorial de la Shoah*, however, does not choose this easy path, offering a very critical view of the country's specific history. Indeed the museum does not solely focus on the persecution of the Jews in Nazi occupied France, but also on the persecution within the "free" south known as Vichy France.

A display panel at the beginning of the exhibition reads as follows: "After years of amnesia, France has finally acknowledged the responsibility of the Vichy government in 1995, thus easing the transition from memory to history. This recent history, so close to us, took place in our country, in our villages, and tragically extended to the extermination camps in Poland, in the heart of Europe. Let us make it our own, let us live and build upon this crime and in spite this crime."

* * *

It was a warm summer in the French capital in 1940. Even before the fall of Paris, a gigantic flow of refugees was set in motion in France. Historians estimate that in May and June 1940, up to ten million civilians fled from the advancing German army towards the south of France.[2]

The German Jewish refugee children in the OSE homes were particularly threatened and should have been brought to safety a long time ago, yet for months the French government refused to issue travel permits for them. "The authorities, who had already clamped on a strict news censorship to hide how badly things were going on all fronts, believed that any mass evacuation of children would have a very bad effect on the morale of the general public," Ernst Papanek noted in his autobiography.[3] Merely a small group of children under eight was allowed to move into the newly opened OSE homes in Central France, as early as spring 1940.

On June 6, just eight days before the German army reached the

French capital, OSE finally received travel permits for all children under 15. One question remained though: where to? The new homes were full, and every hotel and similar accommodations were occupied by refugees.

At the last moment, Ernst Papanek allegedly remembered a conversation he had had the year before with the French Prime Minister Léon Blum, who – Papanek claimed – had told him about a chateau that would meet all requirements as a place of evacuation, namely the *Château de Montintin*, next to Limoges. *Montintin* was said to be spacious, unoccupied, and fitted with a wine cellar that could be used as a shelter during air raids.[4]

In the fall of 2017, I meet with local historian Michel Kiener, who sees things a little differently. Having already opened three homes not far from Limoges in 1939/1940, OSE knew exactly which suitable houses stood empty in the region. "They knew they could flee to *Montintin* in the event of an emergency," he told me.

No matter who came up with the idea of *Montintin*, the fact is OSE sent Papanek to Limoges without further ado, to rent the chateau for the children. Limoges at the time was regarded as France's "red capital" and had a long socialist tradition, which Papanek and the OSE leadership considered a good sign.[5]

Hasty travel arrangements began in Montmorency and Eaubonne, the educators packing bed linen, blankets, and pots and pans in boxes, while the children collected all their personal belongings. In *Villa La Chesnaie*'s kitchen, Amalia Kanner, the cook, spread a mixture of egg and vegetables on hundreds of slices of bread.[6]

Papanek was extremely worried about the Eaubonne children, wondering whether he would be able to provide an orthodox lifestyle for them in *Montintin*. In the end, the orthodox OSE home *Château des Morelles* in Broût-Vernet (near Vichy) agreed to take in 15 children. 15 places were far from enough, though, and after one year of living together, the Eaubonne children were once again faced with separation.

Oswald around 1940, in France. His whole life, Arthur was very proud of that picture, having knitted the sweater himself.

According to his democratic principles, Papanek asked the children to decide for themselves who among them would be sent to *Montintin* and who to *Les Morelles*. The children were completely overwhelmed by this choice: an orthodox home on one hand, Ernst Papanek and their old friends on the other hand. In the end, Papanek himself chose those he thought were the most observant among the children; all the others would be sent to *Montintin*.[7] Interestingly, eleven-year-old Oswald had no difficulty coming to a decision, probably because he was one of the few children who were actually fond of Madame Krakowski and thus wanted to stay with her. He followed her to *Montintin*.

On June 7, 1940, Papanek left Montmorency with his family and a few educators ahead of the children to prepare for their arrival in their new home. *Château de Montintin* turned out to be a quite derelict and run-down chateau outside the village of Château-Chervix, about 17 miles away from Limoges – which quite luckily stood indeed empty. "Jean-Louis de Neuville, the owner, had bought it because of the woods surrounding it," OSE historian Katy Hazan explained to me. "The chateau itself was unoccupied."

In *Out of the Fire*, Ernst Papanek recounts how he rang Jean-Louis de Neuville, who lived nearby, out of bed at six o'clock in the morning to make him a rental offer. When the latter heard *Montintin* was to house Jewish children, he rejected the offer at first. But when Papanek offered him the incredible sum of 40,000 Francs (according to Papanek, it would have been enough to buy an entire chateau), he changed his mind. In just one day, de Neuville removed all his belongings from *Montintin*, leaving behind an empty building. Merely the pool table remained, because it was fastened to the floor.[8]

At the same time, in Paris, OSE engaged in frantic negotiations with the French government, the police, and the railway operators to secure a carriage for the children on the overcrowded refugee trains heading south.

* * *

Oswald tossed and turned, sighing, trying to make himself comfortable on the cold stone floor. A clock struck midnight in the distance and a baby started crying somewhere. Together with hundreds of other refugees, the children had been waiting for hours on the platform for a train that did not come. Snuggled together, they lay on blankets right next to the tracks, their little backpacks tucked under their heads for pillows. Oswald kept feeling his pocket for his most precious possessions, the pictures and letters from his family.

He had had to hand over his passport, Madame Krakowski and her colleagues keeping all the children's identity documents.

Oswald woke with a start. The train had arrived! And that was not all: a note hanging on one of the carriages said: "*Seulement Pour Les Enfants*" (Only for children).

"That such an old train should still be in use," mumbled Erich Grünebaum, as he climbed aboard with his friend. Oswald nodded. Even discarded carriages were used to evacuate the Parisians, as long as they still had wheels and did not fall apart. Oswald managed to grab a seat on a wooden bench, but most of the children had to sit on the floor. However, even the floor offered relatively more comfort than the train's roof a few desperate Parisians had climbed onto, the carriages being hopelessly overcrowded.

The journey was nothing like the well-regulated travel from Vienna to France, one and a quarter years before. Back then, the children had fled the increasing harassment against the Jewish population; today, they fled from an advancing army. The danger was far more tangible this time and did not only concern a minority. All of Paris rushed south together with Oswald and his friends: let's get out of here before the Germans come!

The journey to *Château de Montintin* made a huge impression on the children. Years later, Arthur recalled the details of their flight: "It was just horrendous. The trains were totally overcrowded. On the road, you saw the effects of the war. We passed bombed-out cities. It was the first time that I saw dead people," he said, the expression on his face rigid and stiff. "The roads were just crowded with people trying to get anywhere to get out. It was just a horrendous experience. And of course, there was a shortage of food, we didn't have any – it was the first time that we experienced hunger."[9]

The children traveled a whole day for a distance one would cover in three hours today. The train kept stopping or otherwise had to make detours because train stations and platforms had been hit by German bombs. Things were no better on the streets, where cars drove next to carriages pulled by horses, bicycles, hand-pulled carts, and even baby carriages.

As more and more refugees tried to get on board the train, the children and the other passengers threw quite a lot of bags and pieces of furniture out of the windows. Most of them reached the south of France with a bag of underwear and a blanket as sole possession.[10]

A lot of details in the children's description of the flight coincide: desperately overcrowded trains, people traveling on the roof, and bombed-out cities. Yet in some other details, it appears the children depicted the traumatic experience in retrospect as having been much more terrible than it actually was. Their journey lasted 24 hours, but in Arthur's recollection, for instance, they traveled for at least five or six days.

In the meantime, OSE general secretary, Lazare Gurvic and the rest of the board had remained in Paris until all the children had left Montmorency.

Getting an exit permit for children was difficult enough, but getting such a permit for adult "enemy" foreigners proved an even more complex matter. OSE had to part heavy-heartedly with some of its colleagues, like the cook Amalia Kanner, who did not have valid papers. The organization feared their presence would put the children's rescue at risk in case of a police check.[11] Later, Amalia Kanner managed to get to *Montintin* on her own and reunite with her three daughters.

The situation was even more dangerous for the 23 teenagers over fifteen who were officially considered adults. OSE was about to throw all caution to the wind and illegally send the youths to the south, when they finally did receive exit permits for them on June 10, 1940, merely four days before the Germans reached Paris.

In a letter addressed to Papanek, Gurvic describes the evacuation of the older teenagers, who did not make it on board a refugee train: "We decided to take an extraordinary course of action, ...15 children traveled on a transport carriage, Mr. Pichon took four of them in his car and 6 others, the strongest among the boys, set off on foot. ... There was no other way out of Paris."[12]

By the time Gurvic wrote this letter on June 14, a few children were still on the road. But the escape succeeded. In the end, all the children found their way to *Montintin*.

12. *CHÂTEAU DE MONTINTIN*

Upon their arrival, the children at first mistook the *Château de Montintin* for a medieval castle. Just like in a fairytale, it was situated in a clearing in the forest and surrounded by the farm buildings, farmyards, barns, and stables of a small village. The *Château* itself was quite impressive, with its high towers, winding staircases, and banquet hall, quite the setting one may picture for King Arthur's Round Table.

However, all the rooms inside were completely empty! "When we arrived at *Montintin*, the chateau was completely bare. No furniture, cookware, or beds," Arthur told me. "The first few weeks, we slept on the floors."

Most of the children had reached the south of France with only a bag of underwear and a blanket. They spread their blankets on the floor in the large, empty refectory and cuddled up together. Fortunately, it was summer and they did not get too cold, lying on the stone floor.

Just like Ernst Papanek had feared, keeping the Jewish dietary laws proved quite difficult during the first days in their new accommodation. Food was scarce in the area anyway and in the beginning, the children had to eat pork. Oswald and the rest of the Eaubonne children accepted the situation, as Papanek recalled: "I explained once again that I knew the Bible well enough to know that they were permitted to eat pork in an emergency and that I didn't think anybody was going to deny that this was an emergency."[1]

There were no tables and no chairs and the young refugees had to sit on the floor to eat. Household utensils were scarce too, the children having thrown plates, pots, and pans out of the windows during their journey to make room for even more refugees on board the train. What with the chaos of their hasty departure, they had forgotten to pack knives and forks. They ate their first meals with their fingers.

* * *

The *Château de Montintin* was in the unoccupied part of France, often called *zone libre* (free zone) or Vichy France. On June 17, 1940, Philippe Pétain, a celebrated war hero of the First World War and a veteran of the battle of Verdun, was appointed head of state of the French government that had fled to Vichy. On June 22, he signed an agreement of armistice with Germany and Italy that divided the country in half. From the start, the Vichy regime, which would soon become a totalitarian form of governance itself, collaborated with Nazi Germany. According to article 19 of the armistice, for instance, the new French government committed itself to "extradite on demand all Germans ... living in France, as named and identified by the Reich government." In other words, this meant the French police arrested emigrants who were being pursued and delivered them into the hands of the Gestapo. The German refugees were no longer outside the Nazis' reach, even in the *zone libre*.[2]

This had dramatic consequences for the children in the OSE homes: Ernst Papanek had to leave them!

Only one week after his arrival in Montintin, the socialist mayor of Limoges warned Papanek that his name was on a wanted list. If he intended to protect the children, he would have to leave *Montintin* on the spot, together with a few other educators with links to the German or Austrian Social Democratic Party.

For a moment, Papanek considered hiding in the woods and waiting for things to calm down, but when a special unit of the Gestapo arrived in Limoges, the situation became much too dangerous. Ernst and Lene Papanek, their two sons, and a dozen educators left the refugee children heavy-heartedly and headed towards Montauban, 125 miles away, where the foreign representation of the Austrian Social Democrats had settled. Almost all Robinsons left *Montintin* too and traveled with their Social Democrat parents to Montauban, hoping to be able to emigrate again from there.

In his autobiography, Ernst Papanek gave a very emotional account of his parting with his protégés. When he drove off, the children reached inside the car through the open windows, refusing to let go of him. Many of them felt betrayed, because Papanek, their protector and teacher, their one big constant since fleeing from Germany, was leaving them.

"For while the children knew I might very well be killed if I stayed, They could not help but wonder whether they weren't going to be killed because I wasn't staying," Papanek recalled.[3] "The rumors were going around that he took off and left us kids to our own fate!" Oswald's good friend, Norbert Rosenblum, explained to me.

Parting with the children was very difficult for Ernst Papanek too, who blamed himself for leaving them on their own. With a two-year delay, he was now finally on his way to America. After he had allowed his initial visa to expire in 1939 to stay with the children, he was given one of the extremely coveted *Emergency Visas*. This special emergency-visa program had been brought into being by American President Franklin D. Roosevelt, against the will of his own State Department, in order to help exiled politicians, wanted by the Gestapo, obtain a visa outside the annually approved visa quota.

The visas were shared among several aid organizations, Papanek, and his family receiving one of only 50 visas granted to the American Federation of Labor. 3,000 people in total were nominated for the emergency-visa program, but only 1,000 of them actually secured such a visa; in the end, only 400 people managed to emigrate to the United States. A clear indication of Papanek's important role, but also his luck.[4]

The Vichy authorities refused to issue an exit permit for wanted emigrants, which meant the Papaneks could not leave the country by legal means. The French *Résistance* smuggled them across the Pyrenees to Spain and further on to Portugal, on an escape route that would become famous shortly after, being the same one distinguished celebrities and intellectuals such as Heinrich Mann, Franz Werfel, and Lion Feuchtwanger also took themselves.[5]

The family first took the train to Marseille to collect their American visas, before traveling on to the French border town of Cerbère. The most risky and hazardous part of their journey now lay ahead of them: the crossing of the Pyrenees.[6] For travelers in possession of valid papers, the journey was not such a big issue, as a railway tunnel, built several years ago, enabled one to reach Spain quite easily; without a valid exit visa, however, one was not allowed to board that train.

The Papaneks and their two sons, Gustav and Georg, climbed the *Coll de Rumpissar* (Rumpissar mountain pass) under high summer temperatures, before venturing on the descent into the valley to the Spanish village of Portbou, on preferably narrow paths. As a Social Democrat, Ernst Papanek did not feel safe in Franco's fascist Spain, but the family still managed to reach Barcelona without major incidents, continuing their journey to Madrid from there. Twelve days after leaving Montauban, the Papaneks finally reached the safety of Portugal, where they waited for a ship to America.

* * *

At the end of August 1940, 105 children lived at *Château de Montintin*, which had been made habitable little by little.[7]

Boris Ginodman, the supervisor of the carpentry workshop in Montmorency, had fortunately managed to bring along all the tools. Under his guidance, the teenagers felled trees in the surrounding forest and set up a new workshop. "The older boys and I – I was the youngest in that group – started making tables and chairs and wardrobes," Arthur told me.

The carpentry workshop in *Montintin*:
Oswald too learned to build furniture here.

After two or three months, OSE managed to find beds and the children no longer had to sleep on the floor. "But they weren't masterpieces of beds," Arthur remembered, laughing. "They were these old iron beds with metal springs."

Mid-November, almost six months after the children's arrival, the old furniture from Montmorency, along with a piano, finally reached the *Château de Montintin*. The piano was put in the billiard room on the first floor, which also housed a small library. The children slept on the second floor and in the tower, where the sewing room of the girls had also been set up. The teachers and educators lived in the numerous adjoining buildings and farmhouses belonging to the chateau.[8]

To this day, a stone house stands about a hundred meters from *Montintin: La Chevrette*. A few weeks after their escape to the south, the remaining forty orthodox children moved into *La Chevrette*, together with Madame Krakowski, her husband, and Amalia Kanner, who had already worked as a cook in Eaubonne. Oswald's new home, called "kid goat" in French, was surrounded by chestnut trees. Boris Ginodman had managed to save the Torah scrolls in his car and soon religious services were held in *La Chevrette*.

Oswald developed a close relationship with Amalia Kanner, the cook: "She came closest to being a mother towards me," he declared decades later. Kanner herself mentions Oswald by name in her auto-biography *Shattered Crystals*, recalling how he would always try to wangle leftovers.[9]

Once again the orthodox children lived separated from the rest of the OSE protégés, but they had much more contact with them than they used to have in Eaubonne. While Oswald and his friends ate and slept at *La Chevrette*, they attended classes and spent their free time in the main house. Just like in Eaubonne, not all children in *La Chevrette* were orthodox, but Madame Krakowski nevertheless ran the house as a religiously observant home.

In *Montintin*, the teachers endeavored to establish an orderly daily routine for their protégés as quickly as possible. For twenty minutes before breakfast, the children had to do gymnastic exercises or go for a walk in the woods. True to the old tradition of name-giving, the new sports teacher was soon awarded a nickname, the children call-ing him *Bel Ami* after the hero of Guy de Maupassant's eponymous novel. The children would spend the morning in the workshops – the girls sewing and the boys doing carpentry or repairing shoes – and attend regular classes in the afternoon. In order to prepare the young refugees for possible further emigration, the focus was now on for-eign language acquisition (French, English, and Spanish), and the orthodox children were also learning Hebrew. At the same time, OSE made sure its protégés would remain familiar with German culture, although the latter loudly protested against learning Goethe's *Faust* by heart. Before dinner, the children wrote letters or hung around in the picturesque surroundings of the chateau. The older boys were allowed to go to the nearby village of Château-Chervix to buy stamps or other small items. Unlike during their stay in Montmorency, they no longer needed to wear gas masks all the time, which made walks a lot easier. In the evening, the children played Domino, Monopoly, or card games they knew from Germany. The boys also loved playing chess with Dr. Hirschmann, Lene Papanek's successor as the home doctor.[10]

Exactly like in Montmorency, the children had to tidy and clean their own rooms and help with the maintenance of the chateau and the vegetable gardens. Boys and girls alike also learned how to knit and darn socks. One of the few pictures of Oswald taken during his stay in *Montintin*, in December 1940, shows him wearing a dark wool sweater with a high collar and a zipper. His whole life, Arthur was particularly proud of this picture, always telling me whenever we would be looking at it together, that he had knitted that sweater himself.

Asta Imbert was the new director of *Montintin*. Papanek had designated her as his successor before his departure, because she was French, Catholic, and non-political, and therefore in the best position, in his eyes, to protect the children in the current troubled political situation. Although he describes her in his autobiography as an uninspired teacher, lacking any leadership talent, he saw no other choice at the time, all the progressive educators being foreigners and thus at risk of being arrested.[11]

The children, however, liked Asta Imbert, who would allow them to choose one or two stamps from her personal collection on their birthday; so was Oswald, who turned twelve four months after his arrival in the south of France. Later Imbert married Herman Bodek, a Viennese professor and German teacher in *Montintin*, whom the children did not like because he was the one who had them learn Schiller and Goethe by heart.

In the fall, several OSE members in Montintin were arrested and interned in the *Gurs* camp that served as "a transit camp for emigrants and political prisoners."[12] In Ernst Papanek's papers in the *New York Public Library*, I came across several letters *Montintin* girls had written to Hanna Kaiser, a Robinson girl who had left the home. The girls described what had happened as follows: "Margot, Anni, and fat Käthe were sent to Gurs, unfortunately, and they haven't come back yet. ... What else can we do but hope?" Dörli Löbel wrote in October 1940.[13] One month later, Eva Unikower wrote: "The gendarmes pestered the home in the following weeks... on one occasion, they wrote down all the information and personal details of the German and Austrian children and on another occasion, all those over 15 had to show them their papers." Whoever had children among the female OSE members, like the cook Amalia Kanner for instance, was released quite soon, but for the other women and men things took much longer.[14] Around the same time, the Vichy government issued a so-called "Jewish Statute" that bore a terrifying similarity to the German anti-Jewish laws: Jews had to register with the authorities and shortly after, an "aryanization" of the economy was carried out. Adults were not the only ones threatened by these laws, children over 16 were also in danger. "There was always the problem of the French police coming around looking for some of the older children," Arthur recalled the perilous situation. "The French police knew where we were. But we were isolated and some of the older kids were able to escape into the forest when the police came around... It was unsettling and scary."

Leo Brenner, a Viennese teacher and cousin by marriage of Ernst Papanek, played a very important role in these troubled times. Brenner had already been a fervent supporter of Papanek's pedagogy back in Montmorency and he assumed a great deal of responsibility in *Montintin*. Not being Jewish, Brenner felt relatively safe in anti-Semitic Vichy France, even though he was a foreigner. He organized a lot of activities and lectures and introduced scout groups in

Montintin, dividing the children into three age groups: the Leverets, the Scouts, and the *Club de Jeunesse*, the "Youth Club."

The student co-administration also remained. I was able to read how highly the children valued this system in the letters they sent to friends who had already left the home, describing the different committees in vivid detail. They mentioned for instance the Group Council, the Home Council, and the Sports Committee, as well as a newspaper Editorial Board that wrote the *Echo de Montintin*, a kind of wall newspaper displayed in the chateau. Oswald too carried out a specific function: "Another sports competition will take place in about six weeks ... Felix the monkey, Dörli Löbl and Oswald Kernberg are the members of the Sports Committee," Ernst Valfer wrote to a friend.

A picnic in the spacious grounds in *Montintin*, around 1940. Oswald sits on the left, next to the educator.

* * *

"I'm quite fascinated by the way things continued in occupied France," Austrian historian Gerda Hofreiter confesses when we talk in the fall of 2017. "To think that even in the middle of such chaos, when everything around falls apart, some people still possess the spunk and energy to organize and do things."

A retired elementary school teacher from Tyrol, Hofreiter began to study history when she was sixty. In 2010, she published *Allein in die Fremde (You must go Alone)*, the first book dealing specifically with the *Kindertransports* leaving Austria.

In her research, Hofreiter compared the *Kindertransports* to France with those headed to England or America. The French transports stand out as a particularly successful example because the children "lived together so happily inside the homes" before the war broke out. According to Hofreiter, this was due to the relatively small number of children as well as the presence of extremely committed educators.

The German and Austrian OSE teachers could also make sure the children would not forget their mother tongue. "In England, most of the children forgot their language very soon, especially the younger ones. They could no longer speak with their parents after the war, if they saw them again, that is." Learning the works of Goethe and Schiller by heart definitely made sense indeed.

Another specificity of life in France was the fact that OSE would also look after children who had not arrived on a *Kindertransport*, after a large part of the country was occupied. "There were quite a lot of stranded children in France," Hofreiter tells me.

As a matter of fact, the number of children living in *Château de Montintin* grew significantly within a very short time. After the German invasion, OSE took in a lot of Jewish refugee children from Belgium and the Netherlands in its homes. French Jewish children, whose parents no longer had the means to look after them, also found shelter in the OSE homes. At the end of 1940, OSE was taking care of 1,600 children of different nationalities in eleven homes. There were now French-speaking children in *Montintin*; German was no longer the sole everyday language.[15]

13. "IT *VRAIMENT* SUCKS!"

The *Château de Montintin* is situated near the city of Limoges, famous for its porcelain. At first, I have some trouble finding out the current owner's identity. There is nothing listed on the Internet, even after some extensive research. Luckily though, local people turn out to be extremely helpful: thanks to the librarian of the neighboring village of Château-Chervix, I finally learn that *Montintin* is owned by the De Lamaze noble family. The mayor of the village asks the family for permission to let me visit the chateau, unoccupied for the best part of the year. In the fall of 2017, the administrator of their chateau invites me to *Montintin*. Quite a stroke of luck actually, as I would come to realize later. "I've never been there myself," local historian Michel Kiener tells me during our meeting. In 2006, Kiener published a book about *Montintin*, even though he has not been granted a visit to the chateau for over a decade.[1] The previous owner would not permit any historian to enter his chateau, which had only recently come into his son's and grandson's possession, both of them showing a keener interest in the building's history (including its Jewish history).

Mid-September 2017, I am on my way to Limoges. The De Lamaze administrator cancels our appointment at short notice because of some essential engagement, but Jean-Claude, the *gardien*, will meet me at the train station in his place and show me around. As *gardien* can stand for anything from supervisor to caretaker, I am not exactly sure what to expect, but as it turns out, Jean-Claude is a real sight. In his mid-forties, the black man welcomes me in a blue-checkered three-piece suit with a red necktie and matching breast pocket handkerchief, a signet ring, and leather shoes polished to a shine that would have better fit in a Parisian Salon than on the muddy forest paths we find ourselves trudging along shortly after. The son of Congolese emigrants is a trained porcelain painter, who worked as a taxi driver for over twenty years in Paris because he could not find a job in the Limoges area. He had only returned to Limoges a few months ago, to look after the De Lamaze's property, in the capacity of "Director of Castle Montintin" as he introduces himself to me. Because of Jean-Claude's broken English and my wobbly French, our conversation quickly turns into a weird jumble of both languages.

It is a thirty-minute drive from the train station to the chateau in Jean-Claude's white van, past green meadows and stone farmhouses, the streets getting increasingly narrow the closer we get to the chateau.

In their recollections of *Château de Montintin*, Ernst Papanek and the children always described it as a medieval knight's castle, but it was actually built in the 19th century. Their mistake is quite easily understandable though; the impressive building indeed looks like some fairy tale castle, with its natural stone walls typical for the region and its neo-gothic style elements.

Compared with the imposing *Château de Montintin*, *Villa Helvetia* I have visited only a few days before appears no bigger than a terraced house. Today the *Montintin* property includes over 60 acres of forest and two lakes. It takes three hours for Jean-Claude and me to walk through the immediate surroundings of the place and visit the outbuildings and the chateau's 30 rooms. I cannot help feeling in awe during the entire tour. *"C'est très joli,"* I keep saying again and again,

"It's very nice." – "*C'est magnifique*," Jean-Claude readily replies, "It's splendid."

Merely two doors lead inside the chateau: a small service entrance and the actual entrance gate, surmounted by the De Lamaze's family crest – a lion beneath three cubes – carved into stone. The wrought iron gate of the park and the cellar also bear the crest, conveying the impression that the family has been living here for centuries when the De Lamazes only really bought the chateau in the 1990s.

Once inside the building, one can explore *Montintin* in two ways: either using the great main staircase or the spiral stone staircase that gave the servants access to every room without being noticed. We choose the servants' stairs to take a "sneak peek" at the chambers, namely the white room, the red room, and the clouds' room. None of them are alike. "Each room tells its own story," Jean-Claude says, enthused. "Each has its own personality." A knight's armor stands in the stairwell and portraits of ancestors of the family from the time of the Russian Revolution hang on the walls; merely a television set, or the latest issue of some tabloid here and there, disturb one's feeling of actually having traveled into the past. "Time has stopped here," Jean-Claude declares. After three months in *Montintin*, he still cannot bring himself to realize he traded his stressful life in noisy Paris for this idyllic chateau.

Jean-Claude lives in one of the numerous outbuildings, where in a matter of minutes, he conjures up a meal of veal chops, potatoes, cheese, apple tart, and chocolate éclairs. While the chops sizzle and the potatoes boil, Jean-Claude proceeds to inform me about his troubled love life. Long-distance relationships are difficult, even for chateau dwellers.

As much as I enjoyed visiting *Château de Montintin*, I enjoy even more sitting in the sunlight in front of the building and listening to the complete silence. *Montintin*, with its adjoining forest, is a true paradise. The perfect place to write a book or find yourself cut off from the world.

I cannot help but think Oswald and the other refugee children could have been very happy here, had they not arrived in the chateau at the worst moment in their lives, after a nerve-racking escape throughout France.

* * *

The chateau was now equipped with furniture and cutlery, but food remained a big problem. All the former *Montintin* children I spoke to told me they were constantly hungry. The OSE protégés only rarely ate meat and then only a very little of it. Even potatoes were scarce in the south of France, stricken by famine. *Topinambour* (Jerusalem artichoke) was the staple food in *Montintin*, a highly praised vegetable among gourmets today, yet at the time grown as pig feed. Amalia Kanner, the cook of orthodox home *La Chevrette*, would fry it, or else make soup or mash – every possible dish consisted of Jerusalem artichoke. No matter how hard she tried, though, the children hated the "animal feed" so much they refused to eat it despite being very hungry.[2] The wretched vegetable is deeply etched in the children's memory: no matter how often I spoke with Arthur or his friends about their life in France over the years, we ended up talking about Jerusalem artichoke every single time. "We ate very, very much *Topinambour*, (Jerusalem artichoke)" Arthur told me, sighing and laughing at once.

Kanner and her colleagues tried their best to improve the menu as creatively as possible: the children were sent to collect berries, mushrooms, and sweet chestnuts and started a vegetable garden of their own. They would also be sent to buy milk, as they drew less attention than the adults. Milk was strictly rationed, but the local farmers illegally sold small quantities to the OSE home. To keep the whole thing as inconspicuous as possible, two boys had to get up very early every morning and buy milk from different farmers.

"We used to have to go with the cans and two boys at a time on a bicycle," Arthur explained to me. Only one boy had a bike in

Montintin, his most precious possession. He had even traveled by bike from Montmorency to the south of France so he would not have to leave it behind. However, despite his loud protestations, the home management would confiscate his bike every morning for the purchase of milk. Equipped with a flashlight, the children set off, riding the bike through the darkness over poorly paved forest paths – a big adventure for the boys. "We were always fighting, we all wanted to go with the bike," Oswald's friend, Norbert Rosenblum, told me.

From time to time, Amalia Kanner would send Oswald to buy bread, the boy always returning with a surprisingly light *baguette*: from the outside, the bread seemed perfectly normal, but Oswald was so hungry he had completely hollowed it out on his way back. A lot of children in *Montintin* suffered from the consequences of malnutrition. Diarrhea was a common disorder, the young refugees eating everything they found in nature and considered edible. The psychological strain of their circumstances also weighed heavily on the younger children, who often reacted with bedwetting.

Still, after a few weeks in *Montintin*, the children had settled back into a daily routine. Many of Ernst Papanek's guiding principles were kept even in his absence, such as the Student Council and the practical teaching. But there was growing unrest among the teachers. Because of the frequent change of personnel, there was little cohesion between the staff, and the new director, Asta Imbert. She was described as an uncooperative and headstrong woman, who did not seem to be able to change this.[3]

The rest of Papanek's old guard drew quite a dark picture of their circumstances at the home in desperate-sounding letters sent to the Papanek family. As early as July 1940, one month after Papanek's departure, Margot Cohn, the former director of *Villa Helvetia*, complained about her "incompetent colleagues" in *Montintin*, who possessed no pedagogical skills whatsoever. "I felt like crying all the time: the educational and reconstruction work of more than 1½ years was forgotten," Cohn complained.[4]

In the first days of March 1941, Leo Brenner wrote to Ernst Papanek, saying he feared Papanek's "hair would turn grey" should he ever learn what went on in *Montintin*. "Asta is a nice person, an excellent teacher, and a dreadful director. She has neither the pedagogical nor the organizational skills required to run a children's home," he continued, sharply criticizing Imbert, who refused to collaborate with the educators.

Brenner also mentions "schemers" and "malevolent" persons: one of the workshop supervisors "beats his 'apprentices' with hands and feet, and in *La Chevrette*, the children are deprived of food as a punishment; it is dreadful." It even came to power struggles, according to him: "Everyone works against everyone, people spend their time scheming and plotting, one almost fears for his life, so to speak. It *vraiment* sucks – It *really* sucks."

Many liberal educators having fled with Ernst Papanek, the influence of Madame Krakowski, the orthodox director of *La Chevrette*, grew all the more. In the eyes of the OSE leadership, implementing a progressive pedagogy had always been Papanek's hobby, but Jewish traditions were part of OSE and upheld as such, no matter who ran the home. Krakowski's authority showed especially in the fact that the interactions of boys and girls were regulated in a much stricter way in *Montintin* than they had been in Montmorency. A boy and a girl would be punished for standing too close next to each other. The home management even considered sending all the girls to another home to get rid of the "problem."

The older the young refugees became, the more they also became interested in the other sex, unsurprisingly. Oswald's friend, Erich Grünebaum, described blossoming "romances" between the older teenagers: "Why else would young men voluntarily go out into the woods to gather firewood for some girls' room?"

However, according to Ernst Valfer, one of the oldest teenagers in *Montintin*, most of the children were "far too immature" for such relationships. During his entire time in *Montintin*, he can only remember one couple that was unfortunate enough to get caught kissing by Madame Krakowski. In 1941, Krakowski made good of her threat and sent all the girls to the OSE religious home of *Mas-Jambost*, on the outskirts of Limoges.

Given all these changes, sociologist Hanna Papanek came to the following conclusion, decades later: "Ernst Papanek's and his colleagues' progressive educational practice depended on their actual presence in the OSE homes. As soon as they left, it all came to an end."[5]

In a letter Käthe Bodek, "thin Käthe," wrote to Papanek in the spring of 1941, she noted, more optimistically: "Some say it's a shame about Ernst's work, but I say: if our children are doing fairly well today, then only because of the wonderful groundwork. Our community can't be broken."

The children usually did not know about the conflicts between the teachers. With one exception, though, Ernst Valfer. "There was a very serious split in *Montintin* between two groups of adults," the 92-year-old told me. "I had a strong opinion about it, and because I was idealistic and very naive, I openly sided, as President of the Student Council, with the more liberal group, which eventually lost the fight. The winning side was headed by the French *Directrice*, Asta Imbert, and her lover, Herman Bodek. After the defeat of the liberal educators' group, this lover took me aside and told me that if I ever again put my nose into the business of adults, he would hand me over to the Germans. Not the French police – the Germans!"

Bodek only apologized to Valfer on the eve of the boy's departure to America. "He took me for a walk," Valfer recounted. "He then gave me a little yellow slip of paper, on which he had written a quote from a Greek philosopher: 'Only through suffering can a human being become educated.' And he tried to make peace with me and said that he realized this was a difficult situation, but he hoped I had learned something useful that would help me for the rest of my life."

As mentioned before however, apart from Ernst Valfer, the children were not aware of the conflicts between OSE members or at least did not worry about it. Much more important to them was the issue of the bad food or the lack of food, as their letters and recollections show. OSE experienced great financial difficulties at the time, the problem being how to get international donations to France. In the south of France for instance, banks no longer accepted British checks, fearing the country would fall into German hands next.[6] In 1940 and 1941, OSE's budget was almost entirely financed by the Jewish-American aid organization Joint but even American money could not be transferred directly to France and had to be channeled over Switzerland or Portugal first. In one of her books, Katy Hazan describes the often epic transactions: OSE members smuggled gold, concealed in the false floorboard of a car, or else hid banknotes under a bicycle saddle.[7] The Gunzbourg family continued to support OSE financially, but it would often be months before the money reached the homes. The farmers around *Montintin* were real lifesavers for the children, as they sold food to OSE on credit for months – despite the legions of famished refugees streaming into southern France.

Hygienic conditions were just as bad, the homes lacking toothpaste, toothbrushes, and pajamas. A lot of children no longer possessed proper footwear and had to wear wood clogs instead. There also was no proper heating in *Montintin*, the building being heated by wood stoves. Luckily though, the chateau was surrounded by woods, so collecting firewood was not a problem. Chopping wood was the older boys' task.

Surrounded by thick woodland, the *Château de Montintin* stood very secluded. But it was not a ghetto, as historian Michel Kiener points out. Many support staff came from the area, including several young cooks who were not much older than the oldest home children.[8] Still, fearing the children could suffer from isolation, OSE organized an "Olympics" in the spring, a sports competition between the children of the eleven homes the organization had opened in unoccupied France.[9] Relay races, high jumping, and spear-throwing were on the program. As mentioned before, Oswald was in the sports commission.

Even in *Montintin*, OSE stayed true to its penchant for celebrations, the parties perhaps not quite as grandiose as they had been the year before, but more essential than ever for everyone's morale. In a letter Leo Brenner wrote to Ernst Papanek in December 1940, he reports: "After a rather tense time... we're on holiday, preparing a Hanukkah celebration for the 30th and a New Year's Eve party for the 31st. The older children take part with great enthusiasm in the preparations that can't be too costly, of course. OSE has granted the home 200 fcs [Francs] for the Hanukkah party. But it's going to be great fun and that's all that matters."

The carpenter apprentices made a Hanukkiah (an eight-armed Hanukkah menorah) from chestnut wood for Hanukkah and built a large Sukkah (a hut) for Succoth (Feast of Tabernacles). Madame Krakowski's husband conducted religious services on Rosh Hashanah and Yom Kippur, two of the major festivals in the Jewish calendar.[10] On the French national day, the children sang the "*Marseillaise*" again, diligently composing poetry just like before. On New Year's Eve 1941, the children composed a song about their home they proceeded to sing to familiar tunes such as "*Frère Jacques*" or the German nursery rhyme "*Alle meine Entchen*" (All of my ducks):

Im Montintiner Heime, – In our home in Montintin,
Da ist es sehr famos. – Things are great, undoubtedly.
Doch wisst ihr auch das eine? – But did you know that here, o woe,
Es gibt nur zwei Klos. – There are no more than two small loos?
Und muss man einmal rennen, – So when you need it quick and bad,
Dann ist es schon zu spät. – It's far too late, no need to add,
Ja, da kann man wirklich flennen, – Seeing someone in line already,
Wenn schon einer vorne steht. – Is more than enough to make you cry.[11]

In addition to the various holidays, a dance evening took place in the chateau almost every Saturday. A few boys played the piano, the accordion, and the saxophone, an old gramophone replacing them whenever they got tired.

Oswald's circle of friends, a clique of eleven and twelve-year-old rascals, spent a lot of time outdoors, concocting crazy business ideas. "Some of the farms had fruit trees such as apples and cherries," Arthur remembered later. "Some of us got friendly with some of the farmers and helped out on a farm. I was allowed to play with the rabbits raised on one of the farms. One of my roommates found a small porcupine which quickly became our pet."

* * *

Everything was silent in *La Chevrette*. Oswald and his friends were fast asleep in their room with six beds, the light snoring of a boy in one corner of the room was the only sound. Then suddenly there was a loud explosion! Glass splinters flew across the room! Oswald woke with a start, trying to find his bearings in the chaos. What had just happened?

"A group of us wanted to make wine," Arthur explained to me decades later. "We had several clandestine midnight requisition raids on the farmers' apple trees and different teams squeezed the apples with a little hand press and drained the juice into jars." The apples were left to ferment for about two weeks, the boys already congratulating themselves on their success, until the jars exploded with a loud bang because of the fermentation process, hurling apple slush across the room.

Another enterprise shows how intensely engaged with their (uncertain) future the children were: "We were all convinced that eventually, we would all reach the United States, the land of milk and honey, the land of unlimited opportunities," Erich Grünebaum recounted. "A few of us got together and decided that when we would reach America we were going to be rich. American women loved fur coats and fur was a high-priced commodity. So we started trapping gophers and moles." The plan was to skin them and make furs.

"We did catch a bunch of these little creatures, but everyone was too squeamish to cut them up," Norbert Rosenblum told me, describing the project. "Needless to say that plan fell through, shattering our hopes."

Yet according to Erich Grünebaum, the boys did bring their enterprise to an end: "We skinned the poor little animals, carefully preserving the hides in a loft-like area above the woodshed. ...We wanted the pelts to dry so we procured a large tin container ...and fashioned it into a homemade stove. We had a roaring fire up there for a few days until we were discovered and kicked out, together with our evil-smelling get-rich-quick furs. It was a miracle that we didn't burn the shed to the ground."

Later Arthur would often speak of a "family" the boys who shared his room had grown into. Already in Eaubonne, he had felt the children were more than just friends, rather like siblings. In *Montintin*, the roommates became a real family, comforting each other in difficult times. The boys went on playing a lot of soccer and the twelve-year-olds began learning for their bar mitzvah, the religious coming-of-age ceremony Jewish boys celebrate on their 13th birthday. Oswald's roommate Erich later described the time in *Montintin* as follows: "None of us will ever forget our year at *Château Montintin*. We lived together, we slept together, we were hungry together and we had happy experiences together. It is hard to put into words the closeness we felt for one another during that very difficult time."

* * *

The children's close friendship helped them cope with bad news from home. Letters became scarcer and scarcer, and some children no longer received any news from their parents. Through his relatives in Switzerland, Oswald was still able to communicate with his parents, even though their exchanges were now very sporadic. On August 1940, the eleven-year-old boy received a letter sent from a new address in Vienna: *Nußdorfer Straße 60*.

The Nazis had forced his parents to leave their apartment on *Gussenbauergasse 1* and move to a so-called "Jew-houses," where a lot of Jewish families from Vienna had been crammed together. The house was also situated in the *Alsergrund* area, about fifteen minutes walk from their old apartment. Since the cancellation of the eviction protection for Jews in May 1939, a lot of these collective apartments and "Jew-houses" had sprang up in Vienna, resulting in ghetto-like situations, which was especially the case in the *Alsergrund* area.[12]

Like so often before, Frieda and Hermann kept the seriousness of their situation from their son. "They wrote me a letter to pay attention to them living at another address," Arthur said. "They didn't say what circumstances, except that they're living in that new apartment."

For some time, Oswald did not receive any news from his family at all. And then, in the spring of 1941, a few letters reached him again – from Poland this time!

On February 26, 1941, Hermann, Frieda, and Fritz Kernberg had been deported to Opole, a small town south of Lublin. In February 1941, 2,000 Viennese Jews arrived in Opole in two separate convoys. By March, 8,000 Jews lived in the city, in a newly established ghetto, under inhumane conditions.[13]

Oswald understood what it meant to be deported. Other parents had also been sent to Opole or even to concentration camps and the children talked about it amongst themselves. "I did know there was a problem," he confessed. "And it's one of the reasons why I always used to say, in my letters to them, I wanted my brother and mother to write something. I wanted to see their handwriting. I didn't tell them why, only that I wanted them to write something – so I would know they were still there."

Oswald's parents did not tell him about the situation in Opole, their letters were as optimistic and confident as ever that they would soon be able to emigrate to America together. "We have been living in Poland for 2 ½ months, we're in good health and doing well. We pray to the Almighty to soon be able to leave this place and emigrate to America," Hermann Kernberg wrote in May 1941.

The rest of his letter is also filled with fervent hope and loving concern for Oswald's life: "We're glad to hear you have so much fun with the rabbits and that you take such great pleasure in the game of soccer, and likewise that you've started to learn for your bar mitzvah." And further on: "My dearest child, you've been through a lot despite your young age, please continue to be brave, courageous, and strong, always remember your parents and your brother, who think of you every hour of every day and talk about you; hopefully it will not be too long before we can all sit together at a table and tell each other everything that has happened to us. We hope and wish you've grown to be tall and strong by now; there is nothing we pray the Almighty more ardently for than to be reunited with you very soon, so we can all live together again."

As so often, Hermann Kernberg's letter was driven by the desire to keep the dreadful truth from his son. Frieda's short message to her son, however, sounds a lot more pessimistic: "My dearest *Burli!*" Frieda wrote. "I'm very sad to be here, in Opole, and unable to travel with you to America and help you with your bar mitzvah. ... *Papa* is too weak to work. Many greetings and kisses from your crying *Mama*, who has not seen you in two years."

* * *

Even in the *Château de Montintin*, the situation became more and more dangerous for the Jewish children. About 145,000 Jews lived in "free" France, which did not mean they were safe there, far from it.[14] "The government and institutions of Vichy France were active assistants to the German persecution and later murder of the Jews," historian Stephanie Corazza writes.[15] Vichy introduced anti-Semitic laws as early as October 1940. The transit camps for enemy aliens were converted into internment camps for Jews. Camps like *Gurs* and *Rivesaltes* were known for their "disastrous hygienic conditions, and scarcity of food," causing the death of countless internees.[16] In some cases, the French authorities acted even more harshly than the Germans expected, also detaining children for instance.

OSE now took on many additional tasks in Vichy France, in an attempt to help the Jewish population in distress in all sorts of ways, providing medical care to French Jews in many regions, for instance. When the property of the Rothschild family was seized in 1941 and after the family itself had fled to America, OSE took in the children of the Rothschild homes.[17]

That same year, OSE began to rescue children from the *Gurs* and *Rivesaltes* internment camps, whose release was legally possible under certain circumstances. Firstly, OSE had to assume full financial responsibility for each child and also had to convince the detained parents to part with their children – very often a much more difficult enterprise. Vivette Hermann, who would later become director of OSE, gave a very moving and impressive example of that. At the age of 22, she volunteered to be detained in *Rivesaltes* and spent several months in the camp to organize the children's rescue from the inside. Hermann's duties involved convincing the parents to part with their children, preparing the children for this separation, and handle all the administrative hurdles and negotiations with the camp management.[18]

Within a mere seven months, Hermann managed to rescue all 400 Jewish children from *Rivesaltes*. On the whole, OSE managed to free 1,000 children from the internment camps and send them to homes such as *Montintin*.[19]

Yet even there they were not safe in the long run.

14. AMERICA AS A LAST HOPE

In the spring of 1941, Purim, the most cheerful and boisterous Jewish holiday, was knocking on the door. In keeping with tradition, the children wrote a poem they recited during the celebration in *Montintin*. This time, though, they adopted uncharacteristically thoughtful tones:

Hört mal zu ihr lieben Leute, – Hear ye, hear ye! Fair people
Purim, das bedeutet Freude. – Purim means joy and happiness
Purim, das bedeutet Kuchen essen, – Purim means having cake
Und den Haman nicht vergessen. – without forgetting about Haman.

Dieser Spruch aus Kindertagen, – This saying from childhood years
Kann uns heute nichts mehr sagen. – no longer a thing to us means.
Dies war gestern, was wird morgen? – This is all past, what will
                                                        tomorrow bring?
Das sind unsere heutigen Sorgen. – These are our worries today.

Visum, Affidavit, Konsulat, – Visa, affidavit, consulate,
Brasilien, Cuba, Dominikanerstaat, – Brazil, Cuba, Dominican
Republic,
Bolivien, Haiti, Paraguay, Alexandrien, – Bolivia, Haiti, Paraguay,
Alexandria,
Palästina oder Rhodesien, – Palestine or Rhodesia,
Australien, Shanghai, Südafrika – Australia, Shanghai, South Africa
Und die letzte Hoffnung ist U.S.A – And our last hope, U.S.A.[1]

No matter how many reports I read about the situation of the Jews in Vichy France, nothing helps me understand the gravity of the situation as clearly as this poem. The time of carefree children's fun was over – *And our last hope, U.S.A.*

Despite the increasing harassment by the Vichy authorities, OSE endeavored to provide a regulated life to their protégés. The organization was well aware, however, that it would not be able to protect the children in the long run and thus did everything in its power to get the children out of the country, preferably to America.

OSE hoped for help and support from Ernst Papanek, who had been living in New York since September 1940, as well as from the American OSE branch AMEROSE, created in 1929 and run since 1939 by Dr. Leon Wulman, a Polish Jewish emigrant. AMEROSE was by far not as large as the French OSE, Wulman's hotel room in Broadmoor Hotel, on the Upper West Side, serving as the organization's office for a long time. There were no salaried employees and Ernst Papanek had to wash dishes at night to be able to work during the day at AMEROSE towards the emigration of "his" children.[2]

At the turn of the year, in the winter of 1940-1941, AMEROSE took over the *Union OSE*'s missions worldwide, the latter being no longer able to ensure the coordination of its numerous international branches since the German occupation of Paris. At long last, AMEROSE moved into an office of its own on 24th West 40th Street, just across the *New York Public Library*, where decades later I would find Ernst Papanek's papers.[3]

Shortly after Papanek's departure, the children had hung a picture of him and of US President Franklin D. Roosevelt on a pinboard. Below Papanek's picture, they had written: "He will *get* us a visa," under Roosevelt's: "He will *give* us a visa."

But the children put too much hope in the American President. The United States maintained a very restrictive immigration policy despite the outbreak of the Second World War and the Nazi persecution of the Jews. Roosevelt's commitment towards persecuted politicians – which had allowed Ernst Papanek to emigrate to the US – was the exception that confirmed the rule. Since the *Immigration Act* of 1924, America applied fixed quota regulations to immigration, only allowing entry to a legally prescribed number of immigrants from each country. Racist and xenophobic motives played no small part in the fixing of these quotas at the time, which favored Western European countries, while the quotas for East European, African or Asian countries were very low. During World War II, a maximum of 150,000 visas were issued yearly, among which 27,000 were allocated to Nazi Germany and Austria.[4] Even those who did indeed meet all the requirements for a visa, often had to wait several years before their quota number came up.

After the November Pogroms in 1938, there was a short-lived hope America would allow *Kindertransports*, just like England or France had. A bill to this effect, the *Wagner-Rogers-Bill*, was introduced to the US Congress in February 1939, and would have allowed the immigration of 20,000 unaccompanied Jewish refugee children to the US, in addition to the existing German admission quotas. Although the bill counted a few prominent supporters – first of all, First Lady Eleanor Roosevelt and the US Secretary of Labor, Frances Perkins – it was thwarted even before it came to a vote in the face of a strong public opposition.[5]

America, which would only enter the war after the attack on Pearl

Harbor in December 1941, had very little interest in dealing with European problems. Added to this was a prevailing anti-Semitic sentiment and American Jews' fear that anti-Semitism would only grow stronger if too many Jewish refugees were allowed entry to the country.[6]

Still, the Jewish aid organizations worked tirelessly to organize small *Kindertransports* that fit into the existing quota regulations. As early as 1934, the *German-Jewish Children's Aid* (GJCA) had managed to be acknowledged as the issuer of a so-called corporate affidavit.[7] An affidavit is a sworn statement in which a guarantor guarantees that a potential immigrant will not be a burden on the US community. A private person usually had to take over this guarantee and accept full financial liability. Yet thanks to the corporate affidavit, GJCA was able to act as guarantor in the capacity of an organization, which greatly facilitated the situation. Between 1934 and 1941, GJCA thus managed to bring 589 unaccompanied German and Austrian minors to America.[8]

After the conquest of France and the Benelux countries in the summer of 1940, public opinion in the US began to change, gradually becoming more open to helping and supporting European children.[9] The *United States Committee for the Care of European Children* (USCOM) played a very significant part in the organization of *Kindertransports* – and especially in Oswald's rescue.[10] In December 2017, I meet with Ron Coleman, Chief Archivist of the *United States Holocaust Memorial Museum* to talk about USCOM.

* * *

The *United States Holocaust Memorial Museum* is one of the largest Holocaust museums in the world. 43 million people have visited it since its opening in 1993. It is situated in the center of Washington D.C., close to the Washington Monument and the National Mall, the grand alley of the American capital city.

The museum itself is an impressive stone building, resembling many government buildings in the neighborhood with its elegant white limestone. However, the red brick walls and steel pillars inside make me feel as if I were standing in an old factory building. Many moving artifacts are exhibited in the museum, such as a wooden boat for instance, on which Jews were saved from Denmark to Sweden, or a photo album of the *St. Louis* refugee ship.

An elevator, concealed behind the security gate, equipped with metal detectors and luggage X-ray, leads to the heart of the museum: the archives. The museum holds a huge collection of over 20,000 historical items and over a hundred million document pages, as well as tens of thousands of copies of files from archives around the world, which makes it the ideal place for any research about the Holocaust. Today, for instance, the files of the Viennese Jewish community can be found in part in Vienna and in part in Jerusalem, yet I was able to consult copies of the entire archival fonds in the *Holocaust Memorial Museum*.

Many archives departments, especially in Europe, resemble impregnable fortresses, requiring you to overcome obstacles and go through several ordeals before finally being granted access to the sacred halls. Nothing of the sort, though, in the *Holocaust Memorial Museum*. Even as a twenty-year-old university student, I was allowed to consult original files without difficulty. I remember quite vividly how exhilarated I felt, holding a letter written on war paper or a child's drawing from France. I know Ron Coleman from that time, the uncommonly helpful chief archivist with the wonderful gift of connecting researchers all over the world. Over the past few years, he has focused especially on the US immigration policy in the 1930s and 1940s and on the *Kindertransports* to America, which still remain completely unknown to this day. In December 2017, I return to Washington, D.C. to view a few last files and arrange to meet Coleman in his office, overflowing with books, pictures, and documents of all kinds.

"We here at the Museum help people answer questions that they may have had about their families for decades," Coleman tells me. "We serve these people best by getting their stories right. And I hope I'm helping people like you to get Arthur's story right."

One year after the failed attempt of the *Wagner-Rogers-Bill* to allow 20,000 Jewish children to enter the United States in 1939, it seemed like another push in this direction might finally prove successful. "Once war broke out, the tide shifted of not so much, 'Oh yes, we want to bring in 20,000 children,' but at least, 'we are ready to bring in children that are in danger,'" Coleman explains to me. "So First Lady Eleanor Roosevelt called together a meeting in June of 1940 to found *The United States Committee for the Care of European Children* (USCOM)."

USCOM was a non-sectarian aid organization, acting independent of the American government, even though Eleanor Roosevelt, in her capacity as honorary president, established many connections. "The president of USCOM was Marshall Field III, who was the billionaire heir of the famous Marshall Field department store in Chicago," Coleman recapitulates. "Field announced a large fundraising effort and used his popularity for it. Everybody knew who he was."

Just like the GJCA had, USCOM received permission to issue a corporate affidavit. In order to guarantee no child would become a charity case, the organization had to leave a deposit of fifty dollars for each child as a guarantee sum and agree to assume full responsibility for the refugee children until their twenty-first birthday. "The corporate affidavit made a huge difference in trying to rescue these children," Coleman says to me, emphasizing the word "huge" with a big hand gesture. "GJCA pioneered the idea and USCOM inherited it."

USCOM had not been created to rescue Jewish refugee children, though, the organization attempting at first to protect British children from German air raids. "Legally it was easier to bring British children to America because they had a country to go back to after the war," Coleman explains.

The first 2,000 British children were supposed to emigrate to the USA in the summer of 1940. But only two months after its implementation, a terrible tragedy brought the program to an abrupt end: 77 children were killed during a German attack on the *City of Benares* passenger ship. The British government demanded the immediate cessation of the evacuations.[11] (The daughter of world-famous German author Thomas Mann, Monika, was also on board the *Benares* and could be saved, after having spent twenty hours in the water; her husband however drowned.)

But the Jewish children threatened by deportation in Vichy France were in such danger that even the perilous sea crossing was no argument against their rescue. "In the fall of 1940, 27 children from France reached the US on a test-transport. After that, USCOM decided to try and do larger transports from France," Ron Coleman says, finishing his explanations.

* * *

If USCOM played a significant part in organizing *Kindertransports* to America, it was by far not the only aid organization involved. In reality, it took a dozen groups on both sides of the Atlantic to save Oswald, and the rest of the OSE children, from the Holocaust.

Decades later, Arthur very nicely expressed this in an autobiographical short story, applying the African saying "It takes a village to raise a child" to his own life. "It took more than a village to raise *this* child," he explained. "It took the government of three countries, many people, and many organizations, both Jewish and non-Jewish."

The background and organization of the *Kindertransports* to America are so complex whole books have been written about individual aspects of the enterprise. For months, I have read thousands of files in four different archives in New York and Washington, D.C., so I would be able to reconstruct Oswald's rescue in as many details as possible. Pages and pages of lists, project drafts, meeting minutes, budgets, and letters filled with increasing despair. More often than not, crucial information is hidden in handwritten notes or misfiled documents. The result is a puzzle I have assembled from an utterly gigantic, ungraspable number of facts and information – the odyssey of one child that ended well, despite countless bureaucratic obstacles.

As it appeared, four groups played a major part in the children's rescue: USCOM, the Quakers, GJCA, and OSE.

USCOM created the legal basis for the emigration to America, but it had no employees in Europe and thus had to work with local partner organizations. The *American Friends Service Committee* (AFSC), the largest Quaker relief committee worldwide, acted as its representative in France. The Quakers are a religious group with Christian roots, created in England in the 17th century. In the middle of the 20th century, the Quakers had 150,000 members worldwide and are known to this day for their aid work during the war. Since the end of the 1930s, the American Quakers took care of refugees in the south of France, especially Jewish children, as Donald Davis, the in-house ASFC archivist in Philadelphia, goes on to explain: "They set up feeding stations and medical centers, they were in the camps to help people there and they opened several children colonies."

Cooperating with the Quakers was extremely beneficial for USCOM, as the Quakers maintained excellent relations with the French, American, and even German authorities. The Quakers' greatest strength was their total impartiality. Helping all involved parties gave them access in turn to all said parties.

The Quakers took over the organization of the USCOM *Kindertransports* in Europe, despite being very critical of the rescue action. In the archive of the *Holocaust Memorial Museum*, I find internal letters from the 1940s attesting to the fact. After the organization of the first *Kindertransport*, in the summer of 1941, Allen Bonnell, who was based in Marseille, wrote to the ASFC head office in Philadelphia: "Expenses for the emigration of these children were extremely high and there is considerable question in our minds whether or not the expenses were warranted." According to Bonnell, the money it took to bring one single child to America could provide for a needy child in France for an entire year.[12]

"It's a common tension all of these refugee aid organizations had," Ron Coleman tells me later. "This tension between relief and rescue. Should we take this money and buy a thousand meals? Or should we take that money to help one person to try and get out and there's no guarantee that he or she would be able to do it."

After reading numerous letters from France, I also realize the Quakers had not expected the organization of *Kindertransports* would result in such a huge amount of work. A work that came at the expense of other relief actions.

As soon as the children set foot on American soil, yet another organization took over the responsibility for them: the GJCA, as mentioned before. Although the *German Jewish Children's Aid* had been the only group for years that brought Jewish children to America by means of a corporate affidavit, it was now only responsible for the children's care in the US USCOM vouched for the young refugees vis-à-vis the US government and took over the costs for their support, the actual care for the children being provided by the GJCA.[13]

The GJCA files kept in New York turn out to be a stroke of luck for me: unlike any other organization involved, GJCA made copies of every single letter it sent and received, always keeping both sides of a correspondence in its files, which allows me to gain a comprehensive insight into the organization's work. Most of the letters are – by far – those of Lotte Marcuse, who in her capacity as *Placement Director* was in charge of finding a home for the refugee children. Marcuse was a German immigrant from Berlin, described by her contemporaries as a hard-working, if not always popular social worker.[14] She planned the children's first week in America down to the last detail:

the schedules she sent record everything from the purchase of toys (two days before the arrival of the ship) and the writing of letters (Friday from 1:30 pm to 3:00 pm) to medical examinations (Tuesdays and Wednesdays). I also discover instructions on how to deal with the press (only with Marcuse's express permission) in the GJCA files.[15]

Just like Arthur wrote in his short story, it took more than "a village" to rescue him. Next to the organizations mentioned above, several others also took action. The Joint and the *National Refugee Service* financed the children's transportation costs, the *Hebrew Immigrant Aid Society* secured places on board the ships, the *Children's Bureau*, housed in the US Department of Labor, supervised the children's care in America, and even the *Young Men's Christian Association* (YMCA) and the Unitarians supported the enterprise.[16]

It is very difficult to reconstruct today who exactly gave a kick-start to the children's rescue to America. French historian Sabine Zeitoun writes that Andrée Salomon, an OSE official responsible for the rescue of the children from the internment camps, made the decisive suggestion in the fall of 1940. According to German historian Inge Hansen-Schaberg, it was Ernst Papanek himself who convinced Marshal Field III to take action, while Israeli Judith Tydor Baumel-Schwartz attributes the initiative to USCOM, which wanted to carry on with its work, together with the Quakers, after the abrupt end of the British evacuations.[17]

"All these organizations claim responsibility for saving them [the children] by themselves. But that's not true," American historian Laura Hobson Faure points out during our conversation. "It was really a collaboration."

* * *

I sit in the ultra-modern archive department of the *Center for Jewish History*, reading yellowing, faded letters. After a while, I come across something interesting: no matter who made the decisive suggestion for the children's rescue, on November 8, 1940, a first contact was established between the Quakers in Marseille and the OSE leadership in Montpellier, the two discussing the "evacuation" of 300 children in a letter exchange.[18] A few weeks later, at the end of 1940, Ernst Papanek in person tried to draw public attention in America towards the fate of his protégés. In his papers in the *New York Public Library*, I discover an old edition of the *New York Post* newspaper. An article published on December 26, 1940, under the following eye-catching headline, reads as follows: "Papa Papanek's 500 Children – They Suffer in Europe but he Hopes to Save Them." The kitschy-sounding article draws a picture of a tearful Papanek, attempting to save German, Austrian, and Polish refugee children from Vichy France, together with USCOM, the Quakers, and the Joint, before they turn sixteen and get deported to a concentration camp.[19]

Indeed, on January 1941, the rescue operation became concrete, the Quakers asking OSE to establish a list of 500 potential candidates. Oswald's name is the 35th on that list.[20] More or less around the same time, Ernst Papanek sent the song lyrics and notes of the American national anthem *"The Star-Spangled Banner"* and of *"God Bless America"* to Montintin, to prepare the children for their new life in the U.S.[21]

On January 21, OSE general secretary Lazare Gurvic sent a short-list of 250 children to the AMEROSE office in New York. Oswald's name appears on this list too, his last name misspelled and reading Kornberg. Everything went very fast after that, the first visas were issued only two months later, in March 1941. On March 31, Gurvic personally met with the Quakers in Marseille to discuss further details. The meeting proved quite satisfactory, as I gather from his letters to America, OSE receiving 70 of the hundred visas delivered for the first transport.[22]

While the preparations for the passage of the first 100 children were underway, the aid organizations already began negotiations for further transports with various US government agencies. But then the first difficulties arose, OSE and USCOM learning that only Jewish organizations were allowed to look after Jewish children in America. The non-sectarian USCOM would thus be out of the race. To solve that particular problem, cooperation between USCOM and the Jewish GJCA was planned. Although discussions started right away, a detailed agreement between the two organizations was not settled before June, as I learn from a meeting protocol.

CURRICULUM VITAE

of the child: KERNBERG, OSWALD

Number of the children in the family: 2

Their names, sex, age and present address:
1. K. Fritz, masc., 15 years, Nussdorferstr. 60. Vienne (Autr.)
2. K. Oswald, " 12 ", Château Montintin par Château-Chervix H.V.

Names of the parents:
Father: K. Hermann Age: 51 years Present address: Nussdorferstr. 60 Vienne
Mother: K. Frieda, born Goldfeld Age: 50 years Present address: same addr.

Profession and situation of the family: father is a merchant (without work)

Date of entering France: 14 March 1939.

Place of departure: Vienna

Reason, why the child departed: because of his jewish origin.

By which organisation? Israelitische Kultusgemeinde at Vienna

Successive addresses of the child in France: 1. Château Maubuisson (S. et O.) 2. Villa Helvetia, Montmorency (S. et O.) 3. Eaubonne (S. et O.) 4. Château Montintin par Château-Chervix H.V.

Which organisation supports the child in France? Union Osé.

Course of study: 4 years of "Volksschule" 1 year of "Hauptschule", 2 years of the school of the Home.

Languages: German, French

Pedagogic and psychological observations:

Important observations of the child's character:
Oswald has a lively intelligence and much of imagination. This is an interesting pupil who will be certainly successful.

This curriculum vitae was part of Oswald's application
for the *Kindertransport* to America.

Discussions led to heated debates on whether the children were supposed to go on living together in homes, as was OSE's and most of all Ernst Papanek's wish, or whether they should be placed in foster care, as was usually the case in America, the GJCA being strongly in favor of that second option. This was not the first time, by far, that quarrels, misunderstandings, and complications arose during the *Kindertransports*, what with the large number of – often ideological– competing – organizations involved.

Selecting the children led to many an argument too. In France, the Quakers and OSE decided together who was to be on a *Kindertransport*, the Quakers having the final say in the matter.[23] But it was USCOM that determined the eligibility criteria. Age, health, plight in France, and expected difficulties adjusting to life in America were considered decisive.[24] The maximum age was sixteen, yet children under twelve were to be given priority. Older children would only be taken along so as not to separate siblings. Children in possession of a personal affidavit, or who had a chance to emigrate with their parents, should also not be included in the list, so as not to take another child's place.

By and large, the same procedure as with the French *Kindertransport* was repeated, the main issue being to select healthy, unproblematic, and preferably intelligent children, to make a good impression in America, so further transports would be approved. The pressure to select the supposedly "right" children weighed heavily on all parties involved, yet especially so on the OSE workers in France, who, unlike the Quakers, knew the children personally. I frequently come across internal letters in which the Quakers complain about OSE and the other way around. The Quakers, known for never breaking a rule, strictly followed USCOM's instructions. Younger children were favored in America because it was easier to find a foster family for them. OSE, however, mainly chose older teenagers, threatened with arrest and deportation, as well as orphans.

In some internal documents, the Quakers accused OSE of deliberately hiding specific details about the children that could be seen as exclusion criteria. OSE on the other hand, complained about the fact the Quakers only choose pretty and gifted children.[25] Even decades later, a social worker of OSE complained about the Quakers in an interview: "They behaved very badly, the Americans. ... They went about their job as on the cattle market, feeling the children's muscles and having them sing and dance, it was awful."[26]

The main problem, however, was the fact USCOM, as a non-sectarian aid organization, wished at all costs to prevent the *Kindertransports* to be seen as a purely Jewish rescue operation. The Quakers, therefore, spent much time and energy selecting non-Jewish and non-German children for the transports on USCOM's behalf. The reason given for this was that it would be easier to raise money in America if different social groups could be addressed at the same time. Which was why it was important to cover a wide range of religions and nationalities. This shows how utterly naive and off the mark USCOM as well as the American public were in assessing the situation of the Jewish refugee children in Vichy France.

* * *

"The perception of danger is very different according to which organization you are dealing with," Laura Hobson Faure also affirms.

Hobson Faure comes from Detroit, yet I meet her in a quiet Art Deco café, next to the *Sorbonne Nouvelle* University in Paris, where she teaches American and Jewish history. Hobson Faure is one of the few historians whose research shows that *Kindertransports* were an intercontinental undertaking.

"OSE had a much more keen sense of danger. They themselves fled Nazi Germany as Jews, they knew that the children's lives were in danger," Hobson Faure explains to me. "But that was not the case for any other group."

Just like USCOM, the Quakers underestimated the magnitude of the threat. "Before 1942 and the deportations of children, the Quakers didn't want to recognize that the Jewish children were treated differently than other refugees in France," Hobson Faure affirms.

Even after years of Nazi terror, the Americans still did not recognize the volatile circumstances of the Jewish children in Europe. This is even true for AMEROSE, which was often closer to the American aid organizations than to its sister organization OSE in France. Major differences of opinion seemingly arose within AMEROSE between Ernst Papanek and the organization's general secretary, Leon Wulman, ending with Papanek's sacking in April 1941.

As I read hundreds of letters and internal messages about the American *Kindertransport*, I find myself pausing more often than not. It is terrible to realize how often conflicts arose between these aid organizations, how often one party spoke ill of the other, despite being allies in the fight for the rescue of the children; how often too they tried to exclude specific persons – like Papanek for instance – from the rescue operations, for completely selfish reasons. If one considers, added to this, the significant communication difficulties during wartime – it would sometimes take several weeks before a letter reached its destination – and the various problems with the local authorities, it feels like a miracle that they should indeed have succeeded in bringing even one single child from France to America.

"But we cannot read history backward," Laura Hobson Faure and Ron Coleman both declare when I raise the subject with them. Today we know about the Holocaust. Today we know Vichy authorities started to deport children from the homes to the Drancy camp, from where they would be sent to camps in Poland, in 1942. People back then did not know that. "They did not see what was coming," Laura Hobson Faure says to me.

* * *

The children themselves remained largely unaware of the negotiations and underlying problems regarding their emigration. For them, things only started to become concrete in the spring of 1941, when the preparations for their escape to America were underway. Just like it had been the case with the transports to France, the whole process involved a great deal of bureaucracy. Multiple copies of files, medical and psychological reports, resumes, passport photos, and authorization forms had to be prepared and established for every single child. From today's perspective, OSE's work is a tremendously impressive achievement, the association's members drawing up over one thousand files in war-torn southern France – not knowing how many of their children would be selected. In Oswald's file alone, I discover seven typewritten resumes, established for different purposes.

The US authorities proved especially particular as far as the children's family and medical history was concerned, demanding to be sent very detailed descriptions and reports, which in turn repeatedly caused delays in the planning of the transports.[27] OSE had the health of its children certified by its home doctors, and yes, admittedly, it sometimes came to cheating. "You needed a certificate that stated the child was fine and in good health. Even though such might not be the case," OSE historian Katy Hazan explains, retrospectively confirming the Quakers' allegations that the OSE reports withheld important information about their protégés, always in favor of the latter.

Today, Oswald's original file is kept in OSE's archive department in Paris. The first entry related to his rescue to America is dated March 31, 1941. Dr. Hirschmann certified Oswald's good health in *Montintin*. "The child ... is mentally normal. His general health has been very satisfactory during his stay in our home." Twelve-year-old Oswald was 4'9" tall, with grey eyes and fair hair and he had not received any vaccine in the past six months, the doctor noted.[28]

On April 7, 1941, the Quakers filled out a registration form for Oswald; from now on, he was officially a candidate for a *Kindertransport* to America. In addition to biographical information, this document also includes quite detailed medical information that goes far beyond what was written in the OSE report, stating for instance, that Oswald had been vaccinated against smallpox in 1939 and against diphtheria in 1940, and that he had already contracted following three infantile diseases: scarlet fever, measles, and whooping cough.

Moreover, the registration form also specifies that a request for an America visa had already been made for Oswald – by his parents! Indeed, Hermann Kernberg had registered his family with the American consulate on June 1, 1938, but nothing ever came of it.

At the end of the Quakers form, a parent or Oswald's legal guardian had to agree to the child's emigration to America. Since the terrible ship disaster during the evacuation of British children, the Quakers also demanded a signature of the guardian, absolving them, as well as any other organization involved, of "any liability of any kind and at any time," should anything happen to Oswald during the passage or in America.

On Oswald's form, I see his signature as well as two purple fingerprints. No adult signed the document, though. Also missing is a passport photo along with a big number stamp, such as they appear on the authorizations of other children. Did Oswald's emigration perhaps rest on shaky ground?

In Oswald's OSE file, I also come across several communication errors, possibly due to the war: forms, some of them filled out at the same time, often show different information. The address of Oswald's parents, for example, alternatively reads *Gussenbauergasse 1, Nußdorfer Straße 60,* or Opole, Poland; sometimes the addresses were crossed out by hand and corrected. There also seemed to be some confusion as to Oswald's origin, whose nationality is in turn stated as Polish, ex-Austrian, or Austrian. The mention of a "Polish" nationality is especially surprising, Oswald being by birth an Austrian citizen. The mistake probably arose from the fact Oswald's father was a native Pole. Whether the indication of different nationalities was actually nothing more but a simple mistake (after all, OSE worked simultaneously on the application of hundreds of children), or whether the Quakers deliberately wanted to choose non-German children remains a matter of speculation today. On the last form, the Quakers filled out before Oswald's emigration, he is recorded as being an Austrian citizen.

The core of each file was the resume that was supposed to highlight each child's characteristics. In Oswald's file, I read in the somewhat broken English of the French social workers: "Oswald went to a public school for four years in Vienna and to a high school for one year. In France, he went to school for two years at the children's homes... The boy has a lively intelligence and a great deal of imagination. He gave every satisfaction to his teachers and was considered an interesting pupil who certainly wood [sic] succeed. He speaks German and French."

In another resume, I read: "Oswald is a child full imagination, spontaneous, very sensible, fellow-like feeling. He is very gifted for drawing."

On a sheet of paper just after that resume, I recognize Hermann Kernberg's round handwriting. At the top of the document, the word *Bewilligung* (authorization) is circled. Despite the turmoil of war, OSE tried to obtain a declaration of consent from the children's parents, whenever it was possible. On May 4, 1941, while he had already been sent to Opole (!), Hermann addressed such a declaration to OSE: "I, Samuel Hersch Kernberg, legitimate father of my son 'Oswald Kernberg,' born October 19, 1928, hereby expressly give my acceptance and consent to my son's emigration to the United States of North America."

In my view, this authorization is one of the most extraordinary aspects of Oswald's rescue. Just imagine: Oswald was living as a refugee in Vichy France and his entire family had been deported to a ghetto in Poland. People in Opole were starving to death, as there was practically no food supply. But the mail still worked! It actually even worked so well, Hermann Kernberg was able to send the authorization form for his son's emigration to Switzerland, where an acquaintance of the family then forwarded it to France.

"If my father had not signed the *Bewilligung*, I would not have been able to get out of France." Arthur was absolutely certain of this. "The parents of one of the boys from my room in *Montintin* did not want him to go and called him back to Paris," he told me once with a grave face. "The whole family was deported to Auschwitz subsequently."

As it happens, Arthur was wrong: when OSE did not manage to contact the parents, an OSE member, acting as the legal guardian, would sign the authorization form. Yet if a parent specifically told OSE not to send their child to America, the organization would honor their wish, as in the case mentioned above.

In the middle of May 1941, it was finally time. The American Consul in Marseille received all necessary documents for the first one hundred children. A misunderstanding in a telegram caused big confusion, though, as to whether the USCOM children should be issued regular quota visas, or special visas, which once again led to more delay.

As it was, the visas were not the only problem: organizing the passage also proved more than difficult, the aid organizations learning in March that the ships to America were fully booked until the beginning of July. Even though the issue of the passage was not yet completely solved, the first one hundred children were still sent to Marseille in May 1941. As announced, the OSE children, among them many children from *Montintin* and *La Chevrette*, made for the best part of the group. One child alone was not allowed to be part of the group: Oswald.

Hermann Kernberg sent his authorization for Oswald's emigration to America from the Opole ghetto in Poland.

15. JOURNEY TO FREEDOM

"All the kids in my room were picked to come to the United States at the time," Arthur tells me in November 2013, during one of our interviews for this book. It is the day after Thanksgivukkah and we sit in the plush lounge chairs of a hotel lobby. Arthur tilts his head and leans it on his hand, sighing softly. Then he straightens up, takes off his old-fashioned, round glasses, and puts them on the table in front of him.

"But the day before we were supposed to leave, they told me I can't go," he goes on, swallowing. "I was absolutely traumatized. I mean I cried, and I cried, and I cried. Because all the other kids in my room, all the boys, all my age group, they all went! It felt as if I had just lost my second family. It was absolutely horrendous to me. You have no idea how much I cried."

"Did you ever learn why you were not part of that first transport?" I ask him.

"No." He pauses briefly before resuming: "But what's tragic was another girl was also taken off the list. Ruth Drucker. And Ruth wasn't picked for another transport, because she had turned sixteen in the meantime and was considered too old. She was later deported and murdered in Auschwitz."

* * *

For twelve-year-old Oswald, not being allowed to emigrate to America with his friends came as a huge shock. But as I discover in my archive research, Arthur's selection for the first transport had been very uncertain from the start. On two lists preserved in the archives of AMEROSE, his name is only mentioned as an alternate candidate. On one of these lists, Oswald's name appears in the fifth position out of 25 of these replacement candidates. On a second list, established after the departure of the first transport, there are only seven alternate candidates left, Oswald's name appearing this time in the second position.[1] As mentioned before, the first authorization form of the Quakers did not bear any signature, which leads me to believe that he had never been meant to be part of the first transport. However, no one seemed to have said as much to the twelve-year-old boy, who thus assumed he would be able to travel with his friends.

Parting with their friends was a highly emotional and difficult moment, for those who had to stay behind as well as for the children who were leaving. Erich Grünebaum devotes an entire page in his unpublished memoir to his parting with his best friend: "The day before the big day Oswald and I sat on the hill before the main house and he cried like a baby. He couldn't understand why he was being left behind. There was very little I could say to him, except to reassure him that he would probably be on the next transport." It would be fifteen years before Oswald and Erich, who had sworn eternal friendship and blood brotherhood in Montmorency, would meet again.

A few weeks after the children's departure, Oswald received a letter from five of his friends, sent from a hotel in Marseille, where they were waiting for their visas. Hans Singer began the group message, riddled with spelling errors, as follows: "Dear Oswald, we have received your letter. We're very sorry we had to part with you. We're doing very well this of you we hope too. As we do not know what else to write we write the journey you will certainly enjoy."

"Hans has snatshed away the [journey] so I'll wrighte to you how things are here," Werner continued the letter. "We're wakened in the morning we eat then we are bored until noon. Marseille is so rich there are peanuts on the street. The day before yesterday we made a Trip to the zoo there we saw a mouse birds 3 zebra 1 giraffe 1 elephant 1 camel and a few monkeys."

As fun as going for walks and visiting the zoo was for the boys, they had nothing good to report about their accommodation in Marseille: "It's like a prison here there is a small yard in front of the house surrounded with walls. Apart from that nothing new, best wishes and lots of kisses, Sigi."[2]

While the children were waiting in Marseille, bored or else enjoying visits and excursions, their passage to America was still not secured. There were some problems with the visa delivery, each child requiring not only one but four visas: one to leave France, one to cross Spain, yet another to cross Portugal (from where the refugee ships left), and the last one to enter America.

As I gather from a both tragic and comic letter, the Quakers finally managed to obtain the four different visa types for the children in just 48 hours, running back and forth between the American, Spanish, and Portuguese consulates and the French police station, whilst sewing by hand one hundred photographs on one hundred substitute passports, as it was utterly impossible to get hold of a stapling machine in war-torn Marseille.[3]

In the end, everything went well, though: the children arrived in America on June 20, 1941, on board the S.S. Mouzinho and were warmly welcomed in New York by Ernst and Lene Papanek.[4] From the first contact between OSE and USCOM to the arrival of the first Kindertransport, eight months had passed.

Almost all the Chevrette children had left, and Montintin's orthodox outbuilding was closed. Oswald and the other remaining residents were transferred to the *Château de Mas-Jambost* a little outside Limoges, the religious OSE home Madame Krakowski had sent the older girls to earlier.

* * *

"Artie was one of my best friends," Norbert Rosenblum tells me. "We were more than friends, we were brothers." Norbert was born in Strasbourg and has known Arthur since *Villa La Chesnaie* in Eaubonne. The two boys became lifelong friends. In the summer of 2016, I meet Norbert and his wife Marion at the house of Arthur's oldest son, Aaron, in Seal Beach, California.

"Artie had a very good sense of humor," Norbert Rosenblum remembers, telling me about that time he sat next to him at a party. "Artie took off his glasses and put them in front of him. Then he looked around and talked to someone else. I took his glasses and put my own instead. A couple of minutes later, he put them on. And couldn't see! It's things like that, you know. We all played that kind of shenanigans."

In France, Norbert Rosenblum lived in the same OSE homes as Arthur: *Villa La Chesnaie, Château de Montintin, La Chevrette,* then after the departure of the first *Kindertransport* to America, *Mas-Jambost*. Although Norbert was a few years older than Arthur and thus did not sleep in the same room, he still remembers him very well. It was Rosenblum, for instance, who told me about Oswald's nickname *Papakuss*.

He is also the only one who can tell me about *Mas-Jambost*. As well as about the exciting journey to the place. "One boy and I were told to drive a horse carriage there to bring the children's possessions," Rosenblum begins. "And Artie insisted on coming along too. The three of us knew nothing about horses! But we did ride the whole way from *Montintin* to *Mas-Jambost*. It was quite a distance, 12.5 miles or so! We left early in the morning, and only reached our destination in the evening."

* * *

In *Mas-Jambost*, Oswald was no longer taught by OSE; for the first time, he went to a French public school. A whole new experience for the twelve-year-old. "I suddenly felt stupid," Arthur recalled years later. "I suddenly realized how little I knew compared to what I should have known. Because the French kids knew that. My French spelling was terrible, my arithmetic wasn't very good either."

As Oswald went on speaking German with his friends, it is difficult to determine whether his school problems were due to his missing French language skills or whether he actually knew very little. In the OSE classes, Oswald must have been a good pupil though, his father having praised him in a letter sent a few weeks before: "We were most interested to hear you're doing so well at school and are the third best pupil in your class. Keep up the good work, my darling, we won't fail to reward you for this."

Although Oswald got along fairly well with his schoolmates in *Mas-Jambost*, he didn't make any real friends. "I couldn't make friends with them because I had to always go back to the home," he told me.

Not that Oswald had much time to get to know new people anyway. After just one month in *Mas-Jambost*, he was sent back to *Montintin*. Oswald was on the list of the second *Kindertransport* to America!

Mid-July 1941, USCOM received the approval for another group of one hundred children, who would be traveling to America in two separate groups, as it was still difficult to secure a passage on a ship. It was high time. On June 22, 1941, the Nazis had started the so-called Operation Barbarossa – the invasion of the Soviet Union by the *Wehrmacht*. The war threatened to escalate.

Ernst Papanek received two letters, informing him of the upcoming arrival of the children. "A second *Kindertransport* is leaving right now, with only very few from us [from *Montintin*] (Norbert

Rosenblum, Oswald Kernberg)," Leo Brenner informed him. OSE general secretary Lazare Gurvic wrote: "It was very difficult for us to part with these children, who had almost all been in Montmorency, the first 'pioneers' of our activities."[5]

A few days before the children's departure, Amalia Kanner, the cook, sent a few boys to pick cherries and sacrificed a little of the strictly rationed sugar supplies to bake a pie. "The children leaving for America on the second transport would soon be able to taste all the delicacies they could only dream about here," she wrote years later. "But I wanted them to remember me – and the kitchen in *La Chevrette* – for something other than the unpalatable *topinambour* (Jerusalem artichoke)."[6]

The Quakers and USCOM having stressed once again that it was more difficult to find a home for older children in America, the second transport mainly consisted of younger refugees under the age of twelve. Fifteen-year-old Norbert Rosenblum was only allowed to be part of the journey because his twelve-year-old sister had been chosen for the transport and the organizations usually tried not to separate siblings. Amalia Kanner's daughters were very lucky too: "The day before the second transport was to leave, two children from another OSE home fell ill and lost their health clearance," Kanner's daughter Eve recounts in *Shattered Crystals*, the autobiography she wrote together with her mother. "Ruth and I were the only children who could fill the precious, vacated slots. Our parents alone were on site, able to give instant approval and sign all necessary documents."[7]

By the end of July 1941, everything was ready: Oswald left the *Château de Montintin* for good. On the morning of the departure, almost twenty kids jostled and pushed each other on the steps of *La Chevrette*, laughing, while an older boy, camera in hand, attempted to get them all on the same picture.

"*Mama*, come on, you too!" Ruth Kanner called and the children moved closer together. Amalia stands next to Oswald, in the next to last row, Norbert Rosenblum and his sister Friedl are on his left. As

I gaze at the picture today, it seems to me it was taken in winter and not in the middle of the summer: the children all wore thick coats and hats to save space in their suitcases.

Oswald and his comrades on the day of their
departure from France, in July 1941.

After the picture was taken, Oswald turned around one last time, trying to commit *Montintin* and *La Chevrette* to memory. The chateau and its dense woods had been his home for the past year, but he had experienced so much here that it felt much longer to him. Then the young refugees were driven to the train station to pick up their visas in Marseille.

On the way to Marseille, the train stopped briefly at the station in *Gurs*, where a few children were able to say goodbye to their parents, detained in the camp – OSE having obtained special permission from the camp authorities. Contemporary reports describe tragic scenes during the three-minute meeting. The children had not eaten their breakfast and handed their starving parents pieces of bread through the windows of the train.

Then the train went on to Toulouse, where the children were able to eat their fill at the train station hotel, before boarding the late train to Marseille, shortly before midnight. On the next morning, they ate breakfast at the station buffet, before being taken to the *Hôtel du Levant*, an accommodation for Jewish refugees.

"We stayed in Marseille for about a week or two," Arthur told me. "Children from other OSE homes joined us there from *Chabannes*, *Masgelier*, *Broût-Vernet*, and *Chaumont*." Adolf Löw was one of them; a little younger than Oswald, the two boys knew each other from their time together in *Villa La Chesnaie*, in Eaubonne. After meeting again in Marseille, Oswald and Adolf never parted again, becoming lifelong best friends as "Arthur" and "Aaron."

The children recall with horror the *Hôtel du Levant*, Oswald's friend, Sigi, even going so far as to call it a prison in a letter, while Ruth Kanner described it as a barrack. The refugee accommodation was hopelessly overcrowded and all the children had to sleep in the same room, often sharing beds. Hung across the room, a wide bed sheet separated the boys from the girls.[8]

Hygienic conditions too left much to be desired. The *Hôtel du Levant* was infested with cockroaches and bed bugs and a lot of children got lice. "They deloused everybody," Norbert Rosenblum said, describing the situation to me. "They washed kids' hair with kerosene. They shaved the hair of some completely to get rid of the lice."

There were no classes in Marseille, but OSE would still organize excursions in an attempt to keep up the children's morale. Moreover, each and every one of them had to submit to yet another medical examination and also appear personally at the American consulate. On August 7, 1941, the Quakers in Marseille once again filled out an application form as well as an authorization for Oswald – this time complete with a passport photograph and stamped number: Number 23. Three days later, on August 10, OSE official Andrée Salomon signed the document as Oswald's legal guardian. His parents' address in Opole was correctly indicated. As it is not possible to reconstruct exactly when Oswald was registered for the second transport, I can only hazard a guess as to why it happened at that particular time. His parents' deportation might have been a decisive factor indeed. In any case, he was now one of those children in need the USCOM transports wanted to rescue.

On August 11, 1941, G. McMurtrie Godley, the American vice-consul in Marseille, issued an *Affidavit in Lieu of Passport* for Oswald, as, just like the vast majority of the children, the boy did not possess any valid travel documents: his German passport, delivered on March 9, 1939, had expired. I discover this substitute document in New York, in a box that had been stored in a warehouse for almost seventy years. Apart from a passport photograph, a few details as to Oswald's physical appearance are listed on it: he was now 4'11" tall, but only weighed 77 pounds and had a long scar on his right leg. Oswald's visa for the United States, issued on August 11, appears on the back of the affidavit, as well as his transit visa for Portugal, dated August 12. His French exit permit, as well as his transit visa for Spain, have not been preserved.

On August 13, 1941, 45 of the Jewish refugee children left Marseille together with a Quaker escort. The remaining 55 children – among whom Norbert Rosenblum – stayed a few weeks longer in Marseille, before they too were able to set off.[9]

During the journey, each child had to wear a card showing his transport number around the neck. "My number was 23," Arthur remembered. "And we had to wear this around our neck from the time that we left Marseille until we arrived in the United States." Oswald's name was printed on the card in English and in French, along with the name of the ship and a message from the Quakers: "In case of [an] emergency cable to one of the above addresses. ... Kindly give my name and number and describe my case. ... A reply will reach you immediately and your expenses will be refunded in full."

The exhausting journey through France, Spain, and Portugal lasted several days, taking a heavy toll on the young refugees: many of them took ill, suffering from cough or diarrhea. Norbert Rosenblum's sister Friedl provided a very moving description of that train journey in a letter she wrote decades later: "I will always remember Arthur since that moment, during our childhood, he offered me his coat to sleep on a difficult train ride from Marseille to Spain."

At the French-Spanish border, the children stopped for a few hours. "We had to change trains between France and Spain, because the railroad gauges were different," Arthur recalled. "The trains couldn't run on the same track."

The French border officials treated the group politely, allowing them to move on without any difficulty. Their Spanish counterparts, however, behaved very roughly towards the children, searching them for valuables and keeping their passports for such a long time, the accompanying adults feared they would not get their protégés' papers back in time.[10]

The children crossed Spain on board an exceptionally old-fashioned train that ran so slowly the older boys sometimes got off the moving train to pick some flowers before jumping back on board. The young refugees traveled in third class, equipped with hard wooden benches. So he would be able to stretch in his sleep, Oswald climbed over the seats and lay down on the wobbly luggage net.[11]

The Jewish refugee children spent one night in Madrid during their three day journey through Spain, sleeping in a most unlikely place: the Catholic nunnery of *María Inmaculada*.

The nuns took loving care of Oswald and his friends and the children were able to properly wash for the first time since they had left Marseille. Yet the children had bad memories of their short stay in Spain. The civil war had ended not two years ago and the children saw a lot of bombed-out ruins and house fronts peppered with bullet holes. "The biggest problem in Spain was there were a lot of people who were wearing the *Hakenkreuz* buttons," Arthur explained to me. The Germans had helped Franco rise to power and there were many sympathizers of Hitler in Spain. A shocking sight for Jewish children hoping to have escaped Nazi symbols forever.

Shortly before they crossed the border into Portugal, another problem occurred: it was Shabbat, the Jewish day of rest, on which orthodox Jews are not allowed to travel. But just as they had during their flight from Paris to the south of France, when Oswald and the other orthodox children had exceptionally eaten pork, they recognized it was a matter of emergency and agreed to embark on the last leg of the journey.[12]

On August 16, 1941, the group reached Lisbon at long last – they had overcome the first obstacle on their journey to freedom!

Oswald and a group of OSE children upon their
arrival in Lisbon, on August 16, 1941.

16. S.S. MOUZINHO

"Lisbon was the bottleneck of Europe, the last open gate of the concentration camp spanning across all of Europe," author Arthur Koestler wrote on his flight from National Socialism.[1] Quite a fitting analogy.

In 1941, Portugal was the last neutral harbor on the continent. The last place Jewish refugees could be relatively safe – at least for a limited period of time – and from where ships still sailed abroad. The north of France, the Benelux states, and Denmark had been occupied by the Nazis since 1940 and in April 1941, the German army had conquered and invaded Greece and Yugoslavia. Spain only allowed refugees to cross its territory, Italy was allied with the German Reich, and Vichy France collaborated with the Nazis. Portugal was the only remaining hope.

The arrival in Lisbon was a memorable experience for Oswald: the country was not at war! To the OSE protégés who had just traveled through impoverished and pro-German Spain, Portugal was truly the light at the end of the tunnel. "We left an ocean of hatred and entered a sweet paradise," Dr. Isaac Chomski, who had accompanied the first *Kindertransport*, declared.[2]

"In Portugal, the refugees felt safe for the first time. For the first time here, there was peace," historian Katrin Sippel confirms. She is the managing director of the *Österreichische Gesellschaft für Exilforschung* (Austrian Society for Exile Research) and tells me about her research on Portugal as a transit country for Austrian emigrants, as we sit in the garden of a Viennese coffee house.

Refugees would often spend weeks or even months in Portugal, waiting for one of the coveted passages or trying to purchase tickets on the black market. "Holidays against one's will, that's how one could describe the refugees' stay in Lisbon," Sippel says. "People were on the run, but at the same time, it also was a moment of rest with a beach break."

This also applied to Oswald and his comrades, although compared with other refugees, the children only stayed for a relatively short time in Portugal, arriving in the harbor city on August 16, 1941, and boarding the ship four days later, on August, 20. But as the children received a lot of visits during their five-day stay and were very often photographed, their brief stay can easily be reconstructed today.

"The surroundings are splendid," the Quakers told OSE official Andrée Salomon. "We are living in a villa next to the sea. We had our picture taken twice at Lisbon train station and a short article about us was already published today in the newspapers."[3]

The children had been accommodated in a holiday camp, a little outside Lisbon. The Quakers had desperately searched for accommodation for a long time and had only managed to find a suitable solution on the eve of the first transport's arrival, after having contacted the Portuguese newspaper *O Século* (The Century). The daily newspaper, founded in 1880, ran a holiday camp for destitute children that stood empty at the time, and at which they agreed to welcome the young refugees. The Quakers did not need to pay for the accommodation itself, only providing for the children's food.

The wealthy owner of *O Século* showed great interest in the fate of the Jewish children and came to visit several times. The newspaper published articles and photographs about the *crianças refugidas,* "the refugee children," almost every day – sometimes even on the front page.

"In their future life, all these children will remember Portugal as the first blessed country, in which they have been able to laugh and sleep peacefully," I read in one of these articles. "A great deal of their joy will be returned to *Século,* which considered itself lucky to have selflessly reached out to a few dozen children in their hour of need, at the dawn of their young lives."[4]

The *O Século* holiday camp was located in a villa surrounded by a large Mediterranean garden. Not unlike *Villa Helvetia* in Montmorency, here too was a quite spectacular veranda that led to the entrance door, the children gathering on its stone steps for announcements. The inside of the villa was pure luxury for the refugee children accustomed to privations: they each had their own room, with their own washbasin.

Since the end of the 1970s, the *O Século* newspaper no longer exists, but the holiday camp for needy children, now run by a foundation, still does. Today the villa also holds an affordable hostel for tourists. The *O Século* papers are kept in the *Portuguese National Archives* and contain a few photographs of Oswald. I cannot help but smile, looking at these pictures, because the children look so funny with their number cards around their necks, the small cardboard signs fastened to a cord fluttering behind them as they play catch. I cannot make out Oswald's number 23 on the pictures, because he kept the card hidden under his sweater.

Oswald was magically attracted to a fig tree that stood in the garden of their temporary home. Overwhelmed by the fact he no longer had to suffer from hunger as he had in France, the twelve-year-old devoured so many figs he got sick.[5]

Just like Amalia Kanner, the cook, had foreseen, the children were now able to try all the delicacies they could only dream of in France. "Lisbon was the first place where we had good food," Ernst Valfer told me. "Suddenly there were mounts of white bread, meat, and God knows what… It was paradise."

The owner of *O Século* was not the only one who visited the children. The Jewish community of Lisbon, the American Joint, and wealthy citizens, all came bringing sweets and chocolate. The bodies of the undernourished children were no longer accustomed to such amounts of rich food and sweets, and many of them suffered from diarrhea and nausea just like Oswald. Yet after a few days with lots of sun and walks along the beach in the fresh air, the children quickly recovered.[6]

Sweets and treats were not the only things the children were given in Portugal, though; they were treated like guests of honor and showered with attention, Jewish shopkeepers completely renewing their wardrobe and offering them all new pairs of shoes. The children were taken to expensive hotels and even to a movie theater once: they saw *Pinocchio*, Walt Disney's second full-length animated cartoon, which had premiered a year earlier in America.

Morris Troper was one of the many visitors who came to the holiday camp. He was the European director of the Joint, an American aid organization that covered a large part of OSE's budget and also paid for the costs of the *Kindertransports*. In an open letter published in numerous newspapers, Troper offered his thanks to the First Lady Eleanor Roosevelt for her support and told her about the children.

Troper's melodramatic descriptions were meant to inspire pity in America and generate donations. Yet he exaggerated so much in doing so that his letter bore little resemblance to the refugees' reality. According to Troper, upon their arrival in Portugal, the children looked like "tired, wan, broken little old men and women," their clothes nothing but rags; they first had to be taught how to play again.[7] Even though Troper's descriptions sound like an insult to OSE's educational achievements from today's perspective, his wish to appeal as successfully as possible to the generosity of the American public is perfectly understandable. The *Kindertransports* were indeed expensive! The Quakers paid 3,000 dollars in the summer of 1941 for each group of one hundred children, just for the journey from Marseille to Lisbon via Spain; in today's money, this sum amounts to almost 51,000 dollars.

Before they left Europe, the children wrote one last letter to their parents. It took almost four weeks for Oswald's letter to reach Poland from Portugal. "We have just received a letter from Lisbon, from our dearest Oswald, saying he will board a ship to America in 3 days," Hermann Kernberg wrote to some relatives in the middle of September. "You cannot begin to understand how happy we were to hear about this, but just know that we have wept for hours on end after receiving our dearest and most adorable boy's letter."

Lisbon, August 20, 1941: Oswald and his comrades wait
on the docks, before boarding a ship to America.

* * *

The story of Arthur and me is full of coincidences. If he had not felt the need to see his old apartment again, we would never have met. I would never have researched his mother's biography for the history project *A Letter To The Stars*. No article about our meeting would have been published in a Viennese newspaper, and his long-lost parents' papers would never have been returned to him. And I probably would not have become a historian.

Another of these coincidences occurred in July 2016, in Maryland, right on the border of the capital, Washington, D.C. I spend the summer here, staying at Esther Starobin's, so I can find out more about Arthur's rescue to America in the archive of the *United States Holocaust Memorial Museum*.

I know Esther very well since I interviewed her three years ago for my bachelor's thesis *Ein Leben nach dem Kindertransport* (A life after the *Kindertransport*). A retired teacher, Esther is originally from the city of Adelsheim, in the north of the German federal state of *Baden-Württemberg*. In 1939, she was brought to England on a *Kindertransport*, along with her three older sisters; back then, she was only 26-months-old.

In July 2016, Esther and I sit on her covered porch. It is a mild summer evening and we each hold a nice cup of Darjeeling in our hands. While I dip Esther's homemade cantuccinis in my tea, I tell her about my day.

"I have consulted the Quakers' files today and the papers of a *Kindertransport* child," I enumerate, and then, just as I am about to change the subject, I suddenly remember I also came across the passenger list of the Portuguese steamer.

"What was the name of the ship on which Arthur came to America?" Esther asks me.

I flip through a few papers to find the right list. "The *S.S. Mouzinho*," I read.

"That name sounds familiar somehow," Esther mumbles, getting up and disappearing into the cellar. After a few minutes, she returns with a large envelope.

"These are pictures of my brother Herman in Portugal, in the summer of 1941, shortly before he boarded a ship to America. He was eight at the time and had been rescued from the French internment camp of *Gurs* not long before," Esther explains. "And here… yes, exactly! Here it is!" she says, pointing at a word painted in capital letters on the side of the steamer on the picture: *Mouzinho.*

Esther can hardly believe her own eyes: Arthur and her brother came to America on board the same ship! But that would not be the only surprise. Glancing at the remaining photographs, I notice a picture showing a group of children waiting at the harbor. And there, right in the middle, smiling at the camera, Oswald, wearing a jacket and a tie, and his mandatory orthodox head covering. Next to him, a head shorter and squinting in the bright sunlight stands a boy with a skeptical expression on his face: Herman, Esther's brother.

Oswald and Herman among a group of children waiting
to board the ship *Mouzinho* to travel to the US.

* * *

Oswald and his friends lined up on the pier in more or less neat rows of two, waiting to hand over their luggage, proudly displaying their new clothes and coats; many boys also wore a necktie. The children still wore the small cardboard signs around their necks, with their numbers written on it. "Mo-u-zin-ho," Oswald's friend Adolf Löw read, looking at the ship next to them. The *S.S. Mouzinho* lay so deep in the water the children were able to take a look inside the eight-thousand-ton steamer, as they talked to each other excitedly. The day had finally come; they were going to America!

"*Vá em frente*," a mustachioed policeman called out to the children. "Move to the front." The row moved forward until the travelers reached a group of dockworkers, whom they entrusted with their suitcases. Then the young refugees had to show their substitute passports to a customs officer, who checked their names on the passenger list.

The *Mouzinho* looked more like a converted freighter than an actual cruise ship, but the unmooring ceremonial remained the same: an orchestra played, confetti flew through the air and people waved colorful flags at the refugees as they walked up the railing.

Oswald left Portugal on August 20, 1941, as the exit stamp on his affidavit and a *S.S. Mouzinho* passenger list intended for US immigration authorities show.[8] On the day of the departure, the Quakers headquarters wrote a letter of thanks to their delegates in Marseille, also paying tribute to the strenuous preparatory work: "Let me congratulate you on the speed and efficiency with which your office got together the August group of USCOM children. ... I hope we have not given you grey hair over this job."[9] The Quakers had completed their mission, safely bringing the young refugees from France to Portugal, across two borders, and against all odds. Today they would be called human traffickers. From now on, Oswald no longer had any contact with the Quakers, who played a brief, yet quite an essential part in his life.

There were 625 refugees on board the *S.S. Mouzinho*, among whom 45 USCOM children with two accompanying persons. Despite all contrary instructions, Jewish children made up the majority of the second American *Kindertransport* too (42 of the 45 children were Jewish, 13 among them orthodox). Only two children were Catholic and one was Protestant. 26 boys and 19 girls aged seven to fifteen set off on the journey together.

The passage on board the *S.S. Mouzinho* lasted almost two weeks and was "very comfortable," Arthur would often joke later. "We were lucky. We shared a semi-private cabin. We shared it with three hundred other people."

The *S.S. Mouzinho* was hopelessly overcrowded and most of the refugees were accommodated in the cargo hold, where makeshift triple bunk beds had been set up. Under such jammed circumstances, the passengers had no privacy at all; the only ones who enjoyed the situation were the two USCOM accompanying persons who could thus easily keep an eye on all 45 children at once.

Every evening before going to bed, Oswald checked the contents of his small suitcase: the family pictures he had removed from the photo albums in Vienna, the letters from his parents, as well as a small school notebook filled with self-written stories. The following sentence was written in French under the compass and ruler that adorned the cover of the notebook: "*appartenant à Oswald Kernberg*" (property of Oswald Kernberg).

* * *

Arthur donated this notebook full of stories to the *Simon Wiesenthal Center* in Los Angeles, in the 1990s, his family forgetting about it afterward. Even Arthur's eldest son, Aaron, who accompanies me in November 2017 to the Holocaust research center, named after the famous "Nazi hunter" Simon Wiesenthal, does not know about that notebook.

"Isn't it wonderful?" the archivist asks me, as I slip the notebook out of its protective cover. Indeed it is. And it is the first time I hold

a piece of Oswald's childhood in my hands. None of Oswald's letters has survived the war, no handicraft or schoolwork, none of his
beloved books. Only this notebook. Oswald has filled its pages with
a half a dozen stories, using crayons to draw every capital letter while
neatly writing the rest with a pencil. Surprisingly true-to-life illustra-
tions Oswald drew in colored pencils accompany each story, written
in German. No wonder OSE insisted on Oswald being a very gifted
artist in his registration form for the *Kindertransport* to America.
His stories too reveal an overflowing imagination, along with a sad
touch of reality.

The first story is about the Chinese King Sing-Fo (the two first
syllables of the German word, "*Singvogel*," songbird) and his nightingale, which shares quite a few similarities with Christian Andersen's
fairy tale *The Nightingale*. In Oswald's version, King Sing-Fo wishes
to kill his nightingale, yet at the very last moment, he decides to let it
live and sets the bird free. When the country is plagued by war shortly afterward, the bird returns the favor. "The nightingale gathered all
the birds," twelve-year-old Oswald wrote, "and they darkened the
skies above their enemies so that darkness fell all around them. The
enemies believed the Demon was against them and they left. This is
how a nightingale offers its thanks."

In the next story, we read about the adventures of the four jolly
dwarfs Pick, Pack, Pock, and Puck, who dance around a toadstool
and then, a few pages later, a poem about the "bad boys" Flick,
Flack, and Flock. Yet it is the last story I find the most moving. It
is about a boy named Walter and opens with a drawing of a cliff.
Walter stands on the edge, as far below a locomotive crosses a wobbly
bridge. Walter looks over his shoulder towards an "Indian," wearing
colorful feathers and rushing at him with hatchets. On the next page,
the actual story unfolds, in a sometimes quite imaginative spelling:
"In his fifth year of life, he went to North America with his parents.
The Narcissus, such was the name of the ship, capsized and Walter's
parents lost their lives. Walter had enough presence of mind to hold

on to one of the beams and ten minutes later, he was rescued by a ship heading to North America. He was dropped off in Mexico. For a fugh days, he fed on tree fruits, but he realized he couldn't go on like that. Now he wanted to go to New York. But how? He started walking straight on. After 2 days, Indians caught him unaware. Walter ran and ran, but suddenly he found himself in front of an abyss. He jumped and where was he? You'll be surprised. Under his bed. It was a weird dream."[10]

A drawing from the story notebook showing Oswald's King Sing-Fo.

The parents die, but the child has the presence of mind to save himself. Oswald's story may describe nothing more than a mere dream, but it contains more than just a grain of truth.

Two and a half years had passed since Oswald had left his parents and his brother. He had been ten back then; now he was almost thirteen. Oswald's family no longer lived in Vienna, but in a ghetto in Poland. Despite Hermann Kernberg's repeated assurances, in his letters to his son, they would all soon be reunited, Oswald felt this was not true.

How does it feel knowing your parents are in greatest danger when you are finally safe? How does it feel knowing your brother is in greatest danger and you are on the other side of the world? How does a twelve-year-old deal with the knowledge he cannot do anything to help them? Is it as if the parents would drown, but one has the presence of mind to save oneself? Or is it all but a weird dream?

PART 3 – NEW YORK

17. ARRIVAL IN NEW YORK

"Give me your tired, your poor,
Your huddled masses yearning to breathe free,
The wretched refuse of your teeming shore.
Send these, the homeless, tempest-tossed to me:
I lift my lamp beside the golden door."

Emma Lazarus, *The New Colossus* (1883)
Sonnet on the pedestal of the Statue of Liberty

After a two-week journey, Oswald reached New York Harbor on September 1, 1941. Lined up alongside the railing of the *S.S. Mouzinho,* the children cheered loudly after catching a glimpse of the Statue of Liberty. Just like millions of immigrants before them, they were welcomed by the statue, affectionately nicknamed *Lady Liberty.* From the distance, the children could not see the sonnet by Jewish-American poet Emma Lazarus engraved on the pedestal, but they all knew the history and the meaning of *Lady Liberty.*

Oswald and 44 other refugee children upon arrival in New York.

Vienna, Paris, the South of France, Madrid, Lisbon, and now New York: Oswald's escape came to an end in America, the land of the free, the land of endless opportunities.

* * *

Oswald was 12 years old when he saw New York for the first time. I am 15 – and fortunately traveling under completely different circumstances. While Oswald would always remember the Statue of Liberty as his first impression of the Big Apple, I will forever recall the overly loud Times Square, with its house-size billboards shimmering in the night.

It is April 10, 2007, and I have come to New York with a group of 30 Austrian students. As so-called "Ambassadors of Remembrance," we will spend a week here and meet Holocaust survivors – all of them born in Austria – to talk about their life stories. Having just turned 15, I am the youngest on the trip, organized by *A Letter To The Stars*, the student history project for which I wrote the biography of Frieda Kernberg when I was 11 years old.

Matzo Ball Soup, stuffed cabbage, and Seven Layer Cake – my first kosher meal! Even though Kurt Goldberger reassures me that there is no shortage of Viennese food in New York, he still prefers to show me something new: he and his wife Margaret take me to *Ben's*, a Jewish deli in the heart of Manhattan. Kurt and Margaret (who introduces herself with the famous Kennedy quote *"Ick bin ein Berliner,"* I am a Berliner) both escaped on a *Kindertransport* to England and later emigrated to the US. With the exception of Arthur, they are the first people I ever speak to who owe their lives to the *Kindertransport*.

Two days later, I meet Johanna Trescher, who came to New York as a five-year-old girl with her Jewish mother and grandfather, while her Christian father stayed behind in Vienna. Johanna is a charming lady who still grieves for a teddy bear she had to leave behind in Vienna. The next day, I accompany her to the *Museum of Jewish Heritage*, which houses several collections about Jewish history and the Holocaust. Until now, Johanna never dared to come here, but today, with me, she finally braves her apprehension.

Several more very moving meetings with Holocaust survivors take place during our trip, all leaving a strong impression on us Austrian students. One time, we visit a synagogue in Queens, where the Jewish organization *Selfhelp* regularly organizes a "Viennese Coffeehouse," an afternoon of coffee, cake, and Viennese music. What impresses me most is how much these former Austrians still remember about their old homeland. They immediately start asking us about certain landmarks and want to know which of the "real" pre-war coffee-houses still exist. They remember Viennese music even better, always recognizing quite accurately the songs playing in the background and singing along loudly in German. Towards the end of the afternoon, I waltz with one of the elderly men sitting next to me at the table. When we part, he tells me with great emotion, "I will never forget this moment."

I will never forget this moment – and the whole trip to New York – either. And there is one thing I am sure about: after about one day I want to study here!

A week after my return to Vienna, I receive a letter from Johanna Trescher: "Dear Lilly! It was a pleasure meeting you last week. The time we spent together brought back a lot of memories. Thank you for all the wonderful gifts you brought me. The biggest gift of all was a connection to my past, to my heritage. Even the sad moments were a memory of who I am."

* * *

Oswald and the other refugee children reached New York on September 1, 1941. As it was Labor Day, they had to wait until September 2 to be able to disembark. Ernst Papanek, who by then no longer worked for AMEROSE, did not come to the pier to welcome Oswald and the rest of his former protégés – a decision he came to regret dearly later.[1]

At the pier, the children were welcomed with cookies and milk by the Red Cross before being photographed several times. A couple of days later, a picture of Oswald standing amongst a group of smiling and waving children appeared in a New York newspaper with the caption: "Saved from the internment camps of Europe, where many parents are still confined, these children were pictures of joy on arrival aboard steamship Mouzinho."

During the Second World War, the New York Times published a

daily column about the arrival of (refugee) ships from Europe. It is there that I discover the *Mouzinho* docked at Pier 8 in Staten Island[2] – which is quite interesting, as none of the historians I interviewed for this book seem to have ever heard of transatlantic steamers docking in Staten Island. Usually, immigrants arrived on Ellis Island, the island in the Hudson River that served as the main gateway to the United States for decades.

Arthur disembarked on that pier in Staten Island.

Pier 8 no longer exists, but thanks to an incredibly helpful archivist from the *Staten Island Museum,* who cross-referenced three antiquarian maps with today's *Google Maps,* I am able to find its previous position. Former Pier 8 is located ten minutes by foot from today's terminal of the *Staten Island Ferry,* popular among tourists because the best pictures of the New York skyline are taken from the ferry. These days, the former Pier 8 is a run-down port area, with discarded oil canisters lying around and a few old fishing boats bumping against each other on the soft rippling water, while seagulls circle overhead, screeching. There is no longer any evidence of the ships that used to arrive here, crowded with hundreds of European refugees.

In Staten Island, the children were welcomed by Lotte Marcuse of the *German Jewish Children's Aid* (GJCA), who took them to Manhattan in two buses. The GJCA was responsible for the young refugees from the moment they arrived, and Lotte Marcuse had planned out the first days in their new homeland with military precision. The children were first accommodated in a Jewish orphanage on 1560 Amsterdam Avenue, so they could slowly get accustomed to their new surroundings. For the umpteenth time, Oswald and his friends had to undergo detailed medical examinations; afterward they were interviewed by social workers who decided where each child was to be placed.

On their first morning in the orphanage, the young refugees were served a typical American breakfast: *Kellogg's Rice Krispies* with strawberries, bananas, and milk. "When we finished, one of the kids raised their hand and wanted to know, 'Can we have some more?'" Arthur told me. "They said, 'It's on the table, take what you want.' You should have seen what happened, with all the kids grabbing the bowls all at once! I remember this so vividly."

While their future was being decided behind closed doors, Oswald and his friends were sent out to tour New York. Volunteers took them to Central Park, the *Metropolitan Museum of Art* or to see a movie. Just like the GJCA social workers, these volunteers spoke German or Yiddish with the children, and tried to teach them a few English words. More than once, this resulted in funny misunderstandings, one girl mistaking the word *juice* for *Jews* for instance, and believing that it was a special drink, specifically meant for refugees.

For Oswald, this first week in America brought about an entirely new feeling: "I hadn't really experienced not to be afraid anymore," he confessed to me years later. "When we left France, I worried about being held at the border. In Spain, I was a little afraid because of the *Hakenkreuz* people, the men with swastikas. But in the United States, you didn't see any of this. And when we were taken to the orphanage, that's where I saw a Jewish policeman for the first time. And he spoke some German or Yiddish, and he said, 'You don't have to worry about being Jewish here.'"

* * *

On a windy December afternoon in 2017, I am wandering through Hamilton Heights, in Harlem, in search of 1560 Amsterdam Avenue. The Jewish orphanage was later used as *Army Hall* by the military – and would much later play once again an important role in Oswald's life – before being torn down in the late 1950s. I pass Dominican *bodegas*, cheap laundromats, and hipster coffee shops, where filter coffee costs full five dollars, and finally reach the corner of 137th Street, where the orphanage used to stand. These days it is the *Jacob H. Schiff Playground*, named after a German-Jewish philanthropist.

Fallen leaves swirl in the wind. Right next to me, wrapped in thick winter coats, several men play dominoes. At the far end of the park, a boy is running around a well-maintained soccer field and two moms are pushing their baby carriages. Walking up to a red jungle gym, I spot an African-American park employee picking up trash while listening to music from a set of purple headphones. I ask him if he could take a picture of me and we start talking. Much to my surprise, he knows about the Jewish orphanage that used to stand here.

"I was putting up some signs and I happened to read the background story of the place," the man explains, going on haltingly: "You know, this college here" – he points at a *City College of New York* building across the street – "brings bad memories back to me."

In 1991, nine young people died in the building during a mass panic at an event organized by rapper P. Diddy. "My cousin was one of the people who lost their lives," he tells me. "So, it's bittersweet for me, working here. But recently I found out that this was an orphanage asylum, and that really threw me for a loop. Because I would never have thought that. Somehow it is reassuring to know that young people didn't just die here, but there were also those who were saved."

I tell him about Arthur's story. "Wow. And he was able to get away from Hitler? That's incredible. You don't get many stories like that." As he stores his equipment in a shed, I can see the man is smiling.

* * *

After years of living together in OSE homes, the young refugees believed that the Jewish orphanage on Amsterdam Avenue would be their new home. But this was not the case.

Ever since an American *Kindertransport* had first been planned, an emotional debate raged behind the scenes as to the placement of the children, with Ernst Papanek and OSE on one side, Lotte Marcuse, the GJCA, and the American welfare system on the other. OSE and Ernst Papanek wanted to raise "their" kids in a home run by Papanek. Naively perhaps, they had expected that their Montmorency concept could easily be implemented in America. But in the United States, it was not common to put children into group homes, and (foster) families were considered the optimal solution. So-called institutions housed only "difficult" teenagers or juvenile delinquents, and had a bad reputation among the American public. In the early 1940s, many orphanages were closed for that very reason – including the one on Amsterdam Avenue.[3]

Despite vehement protests from OSE, Lotte Marcuse, who was responsible for the placement and care of all arriving Jewish refugee children, put Oswald and his friends in foster families, per US regulations. Furthermore, the young refugees were scattered to the four corners of the country and forbidden to have any contact with each other. The GJCA acted partly out of fear of anti-Semitism, thus choosing to avoid concentrating too many Jewish children in one place. Lotte Marcuse's main motivation, though, was her strong belief that the children could only assimilate into America if they completely broke with their past. Not only were the refugee children supposed to forget their OSE friends, but preferably their families in Europe as well.[4]

Ernst Papanek and OSE saw the separation of the children as an attack on their values and a threat to the results of years of work – saving the children not only physically, but also emotionally. Papanek and the French OSE held the progressive opinion that the children should not ignore their experiences and their parent's fate, or else they would not be able to overcome their traumatic pasts. It would take until the 1980s for this opinion to become the scientific standard of child psychology.[5]

Nowadays, teachers and psychologists believe group homes to be a better placement for unaccompanied refugee children than living within foster families.[6] This is an important lesson we can learn from the *Kindertransports* – especially in times of the ongoing refugee crisis, which brought thousands of unaccompanied minors to Europe or to the Mexican border.

Even years after the arrival of the American *Kindertransports*, Ernst Papanek still fought to place the children in homes, unable to forgive Lotte Marcuse for her rigorous stance. "Everything we had worked to accomplish at Montmorency was being destroyed. Everything,"[7] he wrote in his autobiography, decades later, in a harsh attack against her.

Historians often use the German word *Kulturkampf*, the war or clash of cultures, to describe the conflict between OSE and the GJCA as a clash between European and American systems and convictions.[8] In France and Austria, collective housing of children had been an accepted practice and Papanek struggled to understand the different US system. Meanwhile, the AMEROSE sided with the Americans, which was met with much incomprehension on the part of the French OSE. The AMEROSE's decision to fire Ernst Papanek is a prime example of this conflict of opinion.

In Papanek's view, the AMEROSE quite plainly ignored their responsibilities by agreeing on the former OSE charges being placed within foster families. After all, OSE, and therefore the AMEROSE, was "juridically and even more so ... morally responsible for the children entrusted to them," he lamented in a letter.

In reality, the creation of OSE homes in the United States had probably been no more than wishful thinking from the beginning. Looking back, sociologist Hanna Papanek wrote that OSE should have tried to open a boarding school instead, which would have been much more socially accepted in America. For the rest of his life, Ernst Papanek struggled with the fact he was not able to do more for the children. "It was a fight he lost," his son Gus told me. "But the biggest disappointment for him was that he didn't manage to save all the children to America."

The former OSE protégés did not know anything about the conflict between the GJCA and OSE. Faced with the sudden and unexpected separation from their friends, the children reacted with shock and incomprehension, many of them suffering greatly in American foster families, and longing for the lost community of the homes.

Ironically though, opening orphanages would have made life easier for Lotte Marcuse and the GJCA. Government requirements for foster families were so strict that finding suitable ones proved quite difficult. In the United States, foster children were only allowed to be placed with families of their own religion, who also needed to prove a high income on top of that. Many Jewish – and particularly orthodox – families, who would have liked to take in young refugees, did not meet these criteria.[9] (In comparison: it had been much easier to rescue 10,000 *Kindertransport* children in Great Britain because many of them were placed within Christian families.)

Even relatives wishing to take in refugee children had to meet the same requirements as regular foster families. In many cases, those relatives were refugees themselves and only had a minimal income, which meant that the GJCA would not allow them to take in a child. This is what happened in Oswald's case.

Three of Oswald's relatives had managed to flee to the United States a year prior: His aunt Erna, Frieda's "old-fashioned" sister; his uncle Sigmund, the director of the knitting factory in Heidenreichstein, where Oswald had spent many a summer; and Oswald's cousin Gina, nine years his senior.

"Now you will be very surprised that I am writing to you from the U.S.A. We have been here for 3 months and as you can see, we are doing very well here, thank God," Sigmund Lieblich had written to his nephew Oswald back in September 1940, when the boy was still living at the *Château de Montintin*.

Sigmund was that uncle who had been taken by the Nazis during the November Pogroms and deported to Buchenwald Concentration Camp. After his release, he had immediately sent his daughter Gina on a *Kindertransport* to England. In 1939, Gina managed to bring her parents to England and the whole family emigrated to America in 1940, where they settled in Kingston, about 90 miles from New York City.

The GJCA knew about Uncle Sigmund and tried to contact him several times before Oswald's arrival, but apparently, they did not have his current address.[10] Oswald himself knew a more recent address, which he gave to a GJCA social worker upon his arrival, but it was still one week before the Lieblichs reacted. In the meantime, the GJCA had started to look for a foster family, in case they would not be able to locate Oswald's relatives.

The GJCA contacted orthodox families in Baltimore, Boston, and Rochester, but Oswald was adamant about staying in New York. "Oswald approached... Lotte Marcuse in the evening saying, *'Ich muss in Ny bleiben'* [I have to stay in NY] most defiantly," a social worker noted in his file. "He repeated that he had to live in an orthodox home. There was such anxiety, but also such stubbornness expressed that I felt one ought to handle his placement carefully."

Oswald's uncle Sigmund and his aunt Erna before their flight from Vienna.

On September 8, the GJCA was about to send Oswald to a foster family in the Bronx when all of a sudden, his cousin Gina walked into their offices. "Miss Lieblich... is a strikingly pretty girl, rather elaborately gotten up for the occasion," Oswald's social worker commented in his file. Gina expected to be able to simply take Oswald home with her but learned to her surprise that the GJCA had to inquire about her parent's circumstances first. She explained that her parents saw themselves as Oswald's "natural guardians" and that the boy "would feel at home" with them, because they used to have a close relationship in Vienna and were orthodox, like him. Nonetheless, the GJCA did not want to send Oswald to his relatives without personally checking their living conditions first. Which was unfortunately easier said than done: As mentioned before, Kingston was more than 90 miles away from New York City. What was more, the GJCA was under pressure to place all the children before the third *Kindertransport* reached New York. The agency decided to stick with the original plan. Gina was allowed to take Oswald for ice cream, but had to return home without him. Oswald left the orphanage on Amsterdam Avenue that very day and was sent to live with a foster family in the Bronx.

His first night there was probably the worst of his life, the feeling of loneliness almost unbearable. "I felt so totally alone. All my friends from France were gone. I did not speak English, and of course, my parents were not there," Arthur remembered. "I went to bed and cried."

18. THE FATE OF FRIEDA, HERMANN, AND FRITZ KERNBERG

Oswald tugged at his jacket, nervously shifting his weight from one leg to the other as he looked around. The entrance hall of Temple Zion slowly filled with worshippers on that Saturday morning, but Oswald stood completely alone. A little apart from him, his foster parents, Mr. and Mrs. Falk, were talking with the rabbi. At the far end of the room, Oswald saw two boys, surrounded by a large group of relatives, smiling and laughing. Both boys wore elegant suits – nothing old-fashioned like the pair of knickerbockers a social worker had picked out for him. "These things have been out of fashion for years!" Oswald thought with despair, fervently hoping no member of the community would gossip about his ridiculous outfit.

It was November 1, 1941, two weeks after Oswald's thirteenth birthday, and the day of his bar mitzvah. In Judaism, a bar mitzvah marks a young man's accession to religious maturity. On that day, he becomes a full-fledged member of the community and from then on must observe all religious commandments and prohibitions. As part of the ceremony, the boy reads the Torah section of that particular day, chanting in Hebrew during the religious service.

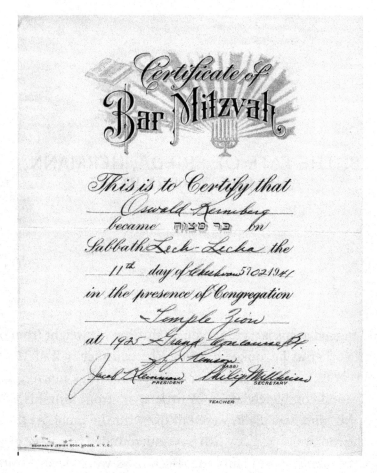

Oswald's bar mitzvah certificate, 1941.

Learning the often complex reading usually takes many months and Oswald had just arrived in America a few weeks earlier. Yet thanks to Madame Krakowski's orthodox education, he was so well prepared the rabbi of Temple Zion had decided to accept him without additional classes.

Oswald's bar mitzvah was on *Shabbat Lech-Lecha*, the Shabbat on which the *Lech-Lecha* Torah section, from the first book of Moses, is read in the synagogue. Whether it was chance or fate, Oswald recited his own story before the assembled congregation: "And the Lord said to Abram, 'Go forth from your land and from your birthplace and from your father's house, to the land that I will show you!'"

Yet something quite different is engraved in Oswald's memory. "Nobody came to my bar mitzvah," Arthur told me. "A bar mitzvah should be a happy occasion, but for me, it was one of the saddest days in my life."

Neither Uncle Sigmund, Aunt Erna, nor his cousin Gina, attended the ceremony. Oswald's foster parents, Mr. and Mrs. Falk, were there, but they would have gone to their synagogue anyway for Shabbat. Oswald was alone in a sea of strangers. Only twelve-year-old Adolf Löw had come to spend the festive day with his friend.

"The two other boys had parents, they had family, friends. They had a party, they got presents," Arthur recalled. "For them, it was a wonderful day. But not for me."

Frieda and Hermann Kernberg were denied the joy of attending their son's day of honor – but they were with him in their thoughts. On October 19, on the actual day of Oswald's birthday, they had sent him a very emotional letter from the ghetto in Poland that reached New York at the end of December. "My dearest darling!" Hermann wrote in his round handwriting. "Today, on the day of your birthday as well as the day of your bar mitzvah, we all sit, your beloved *Mutti*, dearest Fritz and I, in the tiniest room, talking and thinking about you again and again. All our thoughts and longing go out to you alone and our most ardent wish is to be reunited with you soon, in peace and joy."

Frieda and Fritz did not sign the letter – despite Oswald's previous request – and the thirteen-year-old wondered, while reading the letter, whether his mother and brother were still alive. Hermann went on: "And now, my dear, sweet *Burli*, please receive my deepest congratulations and blessings on this most important day. May your luck shine as bright as the stars in the sky and may we soon be granted the joy to hold you in our arms and be able to brighten your life as we have always strived to do. You are all our longing and hope and thus must remain in good health, tall and strong. In spirit, I raise my hands above your dear head and bless you with the biblical saying 'May the Lord bless, protect and keep you and may his right hand be over you always, Amen!!!'"

It was the last time Oswald ever heard from his family.

* * *

Since Oswald's departure to France in March 1939, Hermann had done everything he could to also save Frieda, Fritz, and himself. His increasingly desperate attempts to flee Austria (and later Europe) can only be reconstructed in part from the few letters which have been preserved until today.

On June 1, 1938, even before Oswald's leaving, Hermann had applied for a visa at the American Consulate in Vienna. Yet being born in Poland, he was on the very limited Polish quota list and it could be years before his family would be able to leave. On April 4, 1939, an American cousin, Martin Fleischmann signed an *Affidavit of Support*, in which he guaranteed the Kernbergs would not become a burden to the community should they emigrate to the US. Nine months later, in January 1940, the US Consulate informed Hermann that two further documents, as well as a "friendship letter" from Fleischmann, were missing, so they could not proceed with his visa application. Around the same time, however, Oswald's father learned that his quota number was about to be called and he felt quite confident that the family would soon be able to emigrate to America.

But then the Kernbergs had stopped being selective a long time ago regarding which country they wanted to escape to. "I shall leave at once to wherever the first available and safe opportunity within my reach will offer itself," Hermann wrote to Mr. Reiss, his Swiss financial advisor, whom years before he had entrusted with part of his fortune and who committed himself to helping the Kernbergs emigrate. Apart from applying for an American visa, Hermann also tried to obtain a visa for Panama, Shanghai, Japan, Cuba, Russia, and "Eretz Israel," as he called Palestine in his letters. On January 9, 1940, the Kernbergs applied for a new joint family passport, so they would be ready at any time for a potential emigration. A red "J" stamped on their documents, as well as the additional names "Israel" for Hermann and Fritz, and "Sara" for Frieda, designated them as Jews.

Hermann's and Frieda's passport was issued by the
National socialist authorities in January 1940.

In April 1940, Oswald's family learned Martin Fleischmann's affidavit was not valid and they immediately strove to obtain another one. Six relatives from New York and Los Angeles drew up affidavits, yet there appeared to be some problems with these too. It seems the guarantors could not prove sufficient assets, and the affidavits were thus deemed too "weak," as it was called at that time. In the end, the Swiss financial advisor Reiss tried to speak directly with the

American Consul and offered a guarantee sum of several thousands of dollars for the Kernbergs. Yet his offer was turned down in the absence of any American citizen also acting as a guarantor for the potential emigrants.

On June 1, 1940, Erna and Sigmund Lieblich emigrated to America with their daughter Gina. Hermann and Frieda now pinned all their hopes on the fact the Lieblichs would be able to procure a "strong" affidavit for them. Yet these attempts too failed, the Lieblichs not sending urgently needed additional documents or otherwise proving unable to obtain them in the first place. For the first time, the Kernbergs' letters sounded accusatory and full of incomprehension as to why no one would help them. "To leave and no longer care about siblings and in-laws with whom one has lived and worked together for years is ungodly and irresponsible," Hermann wrote the Lieblichs on December 22, 1940. In that same letter, Frieda asked Erna directly: "Have you forgotten about us? Is this how a sister behaves in such difficult times?"

In December 1940, Hermann had three personal appointments with the American Consul-General, who still found his papers too weak. At the end of January 1941, the Consul informed Oswald's father that "nothing could be done, unfortunately, emigration to the USA is presently virtually closed." As a last resort, Hermann tried to obtain a visa for Cuba via a cousin. Yet it never came to that, all emigration attempts coming to an abrupt end when the Kernbergs received a deportation order.

In February and March 1941, the Nazis deported 5,000 Jewish men and women from Vienna to the so-called "General Government" in Poland. The action, euphemistically called "resettlement," was meant to make Vienna *judenfrei* (free of Jews) and provide more living space.[1] Three or four days before the actual deportation, the Kernbergs were made to gather in a Jewish school building on *Castellezgasse 35*, which served as a transit camp. Each person was allowed one suitcase only. As it was forbidden to bring along valuables, Hermann packed a stack of important documents and brought them to his friend Otto Kürth.

On February 26, 1941, Frieda, Fritz, and Hermann were deported from the Aspang train station to Opole Lubelskie, south of Lublin. A few days after their arrival, a ghetto was officially set up in the small Polish town. Unlike ghettos in bigger cities such as Warsaw, this ghetto was not surrounded by walls, and the freedom of movement of the residents was not restricted. However, whoever was caught outside the ghetto was shot without trial.[2]

The small town of Opole looked back on a centuries-old Jewish tradition. At the start of the war in 1939, a little over 4,000 Jews lived here, about seventy percent of the town's population. Forced resettlements within occupied Poland and the deportations from Vienna doubled the Jewish population, which amounted to almost 8,000 persons by 1941.[3]

"The Jews deported from Vienna were settled in small towns, which increased their population so much that the already threatened food supply was even more jeopardized," historian Jonny Moser explains in his book on the Austrian persecution of the Jews. The Nazis' purpose was to "decimate the Jews by starvation."[4]

From the outset, Hermann, Frieda, Fritz, and the other newly arrived people in Opole were confronted with hunger, an ice-cold winter, far too many people on far too little living space, and appalling sanitary conditions. Heating materials, medication, and food were scarce goods, the prices soaring after the arrival of the Viennese Jews. As there were practically no income opportunities in Opole, the ghetto residents sold the few belongings they still possessed and had to rely on friends or relatives to send them food. In 1941, the official food rations were fixed at 2,310 calories a day for Germans, but no more than 184 calories for Jews.[5] The Kernbergs received support from friends in Vienna and even the Swiss financial advisor, Reiss, sent three packages, which did not reach them for months, though. It is therefore all the more surprising postal services would still work so well that, in spite of the dreadful circumstances, Hermann Kernberg was able to send to OSE his authorization for Oswald's emigration to America, in May 1941.

In his letters, Hermann tried to protect his youngest son from reality and continued to give him optimistic news. But this did not mean he did not face the terrible truth himself. In the summer of 1941, Oswald's father wrote to his sister-in-law: "We're doing well, but our dearest parents-in-law are doing even better." His parents-in-law, however, had been dead since the beginning of the 1930s; Hermann used a code to get around the Nazis' letter censorship.

Although there was little cause for hope, the Kernbergs still tried to emigrate to America from Opole. In the summer of 1941, Hermann found out that all the affidavits that had been issued before July 15, 1941, were no longer valid and he begged his relatives in the USA to try and get the family a new one. "If you were a good brother-in-law and dearest Erna were a sister as required by law, we would not be sitting in this ghetto," Hermann reproachfully wrote in a letter to Sigmund and Erna Lieblich. "But God knows love can't and won't be forced."

Frieda's and Hermann's only ray of hope was Oswald's letter from Lisbon that they received in September 1941, and in which he told them he was on his way to America. Weeping with joy, the Kernbergs immediately wrote to the Lieblichs, feeling certain Frieda's sister would take good care of Oswald, despite all the previous accusations and reproaches: "We assume the child is with you, naturally, and if so, we would indeed feel very happy and reassured, confident you will look after our dearest boy with devotion, love, and kindness, just like after dearest Ginerl."

On October 19, Oswald's birthday, Hermann wrote to his son from "the tiniest room." Oswald's fears Frieda and Fritz were no longer alive at that time, having not signed the letter, proved untrue, both adding a few lines to a letter sent to relatives that same day.

On December 28, 1941, Hermann thanked Mr. Reiss for sending

two food parcels. Nothing more was heard of the family after that date.

It is not possible to reconstruct exactly how and when Frieda, Fritz, and Hermann Kernberg were murdered by the Nazis. The death rate in the Opole ghetto was extremely high: many people starved to death on account of the catastrophic food shortage or succumbed to epidemics. In the spring of 1942, the Nazis started to liquidate the ghetto and deported all the survivors to Sobibor and Belzec death camps. Since there is no record of the Kernbergs' arrival at one of these camps, it must be assumed that they died already in Opole.

Of the 2,003 Viennese Jews deported to Opole, only 28 survived.[6]

* * *

65,000 Austrian Jews were murdered by the Nazis during the Holocaust. Men, women, children. Many of them died far from home. Most of them do not even have a grave.

In 2002, sixty years after the deportation of the Jews from the Opole ghetto, a memorial to the Austrian victims of the Holocaust was unveiled in the entrance hall of the main synagogue in Vienna, on *Seitenstettengasse*. The names of the 65,000 dead are engraved on rotating slate tablets, among them those of Hermann, Frieda, and Fritz. A quotation from the Lamentations of Jeremiah appears in the middle of all the names: "For these things I weep; my eyes, ah my eyes flow with tears, for the Comforter to revive my soul is removed from me."

Four years later, I take part in another kind of commemoration for Oswald's family, a less permanent perhaps, yet much more public remembrance ceremony, nicely named "Flowers of Remembrance." On May 5, 2006, tens of thousands of people throughout Austria bring white roses to all the houses in which Holocaust victims lived before being deported. The flowers are meant to remind us that people like Frieda, Fritz, and Hermann were more than nameless victims. They were neighbors, acquaintances or friends, forcibly torn from society before being murdered in foreign countries.

I myself lay three white roses in front of *Nußdorfer Straße 60*, Oswald's family's last home address.

19. A YOUTH IN NEW YORK

"Was there any specific moment in your life you realized your family was gone?" I ask Arthur once.

"No," he replied. "But that was a good thing. My suspicion grew stronger and stronger until at some point I realized they had to be dead. It was a very slow process; So I didn't have any mourning that way."

Yet there was one thing that did cause him pain. "Growing up, I felt guilty when I realized that I didn't have any parents. There was a certain amount of freedom I had, things I could do that other kids could not, because they were restrained by their parents. So I felt sort of guilty about that, but that's the only time, the only guilt feelings I've had."

* * *

After his bar mitzvah in November 1941, thirteen-year-old Oswald went on living in New York. I wanted to do the same. Eight years after my first visit to the city as part of the history project *A Letter To The Stars*, I make my wish come true and move to the city that never sleeps. From 2015 to early 2017, I live in Brooklyn and study journalism at the renowned *New York University* (NYU). These were exciting times for a journalist in New York, what with the presidential campaign taking place and ending with Donald Trump's unexpected victory. For one and a half years, I follow the election campaign up close, interviewing politicians and volunteers, meeting Hillary Clinton, writing articles, and shooting videos for the university, as well as for *The Forward*, a long-established Jewish newspaper. On the evening of the election, I produce the NYU live election broadcast. Shortly afterwards, having finished my master's degree, I return to Europe.

Yet a few months later already, in December 2017, I am back in New York, embarking on a search for Oswald's youth. I set off in the Bronx, at 1925 Grand Concourse. Temple Zion, where Oswald celebrated his bar mitzvah in 1941, is located at that address. Or more precisely: what was formerly Temple Zion. The building still stands, but it no longer houses a synagogue. It has been turned into a Catholic kindergarten instead!

The *New Covenant Christian Day School* is painted a bright light blue, a striking sight among the grey and brown neighboring houses, much like a colorful bucket in a sandbox. The blue color is supposed to stand for the sky, the lower half of the house adorned with a landscape scenery: children solving arithmetic problems in lush green meadows, while flower-like letters sprout out of the ground next to them. It is only at second or third glance that I realize Jewish symbols lie concealed under the thick layers of paint. Above each of the eight windows on the second floor, for instance, a relief-like protruding Star of David is covered with pale blue paint, and under a larger-than-life purple bee a Jewish date is carved into the stone.

"Inside there is really no Judaica left," Ellen Levitt, the author of the book *The Lost Synagogues of The Bronx and Queens*, tells me. "Where I thought there would have been the holy arc of the synagogue, there was just an empty space and it had been covered with a curtain." On her quest for lost synagogues, Levitt comes across a lot of converted temples. "Synagogues are tailor-made buildings to become churches; after all many of the architectural elements are similar," Levitt declares.

From Grand Concourse, where Oswald celebrated his bar mitzvah, I walk towards 2075 Morris Avenue, Oswald's first home in New York. It is just a short walk, no longer than ten minutes. After all, one is not allowed to use public transportation on Shabbat and Oswald's foster home thus had to be in the vicinity of his foster parents' synagogue.

2075 Morris Avenue is a five-story building of light brown brickwork, quite a popular building material in New York. 48 apartments are listed on the doorbell, almost all of the names Latino-sounding. Luckily for me, a young woman just comes out of the house and lets me in. Left and right of a great tiled entrance area, narrow flights of stairs lead up to winding stairwells. The windows, stairs, and apartment doors are painted bright red. It is an odd feeling to be walking through an unfamiliar house and although I come across a few ladies decorating their doors with Christmas ornaments, I approach no one.

* * *

Since early September 1941, Oswald had been living on 2075 Morris Avenue with his foster parents Hannah and Harry Falk.[1] Little is known about the Falk family. According to census data, Hannah was 49 and Harry 55 when they took in Oswald. Austria or Galicia are alternately indicated as the couple's country of birth, which means they come from the northeastern part of the former Habsburg monarchy. The Falks had been living for over twenty years in the US, having received American citizenship sometime between the 1920s and 1940s. They spoke English and Yiddish, which was close enough to German for Oswald to be able to communicate with them in the beginning. Harry Falk worked as a second-hand textile fabric merchant, and Hannah was a housewife. Besides Oswald, the Falks' two biological sons also lived in the three-room apartment on Morris Avenue: fifteen-year-old Averon and seven-year-old Sheldon.[2] The three boys shared one bedroom.

Hannah Falk acted as a guarantor vis-à-vis the GJCA and USCOM for Oswald's well-being, signing all necessary documents as his official foster mother; in the eyes of the authorities, Harry was "merely" the husband. Arthur later described his foster parents as "nice people," yet not exactly "the brightest people in the world." On his first night at the Falks' for instance, Harry beckoned Oswald over to him and pointed to the light switch. He pressed it and the light went on. He pressed it again and the light went out. Oswald gave his foster father a puzzled look. "But you know, he had come from a small *shtetl* in Russia or Poland, where they had no electricity," Arthur told me years later, grinning. "So he thought I wouldn't know what a light switch is. But I came from a big city! I came from Vienna!"

The Falks treated Oswald well, but he did not feel quite at home with them. "It wasn't necessarily my foster parents' fault," Arthur explained to me. "But for most of the OSE children I know and who went into foster homes, it did not work out. The Falks treated me nicely – I was not abused or anything, but I was treated differently than their children and I felt it. There were little things, like their own kids could go to the refrigerator without asking, any time they wanted, and I could not. Not that they didn't feed me, I got room and board – but I wasn't part of the family. And I could feel it."

After a short pause, he added: "But you know, you live through these things."

* * *

You live through these things. Arthur never said this about his time in war-torn France, where he suffered from hunger and deprivation. Yet when describing his first years in New York, he would frequently use these words, although he was better off at that time than he had been before, at least according to his external circumstances. His lonely first night at the Falks', his bar mitzvah, one of the saddest day of his life, reading his father's last letter – Arthur would tell me about all this and always add right away: "But you live through these things."

Arthur generally spoke very little about his youth in New York. Even when I asked him directly about it, he would only tell me some details and anecdotes before changing the subject. Very little would have been known about Oswald's teenage years, had I not found his "secret" foster care record. Even decades after a person's death, access to foster care records is restricted to protect people's privacy and the files can only be consulted with the assent of the next of kin. Of course, one first needs to locate said files.

After months of research, I learn Oswald's file is kept in the YIVO archive in New York. The *YIVO Institute for Jewish Research* (formerly *Yidisher visnshaftlekher institut*) runs together with four other Jewish institutions the *Center for Jewish History* in Manhattan, where I research for this book in the winter of 2017. YIVO also keeps the public files of GJCA, which I have long known about, yet no one breathes a word about there being hundreds of personal files of former GJCA protégés in a warehouse in New Jersey. The knowledge about these foster care records is passed on like a secret among Holocaust survivors and this is how I too finally get to know about them. Yet even though Arthur's son, Aaron, has provided me with an official authorization to consult his father's file, it is months before YIVO hands over a copy to me.

The 133 pages of the record prove to be a wealth of information – for me, but most of all, for Arthur's family, who knows just as little about his teenage years as I do. Like every Jewish foster child at that time, Oswald received a monthly visit from a social worker of the *Jewish Child Care Association*, who sent quarterly reports about his development to GJCA and USCOM. Besides school evaluations and forms, these reports also include medical information from bi-annual routine examinations. Oswald, for instance, received a pair of glasses in December 1942 and was still slightly undernourished in 1943, after two years of American food. In 1944, puberty set in, as I gather from the file. Oswald had to be officially registered as a foreigner in America and thus had his fingerprints taken on his 14th birthday. Expenses or financial matters were just as painstakingly recorded in his file: the Falks received 25 dollars a month as support for food. Oswald himself received a monthly one-dollar allowance from the foster care authorities, from mid-1943 on.

In the first months after his arrival, the reports about Oswald's new life in America were still quite succinct, yet later I find much more detailed descriptions. In December 1942, the social worker responsible for him wrote to USCOM, saying that "Oswald seems to have adjusted well in the foster home. ... He made excellent school progress. ... At present he is in the 7th grade, doing better-than-average work. Oswald mastered English very quickly and speaks and understands the language completely."

Immediately after his arrival in America in September 1941, Oswald was enrolled in 5th grade, because the teacher spoke Yiddish – according to his age, though, he should have attended 7th grade. He was moved to 6th grade only a few weeks later, having learned English very quickly. Even later, Oswald often skipped school terms or attended extra classes, so he would be enrolled in higher grades. By the time he graduated from high school, he was an Honor Roll student and only six months behind his age group.

* * *

"Touchdown," cheered a boy from the neighborhood, running towards his comrades, all smiles. Oswald's team was losing. I wish kids would play soccer in America too, Oswald thought for the umpteenth time, as he scrambled to his feet. After all, the thirteen-year-old was an ace when it came to soccer, but what use was it in New York if headers were your specialty? At first, he had tried his luck with stickball, the street version of baseball. But no matter how often he tried, Oswald just would not manage to hit a small ball thrown at him from a 16-foot distance with a broomstick. Football it was then; at least he could run fast.

"Hey, you're bleeding! Everything OK?" a boy called out to him. Oswald looked down and froze. He did not care about his bleeding knee, but he worried about the seven-inch-long tear in his trousers. The fabric must have got caught somewhere in his fall, the trousers were ruined. Oswald trudged home, his head low.

As a foster child, he possessed very few clothes, which he could purchase on a fixed allowance provided by the *Jewish Child Care Association*. He hated these shopping trips with his social worker that would always make him feel like a beggar being given alms. After the business with the ripped trousers, Oswald had to wait six months before he received a new pair. He decided never to play football again.

While Oswald got used to his new home, learned new kinds of sports, and tried to make new friends, the war still raged in Europe. On December 7, 1941, only three months after Oswald arrived in America, the war turned into a world war when Japan, allied with Hitler's Germany, unexpectedly attacked the US naval base at Pearl Harbor. The next day, the USA declared war on Japan and on December 11, 1941, on Germany and Italy. Thirteen-year-old Oswald hoped America's entry into the war would be the end of the Nazis. Perhaps there was still a glimmer of hope for his parents.

Oswald spent two years with Hannah and Harry Falk, even though it had always been his parents' express wish he should live with his uncle Sigmund and his aunt Erna. Oswald too wanted to move in with his relatives and from today's perspective, why this did not happen – at least at first – seems incomprehensible.

Possibly, the accommodation only failed at first because of GJCA's tight deadline, the association striving to find foster families for the refugee children as quickly as possible. Later though, there was no longer any valid reason why Oswald was not allowed to move to his relatives. Former factory director Sigmund had not been able to bring his fortune to America and the family was poor, but then the Falks too received a contribution from the foster care agency for the boy.

One sentence may provide a clue as to why the child welfare authorities seemed reluctant to give Oswald's custody over to the Lieblichs. I read the following comment on a typed phone message in Oswald's foster care file: "There is still real doubt about the offer from the relatives [to take in the boy]."

The Jewish social workers knew Oswald wanted to leave the Falks and seemed to have given his wish a great deal of thought. "Before considering replacement with Oswald, we feel it necessary to give him an opportunity to discuss his feelings about separation from his family and his feelings about being under foster home care," I read in a letter addressed to Lotte Marcuse. "During the year there was much discussion ... to his going to live with his aunt and uncle. He was eager for this, but also hesitant because it would necessitate school change," it says in another report.

In September 1942, Sigmund and Erna moved from Kingston to Manhattan, where Sigmund became the joint owner of a candy store. Oswald began to visit them frequently, and also spend the holidays with them. Gina had already married and no longer lived with her parents. The Lieblichs had a four-room apartment and thus enough space to accommodate Oswald, but their financial situation was still precarious. When GJCA finally agreed to provide the family with a monthly 20 dollars allowance, nothing stood in the way of Oswald moving in with them. Yet it was decided Oswald would remain with the Falks until the end of the school year, to ensure leaving his familiar environment and parting with his new friends would not be too hard on him. On September 24, 1943, two years after he arrived in

America, Oswald moved to Aunt Erna and Uncle Sigmund on 349 Amsterdam Avenue.

* * *

The Jewish orphanage where Oswald spent his first days upon his arrival in New York formerly also stood on Amsterdam Avenue. Which does not mean the Lieblichs' apartment was just around the corner. Manhattan's straight avenues are so long the two addresses are actually over three and a half miles apart. By subway, though, it just takes me twenty minutes to get there, during my search for clues in December 2017.

Evening has come as I reach number 349 and the whole street glows red in the sunset. Oswald's former home is on the Upper West Side, one of the most expensive areas in New York today, surrounded by trendy shops, overly expensive gyms, and small restaurants. The five-story brick building is relatively low compared to the rest of the houses in the area; on the left, a building, almost twice as tall, rises high into the sky. With its reddish-brown stone and the fire escape on the façade, 349 Amsterdam Avenue is the epitome of a New York building.

* * *

Since his 13th birthday, Oswald worked after school and during holidays to earn a little extra pocket money. During his teenage years, he thus did all manners of odd jobs: newspaper boy, egg-packer, laborer for a textile factory and a paper factory, seller in a five-cent shop, dance teacher, and during the summer, bus boy in a hotel. With his very first wages, Oswald bought himself a pair of tennis shoes he was unfortunately only able to wear for three months, having had a huge growth spurt shortly afterward. He also invested money in war stamps. Oswald "has shown maturity in handling money, and is definitely saving towards a college education," his social worker wrote, praising him in her quarterly report.

After moving to the Lieblichs, Oswald settled well in Manhattan. The fifteen-year-old had a very close relationship to his uncle Sigmund and his aunt Erna. An entry in his file dated 1944 shows he called them "Mom" and "Pop," no one believing at that time that Frieda and Hermann could still be alive. Yet the older he became, the more critically Oswald viewed his relatives, considering Erna and Sigmund old-fashioned and complaining they would cling to Austrian traditions instead of embracing the American ways. He also terribly missed the community life he had known in France.

"I was happier in the children's home in France than I was with my aunt and uncle or with my foster parents," Arthur told me. "I think it was because we had become a family. We had lived together in the same room, eating together and doing the same things, playing sports, going to school. We were a family."

A family Oswald was only occasionally able to have contact with. Lotte Marcuse had scattered the former OSE protégés across the whole country and refused to communicate to the children the addresses of their former friends, holding the opinion that the young refugees could only truly settle in America if they completely broke with their past. However, Oswald and six months younger Adolf Löw somehow managed to get each other's address and met once a month. Marcuse did not want the children getting in touch with each other, and particularly disapproved of OSE's attempts to exert influence on its former protégés. As an extreme example, the GJCA refused to provide OSE or AMEROSE with the children's addresses. When parents in Europe tried to write to their children with OSE's help, the latter was now forced to forward the letters to GJCA, because Marcuse would not allow them to have any contact with the children. Specifically, Ernst Papanek, who lived in New York and would sometimes meet with Oswald and other OSE children, was a thorn in Marcuse's side. "It is important that we get him away from here," she wrote in an internal memo.

Marcuse also believed it was important not to urge the children to write to their parents in Europe, refusing to admit the fact that the desperate parents in Germany or Poland longed for nothing more fervently than to see their children's handwriting. The OSE children who had remained in *Château de Montintin* felt likewise betrayed by their friends, as Lazare Gurvic deplored in a letter to Ernst Papanek: "Children, who did not leave France and to whom their little friends had promised to send letters and news, are very disappointed, feeling they have already been forgotten."

* * *

Oswald had made it out of France just in time. After he arrived in New York, only two other USCOM transports reached America, the last in May 1942.[3] In the meantime, the Nazis had decided on the so-called "Final Solution," the murder of all European Jews. In the summer of 1942, the collaboration of the Vichy regime with the Nazis was confirmed, and France started to deport not only adults but also thousands of children, to Poland. French police raided some OSE children's homes, at times even taking toddlers under the age of two.

Shocked by the reports and news from Europe, the American government finally approved 5,000 emergency visas for Jewish children in France.[4] Based on the deportations, the Quakers too had reconsidered their attitude and now fully supported the *Kindertransports*. A ship for the first group of children was already on its way to Europe when the Allies invaded French North Africa – that collaborated with the Germans – on November 8, 1942 (*Operation Torch*). As a reaction to the lack of resistance on the part of the French troops in Africa, Hitler ordered the occupation of the whole of France. On November 11, the German army marched into Vichy France and sealed all borders, one day before the children would have left Marseille.[5]

"And all because of bad timing," archivist Ron Coleman declares, sighing, during our meeting. The US State Department issuing the visas did not know about the upcoming invasion of North Africa. "The military effort was on a completely difficult track. And they had a completely different war to try to win. So this is just a case of the larger war stories completely consuming the smaller human stories," Coleman explains to me.

In the end, "only" 253 Jewish children from the OSE homes came to America on a *Kindertransport*. Estimates assume that 100 other OSE children managed to reach the country by other means (often together with their parents). GJCA's and USCOM's corporate affidavits brought a total of 1,035 unaccompanied minors to the United States (today the group is referred to as the *One Thousand Children*). A shockingly low number, given the size and resources of the United States.

After the German occupation of southern France, OSE hastily closed its homes and launched a last big and extraordinary rescue action. With the help of the *Résistance*, the French resistance movement, OSE hid 2,000 children under false identities in French families, on farms, and in convents. OSE managed to sneak about 1,000 more children over the border to Switzerland.[6]

69 children from OSE homes were deported – most of them to Auschwitz – among them 11 from *Montintin*.[7] Over thirty OSE members were murdered by the Nazis during the war.

Arthur's biography tells the story of an extraordinary rescue. "Thousands of children did not get chosen for any *Kindertransport* and perished. I was chosen for two," he wrote decades later in a short story entitled *Luck*. Even if "only" a little more than 1,000 children made it to America, it does not minimize in any way the tireless commitment of a large group of people on two continents, who strived against all odds to bring every single one of these children to safety. The Quakers were awarded the Nobel Peace Prize in 1947 in recognition of their assistance to war victims.

In his autobiography *Out of the Fire*, Ernst Papanek drew quite a nice conclusion about his work for OSE: "Epic stories are born only in retrospect. While the Montmorency Homes were in operation, it was no more than a modest story of children who wanted to survive, and whom I thought I could help to survive. Nothing so remarkable about that. ... I didn't do enough because nobody did enough. But some things were done."[8]

20. OSWALD BECOMES ARTHUR

Oswald was an exceptionally gifted student, I very rarely read otherwise in his foster care record.[1] As soon as 1942, after only one year in America, his progress at school was deemed "excellent," as his social worker wrote in praise. In the following years, she would time and again refer to Oswald as "College material," at a time when more than half of the American population did not even graduate from high school.

Oswald was especially good at math and natural sciences. He attributed his love of numbers to his algebra teacher, Miss Bowden. "She made a game out of algebra," Arthur wrote dozens of years later in a short autobiography. "And I loved playing that game almost as much as I loved making the class laugh by making absurd comments whenever the opportunity presented itself."

In January 1945, Oswald graduated with distinction from Junior High School. He was supposed to transfer to Senior High, the whole question being which one? Seventeen-year-old Oswald was not at all sure what exactly he wanted to do in life, even briefly considering registering in a yeshiva, a Jewish religious school, where male students devote themselves to the study of Torah and Talmud. In the end, though, he chose a different path. "Most of the really bright kids from my Junior High School went to a specific High School where you needed an entrance exam to get in," Arthur explained to me. "So I went to that school too – to be with my friends."

And so it happened that Oswald attended *Stuyvesant High School* in Manhattan, a very renowned technical high school, ranking to this day among the most famous schools in America. In Oswald's days, the *Stuyvesant* campus was on 15th street in Manhattan, right next to Union Square, where I too had to change subways on my way to university. At the time, the all-boys school welcomed 2,600 students.

"In Stuyvesant, they are given every opportunity to explore the realms of mathematics, physics, chemistry, biology, and allied technical and scientific subjects to an extent undreamed of in ordinary high schools," I read in the yearbook of Oswald's graduating class.[2] Besides theoretical lessons, the students also attended a lot of practical classes, the numerous chemistry, physics, and work rooms far better equipped than the workshops in the OSE homes, yet operating with a very similar approach. Thanks to his excellent grades, Oswald was considered an honor student in *Stuyvesant*, an exceptionally gifted student. He had also joined the swim team and the math club.

The Second World War ended during Oswald's first year at *Stuyvesant High School*. Unlike Europe, the war in the United States did not end on May 8, 1945. On August 6, the Americans dropped a nuclear bomb on Hiroshima and another one, a few days later, on August 9, over the city of Nagasaki. On September 2, 1945, Japan's capitulation put a definite end to six years of war that had claimed approximately 50 million lives worldwide.

Oswald's uncle Sigmund, with whom he had lived for two years, did not live to see the end of the war. He died of a pulmonary embolism shortly before, on August 12, 1945. Aunt Erna wanted Oswald to drop out of school and take over Sigmund's candy store. "I wanted to do something with my life," Arthur told me later. "I didn't want to have a candy store." The *Jewish Child Care Association* and GJCA, therefore, doubled Erna Lieblich's monthly allowance, giving her 40 dollars, so Oswald could continue to live with her and attend school.

In 1947, Oswald graduated from the renowned *Stuyvesant High School*.

Oswald still had a good relationship with his aunt and cousin Gina, as ever, his care record describing him as being "devoted" to them. In 1947, Oswald graduated from *Stuyvesant High School*. The school graduation ceremony took place in the prestigious Carnegie Hall. The following summer, Erna married her late husband's business partner – and kicked Oswald out of the house.

The eighteen-year-old was deeply shocked. "In the summer I worked as a waiter in a hotel up in the Catskills," Arthur recalled. "And then she said I couldn't come back to live with her."

Forced to find a room as a subtenant, Oswald moved to Mrs. Jennie Frank's place on 1467 Taylor Avenue, in a tenement house in a quiet neighborhood of the Bronx. For 50 dollars a month, he rented a room and was served two warm meals a day. "Mr. and Mrs. Frank were very nice people," Arthur told me, "I wish I'd had them as foster parents to start with. I would have stayed with them." Yet, it was not only on account of the Franks that Oswald so much enjoyed living on Taylor Avenue; it was mostly because of his neighbor, Adolf Löw, who rented a room in the house across the street. The two friends now spent every free minute together.

In the fall of 1947, Oswald and Adolf started to study, both of them benefiting from a monthly scholarship allocated by the *Jewish Child Care Association*. The prediction of Oswald's social worker had come true: he was indeed college material. But he was once again tormented by doubts about his future. After his uncle's death and his aunt's second marriage, he started wondering whether there was anything that actually kept him in New York. Adolf and he began entertaining the idea of emigrating to the future state of Israel. "I liked the idea of working on a kibbutz, on a farm. Because when I was in France, in *Montintin*, there were farmers around and I always sort of liked being in that atmosphere," Arthur said to me. "But then we both got scholarships and we decided to go to Israel after our studies."

The social workers at the *Jewish Child Care Association* tried to actively support Oswald with his planning for the future, sending him, among other things, to a psychologist for career counseling. The psychologist found Oswald had an IQ of 121 and confirmed that he possessed a "superior capacity in general intelligence as well as in specific aptitudes required for engineering." Oswald would have loved to go to medical school, but his scholarship was not large enough to allow him to. In the end, he took the same decision as previously. "I wanted to be with my friends," Arthur explained. More than half of the *Stuyvesant* graduates enrolled in electrical engineering and Oswald followed their example. After getting a bad grade in his first physics seminar, he switched to another discipline within the engineering sciences: mechanical engineering.

Oswald studied at the *City College of New York*, attending lectures in a building that was more than familiar to him: 1560 Amsterdam Avenue. The university had bought the former Jewish orphanage building. Several times a week, Oswald would now study in the very same rooms where he had spent his first days in America.

Studying at the *City College* was free for students at that time. Oswald received an annual grant of 500 dollars from the *Jewish Child Care Association*, which allowed him to pay for his rent and food. But he still needed to do side jobs to buy textbooks and cover his other expenses.

* * *

Even though the nineteen-year-old was officially enrolled at the City College as Oswald Kernberg, his professors and fellow students only knew him under another name: Arthur.

"Oswald was an unusual name over here," Arthur explained to me. "They don't use that name over here. And the kids in school used to tease me, calling me 'Oswald the rabbit.'" This a reference to Walt Disney's cartoon character *Oswald, the Lucky Rabbit*, considered as the forerunner of Mickey Mouse. "They were always after me with this 'Oswald the rabbit'-thing. So then I decided I'm gonna take a more American name. When I was still with my foster parents, there was a kid named Arthur living in the same house. He was very nice to me and had defended me a couple of times when somebody picked on me. When the USA entered the Second World War, he enrolled voluntarily in the Navy. He was some kind of role model for me. So I started calling myself Arthur."

Oswald, Ossi, Putzilein, Papakuss – and now, Arthur. Arthur had had quite a lot of names in his young life; he would stick with the last one. I have only ever known Arthur by that name. Many of his friends also used the short forms, Art or Artie.

Arthur was not the only one to choose a new name. "We once went bowling and everybody had a different name! Siegfried was Fred and Julius used Jay. Artie was no longer Oswald and I was Aaron," Aaron Low – now no longer called Adolf Löw – told me. The former refugee children would often Americanize their German names or else use their Jewish names from now on. But Oswald did not want people to recognize him as a Jew by his name. This is also why he later shortened Kernberg to Kern.

Around the same time, another fundamental change occurred in his life: Arthur stopped being orthodox. The subject of his extreme religiosity frequently came up in his foster care record. During his first weeks in America, Oswald had not even taken off his head cover to sleep. Over the years though, a slow inner process had taken place, religion moving more and more into the background.

After the young man moved out of Aunt Erna's apartment, he stopped eating kosher.

Arthur had not been raised orthodox during his childhood years in Vienna and he did not live an orthodox life as an adult. The imposed stage of strong religiosity – after having been wrongly accommodated in the religious OSE home in Eaubonne – proved rather short-lived. Former Eaubonne children Ernst Valfer and Aaron Low also stopped living an orthodox life a long time ago. Madame Krakowski's attempt to proselytize the boys had failed.

* * *

In 1948, no longer content with being mere neighbors, Arthur and Aaron moved in together in a furnished one-room apartment on 308 W 94th Street in Manhattan, just two minutes from the Hudson River. The rent, which had to be paid every five days, cost each of them $9.62 a week.

When I moved to Munich in 2011 for my studies, I sent Arthur an email with a picture of my small 215 square feet apartment. "If you think that is small, you should have seen the room Aaron and I shared in our first year at Uni," Arthur replied right away. "We had one room which had two beds, two night tables, and a two-burner stove in one corner. It had one other tiny room with only a sink to wash up. That was it. The bathroom was shared with four other tenants."

Despite the narrowness of their lodging, the two students had a lot of fun. Arthur constantly came up with new pranks to pull Aaron's leg. He was once again the light-hearted rascal he had been in his Viennese years, known for his jokes and tomfoolery. One day, for instance, Arthur placed an empty bottle of milk in front of the door, a secret code the two friends used to inform the other whenever they received the visit of a lady. Noticing the empty bottle of milk, Aaron spent the entire night in the subway, discreetly leaving the room to Arthur. On the next morning, Arthur removed the bottle and acted innocent, as if nothing had happened.

And yet "it was wonderful living with Artie," Aaron recalled nostalgically. "We had all kinds of wonderful experiences."

* * *

In November 2015, I am back in California to spend Thanksgiving with the Kerns. This time, I also pay a visit to Aaron Low and his wife Ellie. I have known Aaron since my first visit to Los Angeles when I was sixteen. After all, it was impossible to spend some time with Arthur without getting to know his best friend sooner or later. Throughout their adult lives, the two men never lived far apart, whether in New York or later in Los Angeles. It is thus only a short drive to the house of the Lows.

As we sit in their pastel kitchen, nibbling cookies and sipping tea, while looking at some photographs, Aaron tells me about his life, a purring cat rubbing against our legs. Aaron's hearing-aid and his medical emergency bracelet betray his age – he is 86 – but every time he starts to talk about Arthur, his face brightens so much that it is quite easy to picture him as a young man.

Born in Berlin, Aaron was four when his namesake – Adolf Hitler – rose to power. Oswald and Adolf met in Eaubonne, but did not spend much time together there; being six months younger, Adolf belonged to another cohort of children. While Oswald learned carpentry, Adolf knitted. During the evacuation of Paris, they were sent to different homes, only meeting again in Marseille: both had been chosen to be part of the second *Kindertransport* to America. "I was supposed to be on the first one," Aaron says. "And all my friends left on the first one. And the same thing happened to Artie!"

The same fate had befallen both boys, their shared experiences quickly turning into a close friendship. "When I met Artie in Marseille, I was so happy to see him," Aaron recalls. "We became friends immediately. We have been friends ever since that time 74 years ago."

Arthur once told me finding Aaron had been the greatest luck in his life: "We were each other's mother and father, we consoled and helped each other – to this day."

When Aaron's scholarship was canceled, Arthur convinced his social worker to reverse the decision. Three years later, when the same thing happened to Arthur, Aaron stood up for his friend too. It was also Aaron who got Arthur a summer job as a waiter in a hotel.

* * *

"Could I have some more bread, please?" – "Some more water!" – "Don't you see my glass is empty?" – "That is regular butter, I ordered salted butter."

Arthur's head was spinning with all the orders and calls. Even though it was his fourth summer in a row as a waiter at the *Alamac Hotel* in the Catskills, he still felt, every time, as if he was in a madhouse, although he did not even have to take the meal orders, being only responsible for serving bread, butter, and drinks and clearing the table. Talk about "only!" Arthur thought, hurrying on.

One hour and a half later, his spotless white shirt was soaked with sweat. The same scene took place three times a day at every meal, seven days a week for three months. Yet however stressful that summer job was, Arthur enjoyed the change from his studies. Between the meals, Aaron and Arthur were allowed to use all the hotel facilities: the pool, and the basketball court, they even went to ride horses. In the evenings, there were Casino nights, where they would always find girls for a dance (or more).

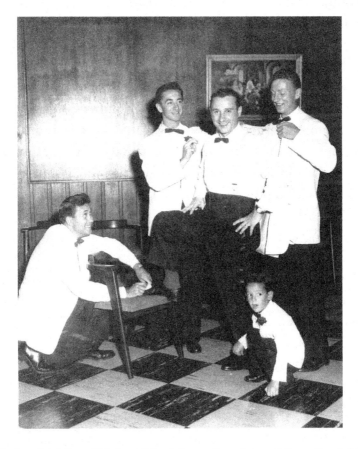

Arthur (right) and his best friend Aaron Low (second from the right) worked as waiters for several summers, in a hotel in the Catskills.

Tips included, Arthur earned up to one thousand dollars every summer – money he used to improve his scholarship during the rest of the year. But the young man also worked during the semester, as a dance teacher of all things, teaching rumba, foxtrot, samba, tango, swing, and of course, as befits every native Viennese, waltz.

Waitressing and dancing were by far not the only jobs Arthur took to keep his head above water. Sometimes he would even work five different odd jobs at the same time, although he was really supposed to study!

"I am glad that you are enjoying your studies. I can only say that I did not like University," Arthur emailed me after my first year at university. "I never had time for anything. I was always either in class, doing homework, or working." This was also reflected in his grades. In contrast to his brilliant school years, Arthur's grades in college were average, sometimes even less than average. At times he even was on the verge of being kicked out of college, because his grade point average was too low. "The engineering course is admittedly a difficult one," Arthur's social worker wrote in his defense to the GJCA that wanted to cut his scholarship. She also added he was living on a minimal budget and had practically no social life at all. "Arthur is a studious and ambitious young man, who is willing to make sacrifices to complete his schooling," the social worker wrote.

In the end, Arthur's grades improved to such an extent that he was allowed to pursue his studies and keep his scholarship. He never became a truly successful student, though. "When I graduated, I ranked 35th among all mechanical engineering students," Arthur told me once, laughing. "Which would have been great, if there had been 500 of us. But we were only 36."

* * *

By now Arthur had firmly settled in America. There was no longer any talk about emigrating to Israel. Arthur also no longer had any contact with Austria – until he received a letter from Vienna that is.

"In August 1945, I was appointed by the then state office for industry, business, trade, and transport as the public administrator of a medium-sized knitting factory *Dr. Heribert Zedlacher*, ... that had been recorded until 1938 under the name of Goldfeld & Kernberg Company, Vienna XIX, Hardtgasse 32 and owned solely by your father," a man called Egon Col wrote to Arthur in the spring of 1948. "I will only consider my voluntary and additional work as manager of the *Dr. Zedlacher* factory as completed, my dear young friend, when I will be able to hand over to you the company that was entrusted to me."

That letter was the result of a year-long search on the part of Egon Col.

Heribert Zedlacher, the "aryanizer" of the Kernberg's family factory had fallen in Stalingrad, in 1943. After the end of the Second World War, his widow had claimed the factory, but the postwar authorities took it away from her, appointing Egon Col – who owned a textile wholesale company and was considered a political opponent of the Nazis – as a public liquidator to restore the business until Hermann Kernberg or his heirs could be located.

The first months, Col waited in vain for someone to contact him. "How many times have I heard my husband say, should Kernberg walk through the door, I would be so happy I would fling my arms around his neck," Col's wife, Friedl, wrote to Arthur in a letter, describing that period. Yet no one came and the Cols began to make inquiries of their own.

After hearing about the Kernbergs' deportation, they were about to give up when a long-term employee of the factory told them "that there had been a boy, Ossi." But the lady mistakenly believed Oswald had been sent to England on a *Kindertransport*. The Cols then wrote to Jewish organizations in England, also turning to the local Red Cross office, yet all in vain. In the end, Friedl Col went to *Gussenbauergasse 1* to ask the neighbors. An old woman told her "little Oswald is said to have been sent to France." The clue turned out to be correct this time: the *Service Européen des Recherches des Juifs Déportés et Dispersés* (European Tracing Service of Deported and Exiled Jews) in Paris informed the Cols that Oswald had indeed been in France, but left the country on a *Kindertransport* to America.

That is what the Cols told Arthur in their letters and from there I can reconstruct their search myself: in Oswald's file at OSE, in his foster care record, as well as in a file specially compiled by the Quakers,[3] I find numerous letters sent by and concerning Col, who by then had been searching "for over two years for one of the many unfortunate victims of Nazi barbarism."

The *Service Européen des Recherches* wrote OSE, which in turn contacted AMEROSE who could not offer any help either, as they did not know Arthur's current address because of Lotte Marcuse's strict directives.[4] At the same time, Egon Col himself contacted the Joint in America, which turned to the *Central Location Index*, an American tracing service. The *Central Location Index* thereupon wrote to the Quakers, who turned to USCOM, which contacted GJCA, every time forwarding the previous correspondence, a fact that enables me today to find all these letters in Oswald's foster care record. The whole procedure lasted for months on end; time and again it came to delays because the lawyers of the aid organizations were unsure whether they were allowed to disclose Arthur's personal information to a foreigner, let alone an Austrian. In May 1948, much to their "boundless joy," the Cols finally obtained Arthur's address.

The Cols had managed to find Arthur right in time; the deadline to apply for a restitution of the company expired on December 31, 1948. In a five-page letter, Egon Col informed Arthur about his inheritance and the necessary legal steps to recover it. Friedl Col also sent him a very moving letter: "As a woman, I would like to be the interpreter of his feelings," she explained concerning her husband's rather matter-of-fact tone. Other letters followed, the Cols repeatedly inviting Arthur to visit them in Vienna.

"The Col couple had no children and I had a feeling that they wanted to adopt me," Arthur told me years later. "But I decided I didn't want to go back to Vienna. I've got nothing lost over there and I didn't know anybody over there anyway. So I told Col I was going to sell the factory and he said he would buy it."

For Arthur to be able to sell it, the factory first had to officially belong to him. The legal prerequisite for this was to have his parents and older brother declared dead. In March 1949, Arthur submitted the corresponding application at the Vienna regional court, which was granted on January 7, 1950 – after a mandatory waiting period. Frieda's, Fritz's, and Hermann's actual date of death being unknown, as usually in such cases, the date of the end of the war, May 8, 1945, was written on their official death certificates "as the day the long-lost person did not survive."

On June 7, 1950, his father's factory was officially returned to Arthur and once again renamed Goldfeld & Kernberg, as I gather from the Vienna Trade Office files.[5] For the following four years, the factory belonged to Arthur, at least on paper, until all formalities regarding the sale had been clarified. Then the knitting factory was renamed *Egon Col*. It operated until 1961, and today it no longer exists. Despite the Cols' long-held wish, Arthur never met them in person. The couple died without an heir.

Because of the tense economic situation and years of bad management under the direction of "aryanizer" Dr. Zedlacher, the business was worth much less than before. 70 employees used to work in the knitting factory in Hermann Kernberg's days, in 1950 there were only 20. Egon Col thus purchased the factory for 5,000 dollars, roughly 50,000 dollars according to today's value.

* * *

On October 19, 1949, Arthur celebrated his 21st birthday. According to the law at the time, he had thus come of age. Eight years after his arrival in America, he no longer was a ward of the state.

The last entry in his foster care record is a letter USCOM sent to Lotte Marcuse at the GJCA: "You will be interested to know that under date of October 28, 1949, the Justice Department has granted the release of all responsibility in the case of the above named [Oswald Kernberg]. This means that you, and we, have no further responsibility in connection with this young man. We are grateful for all that has been done to assist with his care while he has been under supervision."

Being now of legal age, Arthur could apply for American citizenship, which he obtained on December 18, 1950,[6] officially changing his name at the same time. He signed his certificate of naturalization as Oswald Arthur Kern.

Arthur as a young man, playing the ukulele, around 1948.

21. A VIENNESE GIRL

Arthur's grades slowly improved, but he still struggled a lot with mathematics, although he had never had any difficulties in that subject at school. But an unexpected stroke of luck would soon change this – also changing his whole life in turn: an attractive young woman sat next to him in a seminar on differential equations, always earning A grades in the exams when he would only manage a lousy C. In his distress, Arthur asked the young lady – Trudie – for help. Much to his relief, she agreed to study with him and at the end of the semester, Arthur and Trudie both got a B. It was the best grade Arthur had ever got in maths – and Trudie's worst.

"Trudie helped me with a math examination and I found that so amazing that I fell in love with her right away," Arthur told me many years later, a mischievous smile on his face. It did all come to a happy ending for Trudie too, though, in spite of her not so good grade: two years later, the two of them were married.

In a life full of coincidences, meeting Trudie probably was the greatest coincidence of all. What Arthur did not know at that time, was that ten years before, in another life, Trudie had lived only a few streets away from him – in Vienna.

* * *

Gertrude and Lisl Katz shortly before their departure from Vienna.

Gertrude Rebecca Katz was born on June 2, 1939, in *Floridsdorf*, a district of Vienna. Shortly afterward, the Jewish girl moved with her mother Anna, her father Geza, and her sister Alice into a house on *Nußdorfer Straße 4A*, in *Alsergrund*, a mere ten-minute walk from *Gussenbauergasse 1*. It is quite possible little Oswald and little Gertrude (called Gertie) met as children, without their knowing. I for one have walked the short distance quite often in their age; for four years, I attended elementary school right around the corner of *Nußdorfer Straße 4A*, walking from Oswald's home to Gertrude's house on my daily way to school.

The house in which the Katz family lived was, and still is, an impressive building, its facade adorned with an exuberance of turrets, corbels, and ornaments. The house is known in Vienna as the *Colosseum*, because it housed, from 1925 on, the famous *Colosseum* movie theater. Until its closing in 2002, that movie theater was my absolute favorite in Vienna; I was ten when I was first allowed to watch a movie there with a friend, all by ourselves.

As an adult, Trudie had no recollection of her childhood years in Vienna. "I have absolutely no memory at all; I've suppressed them all," she would often explain to me. Her five-year-older sister, Alice "Lisl" Terner, who lives today in the greater New York area, can provide me with more reliable information. The parents of the two girls were even wealthier than Frieda and Hermann Kernberg. "We had a car," Lisl tells me proudly. "There were not that many cars in Vienna then."

Their mother, Anna Katz, a "second generation Viennese," was a well-known artist and a graduate of the *Kunstgewerbeschule* (school of applied arts), who regularly exhibited her work in Vienna and was considered an avant-garde painter. Geza Katz was a trained agricultural engineer, who possessed his own animal feed business. Geza was among the first to mix vitamins with the food, so cows and pigs would grow "nice and fat."

Gertrude started school in a normal elementary school, yet after a few weeks she switched to a *Montessori* school until third grade. Then, her perfect peaceful world was shattered to pieces.

In 1938, the Nazis arrested Gertrude's father and confiscated his business. "My father was a Romanian citizen," Lisl told me. "Later on, they would have just taken him and thrown him in the concentration camp, but in 1938 they were treading a little lightly with the *Ausländer* [foreigners]. But they wanted his business. So they trumped up some false charges and gave my father a one-year jail sentence. And they just took the business away."

After her husband's arrest, Anna Katz decided to take action and brought her daughters to safety: Gertrude and Lisl left Vienna in February 1939, fleeing only one month before Oswald's departure, yet under completely different circumstances. "I came here in style," adult Trudie liked to say. "I came on the *Queen Mary*."

Anna Katz had gotten a ticket for herself too, but she did not want to leave her husband behind and so the sisters traveled alone, on board the luxury cruiser, to join their uncle and aunt in New York. Gertrude was eight and a half years old back then, her sister Lisl thirteen.

* * *

"It didn't feel like being saved," Trudie says to me.

It is August 2016 and we are sitting in her study in Los Angeles, surrounded by dozens of family pictures and colorful figurines. Trudie pulls out a photo album she wants to show me and opens it. She points at a black and white picture of herself and her sister, taken shortly before their departure. The girls both wear dresses with a lace collar, Lisl's is black, and Gertrude's checkered. Both look into the camera, smiling. A few weeks later, they reached America.

"It really didn't feel like being saved," Trudie repeats. "I was one of these children who felt their parents were trying to get rid of them. The last words I remember from my mother were, 'You better behave because your aunt is the devil.'"

Anna Katz hated her husband's sister to whom she now sent her two daughters. No wonder young Gertrude believed her mother sent her away to punish her.

* * *

"Gertie was a child," Lisl pointed out during our conversation. A child that did not understand what was happening. "In today's vision, I guess I was a child too. When I look at my great-granddaughter who is exactly the age I was when I came to America, I can't believe it. I had helped my mother get documents and visas. My goodness, I had to grow up so very fast. I wasn't a child anymore, that part of my life was over. But Gertie was allowed to be a child, because at eight years old, what else was she going to be?"

One year after the departure of his daughters, Geza Katz was released from prison. Until today, Trudie does not know the exact circumstances of his release: "My father never talked about his internment." Anna Katz tried to emigrate legally together with her husband – regardless of the destination: Cuba, America, or Italy, yet all in vain. In the end, because Geza spoke Hungarian, they fled to Budapest and lived there for several years in hiding. It would be ten years before Gertie and Lisl were reunited with their parents.

In 1939, the two girls were living in Manhattan with their aunt Serena and their uncle Imre. "My aunt said that when I came to this country I cried for three weeks, and when I stopped crying I spoke English," Trudie recalled, laughing. Contrary to her mother's fears, Gertie got on well with her aunt Serena. Quite unlike her sister. The older Lisl often upset her aunt and later on greatly suffered from not having been allowed to study, as she had to support the family financially.

Gertie – whom her American friends called Trudie – was a real tomboy. She loved adventures, enjoyed scaring her aunt and passing tests of courage. "I really was a daredevil," Trudie often told me with obvious pride.

As a young woman, Trudie did not wear any make-up, showed no interest in boys, and never sat in a lady-like fashion, all things that would drive her aunt to despair. "What will your mother think about the education I gave you?" Serena frequently complained, sighing. During the summer after her niece had turned 15, she sent her to a *finishing school*, where Trudie was supposed to learn how to sit and walk decently, and also apply make-up properly. Twelve weeks later, Trudie knew how to behave like an accomplished young lady, yet chose never to put these lessons into practice.

Trudie was an exceptionally hard-working and brilliant student with a special talent for mathematics. In 1947, she started studying at *New York University* – the same university I would graduate from in journalism decades later. "Never before and certainly not since, but at the time, I resented Trudie because she was allowed to go to college," Lisl told me.

Trudie spent most of her childhood and her entire youth with her relatives. Even though she did not call them *Mama* and *Papa*, Serena and Imre still felt very much like parents to her in every possible respect, so much she did not want to move in with her real parents when the latter arrived in New York.

Anna and Geza Katz had hid in Budapest until the end of the war, in 1945, many times escaping air raids or being arrested only narrowly. It would be another three years after the end of the war before they would be able to follow their daughters to America, in May 1948. Gertrude and Lisl had not seen their parents since February 1939! Still, their parents had survived the Nazi period and the war. In the father's close family alone, 164 relatives had been murdered during the Holocaust.

For eighteen-year-old Trudie, meeting again with her parents came as a shock. "My father looked like my grandfather. He had aged unbelievably," she remembered. "Geza himself had also problems accepting this now adult daughter. He expected a little girl and now, all of a sudden, there was this young woman who was going to college," Lisl continued, describing her father's reaction to me. As a gift, Geza presented his Gertie with a doll. An original Shirley Temple doll he had managed to salvage throughout the war years. The doll was gorgeous, yet not quite a suitable gift for a college student. "That was not a good start," Trudie commented flatly. There was however a much more serious problem: Trudie had forgotten all her German and therefore could not talk with her parents.

Something else further shook up the family structures. Anna and Geza had not traveled to America alone! They had brought along a little boy: five-year-old Tommy, Gertie's and Lisl's brother, who had been born in hiding in Hungary.

Trudie did not know how to handle all these changes and would have much preferred to stay with Aunt Serena and Uncle Imre. "But they told me 'you can't do that. It would kill your parents,'" Trudie told me. And thus she moved in with her parents and her little brother in an apartment next to Lisl's flat, who had married in the meantime and had a small son of her own.

One month after his arrival, Geza decided he would change the family name because he feared the Jewish-sounding name "Katz" would cause problems in America. Together the family chose the neutral-sounding name "Karen."

On the morning before Trudie's father went to the court for the name change, he had cornflakes for breakfast. *Kellogg's* Corn Flakes, to be more precise. In the eyes of the agricultural engineer, *Kellogg's* was an extremely well-renowned crop production company; and so it came that he decided at the very last minute not to change his name to Karen after all. "He came home and said, 'now we're called Kelloggs,'" Trudie recalled. "I guess it's needless to say that everyone except my father thought it was a terrible name."

1952: Arthur and his wife Trudie graduate from the *City College of New York.*

Trudie's mother, now bearing the name of Anne Kellogg, tried to learn English as quickly as possible and earned the family's living as an art therapist. She had also resumed her artistic career and began to exhibit her work in America. Geza on the other hand, never learned more than a few words of English and had problems finding a job as an engineer in his new home. For the rest of his life, he would not be able to have a proper conversation with his daughter and his relationship with Trudie remained distant.

After one year at *New York University*, Trudie decided to focus on mathematics and physics, two subjects that were only taught on a remote campus at NYU at that time. So she switched to the *City College of New York* and enrolled in electrical engineering, one of the few women studying at the technical institute.

* * *

"Lilly, we're very proud of you, that you are such a good student," Arthur once wrote to me in an email. "You will become just like Trudie. Perhaps you can find yourself a stupid boy who would like to study with you."

It was Arthur's great fortune that Trudie had agreed to study with him. For his future life, as well as for his grades.

"Do you think it was a coincidence that you married a Viennese boy?" I once asked Trudie.

"It was pure coincidence!" Trudie exclaimed. "I used to tell my aunt 'I would not marry anything but a pureblooded American' and she kept telling me she didn't know any Indians."

Well, admittedly, it did not have to be an Indian, but at least someone whose family had lived in America for several generations. "I was not gonna marry anybody from Europe. But when I met Artie, he didn't have an accent to speak of and I thought I was dating an American. My mother and father wouldn't let me study anywhere with a young man except in our house. So the first time he came to my house and heard my parents talking in German, he started to talk to them. That's when I found out! I didn't know anything about his past before!"

No wonder Trudie had been misled by Arthur's lack of accent when she still speaks to this day with an incredibly strong German accent. Every time I see her again after a few months, I cannot help but wonder how "German" Trudie sounds. One could almost believe she came off the boat four weeks ago – not eighty years. And this despite her not remembering one single word of German. Arthur, on the contrary, spoke English without an accent and was also fluent in German, even as an eighty-year-old. Although he used to joke about possessing the German of a ten-year-old, referring to his childish vocabulary.

After a few learning sessions, Arthur became less and less interested in math and more and more interested in Trudie. One thing led to another, and Trudie and Arthur began dating.

In her very lovingly designed family photo album, Trudie has dedicated one page to the beginning of her relationship with Arthur. Under a quite conservative picture of herself and a picture of Arthur, posing casually, Trudie wrote: "Opposites do attract." As proof, Trudie assigned Arthur and herself specific qualities, writing "extrovert, jokester, fast, flirtatious," under Arthur's picture and "shy, serious, naïve, daredevil," under her own.

Trudie and Arthur were now a couple. Yet one would not necessarily have described their relationship as an intimate twosome at first. "For a while, Trudie didn't know who she was dating, Aaron or me," Arthur told me, laughing.

As best friends, Arthur and Aaron were inseparable, even when it came to girls. Sometimes Aaron would bring along a girlfriend, very often though, the three of them would be on their own. "I don't think I ever went on a single date with Artie alone," Trudie declares today.

Aunt Serena did not like Arthur, whom she called a gigolo, because he worked as a dance teacher. Trudie's parents, however, were quite fond of their future son-in-law from the very start. Not least because he spoke German.

Once when we all sat together, I asked Trudie whether her parents had accepted Arthur. "Oh, they loved him," Trudie replied, adding mischievously: "I mean I only married him because they wanted it."

"I didn't want to marry her, I wanted to marry her mother," Arthur interfered, trying to suppress a smile. "But she was already married, so I thought 'Ok, I'll go for the sister.' But she was married too, so I had to take the leftovers."

Arthur barely managed to finish his sentence before bursting out laughing. Trudie started laughing too – all the while thinking about the best way to get back at him.

* * *

Trudie's and Arthur's different life stories, which became one, really are an extraordinary love story: two people, practically neighbors in Vienna, going through so much pain and suffering and fleeing to America only to meet by chance in class and fall in love. Trudie and Arthur got engaged during their final year at college. Trudie's engagement ring was set with three diamonds that had once belonged to Hermann Kernberg.

In the summer of 1938, Arthur's father had traveled to Switzerland, entrusting a distant relative, Leon Tempelhof, with a few valuables. In 1947, Tempelhof contacted Arthur to return Hermann's belongings to him. Among other things, Arthur now possessed a golden watch, a ring, eight silver coins, a silver cigarette case, and three cufflinks set with diamonds. Arthur had Trudie's engagement ring set with these diamonds, so she would always wear a keepsake of his beloved father.

Their wedding took place on September 9, 1951, in a small synagogue in the Bronx. Trudie's Aunt Serena organized the ceremony and the festivities. "I don't know how we managed to find the time to date and get married in our last year at university," Arthur said to me once, sighing.

It was a very private ceremony because the young couple could not afford a bigger party. On Arthur's side, Aunt Erna and her new husband, as well as cousin Gina, attended the wedding. Frieda's brother, David, who had survived the war with his family, also came. On Trudie's side, her parents and sister, as well as her uncle and aunt, and her cousin, were all present. Of course, Aaron Low was there too and Trudie had also invited a friend. All in all no more than twenty persons.

Trudie and Arthur Kern's wedding picture, September 9, 1951.

Out of respect for Arthur's relatives, the wedding ceremony was orthodox and held at Beth David synagogue, which no longer exists today. Trudie wore a short, silver cocktail dress with sewn-on fabric flowers; Arthur wore a black suit with a flower on the lapel.

The orthodox ceremony led to a few misunderstandings, though. Trudie had not been raised in a religious household and did not always know what she was supposed to do. She was not the only one. As part of the wedding ceremony, the bride must circle the bridegroom seven times, under the *chuppah*, the Jewish wedding canopy. As Trudie began doing so, her father jumped to his feet and followed her. Trudie's mother, Arthur's aunt, Erna, and her husband also joined along at once. "It was a circus," Trudie recalled. "Needless to say the Rabbi was bewildered and there was a lot of giggling in the congregation. Yet despite this, we were pronounced man and wife."

At the end of the ceremony, the rabbi wrapped a napkin around a wine glass and Arthur stamped on it, shattering it to pieces. "Mazel tov!" cried the assembled congregation. Congratulations!

* * *

The newlywed couple spent their honeymoon in Atlantic City, New Jersey, before moving into their first shared apartment. Finding an apartment in New York was difficult, even back then, and Trudie and Arthur considered themselves very lucky to be able to afford a one-room apartment in the basement of a semi-detached house. The house stood in a quiet and peaceful part of the Bronx, on 1048 Stratford Avenue.

Standing in front of the brick-built terraced house on a sunny day in December 2017, I can hear children laughing on a playground nearby, as an Italian opera aria echoes from an open window. A pleasant change to the constant traffic noise that dominates so many areas of New York.

White lacquered windows and fences make for a nice contrast to the reddish brown of the bricks and lend a peaceful look to the whole row of houses. Trudie and Arthur spent the first nine months of their marriage here.

"It was one big room with a steam pipe running through it," Trudie explained to me. "We used to play volleyball over that pipe." The young couple divided the space into several "rooms," one corner becoming the bedroom, another the study, and the rest the living-room. The bathroom was tiny – when Arthur used the toilet, he had to put his feet in the shower. In comparison, the kitchen was rather large and offered real luxury: a washing machine that belonged to the owners of the house, but which Trudie was allowed to use. "The people who owned the house were very good to us. I was allowed to go upstairs and take a bath in their bathroom," Trudie recalled.

* * *

After five years of study, and nine months after their wedding, Arthur and Trudie graduated from *City College of New York*, in June 1952 – Trudie in electrical engineering and Arthur in mechanical engineering. Both of them being now engineers, they felt ready to go out into the world.

During their last semester, headhunters from various engineering companies regularly came to the university to attract and recruit students. Trudie and Arthur were offered jobs at *Lockheed Aircraft*, an aerospace company in California.

A few days after their graduation ceremony, the Kerns packed their belongings and drove the nearly 2,500 miles to the other end of the country. "We felt very bad that they left," Trudie's sister, Lisl, told me. "At that time, none of us had money to travel and we knew it would be a long time before we would see them again."

PART 4 – LOS ANGELES

22. THE KERN FAMILY

"*Es ist schon lange, dass wir einen Teenager im Haus gehabt haben* – It's been a while since we had a teenager in the house," Arthur writes to my mother in a somewhat broken German, after driving me to the airport. "*Das Ganze war für uns sehr geniessbar* – The whole thing was very palatable for us. Lilly understood our sense of humor very quickly. We spoke English the whole time and Lilly met almost all of my family, and also a couple of our friends. They were all very impressed with Lilly."

It is the end of March 2008. I am 16 years old and I have known Arthur and Trudie for five years now. They visited us twice in Vienna since then and we exchanged birthday greetings, Christmas cakes, and e-mails across the ocean. At first, it was my mother who kept in touch, but now I am the one writing to the Kerns most of the time. We have long become far more than just friends. "The dear card you sent us warmed our hearts," they once answer a letter from me. "We have 3 granddaughters and since we wanted 4, you are now the fourth."

In March 2008, I am 16 years old and have thus finally reached – in the eyes of my parents – the magical age where I am allowed to fly to America all by myself. It will be my first visit of many. And at the same time the one visit I will remember the best, even years later, mostly because of a beige folder that Trudie gave me: tickets, brochures, postcards, printed directions, everything neatly labeled and stapled. Trudie planned my two-week visit as thoroughly as Lotte Marcuse planned the arrival of the young refugees in New York.

On the first day, we drive to the *San Diego Zoo Safari Park*, America's most visited zoo. Arthur and Trudie's house is on Liggett Street in North Hills, a suburb of Los Angeles. It is a three-hour drive to San Diego – quite a substantial distance for a European, but no more than an afternoon trip for a Californian. All in all, we spend almost seven hours in the car that day – in good traffic conditions, you could cross all of Austria in the same amount of time.

A tour of the famed *Universal Studios*, posing with Jack Sparrow on Hollywood Boulevard, strolling on Venice Beach, the *Kodak Theater* (nowadays called the *Dolby*), where the Oscars are being awarded – in the next few days, I complete the typical tourist program with Arthur. It is not always easy to tell which one of us is the teenager: Although he has promised Trudie he would take it easy, the 80-year-old rides every single roller coaster at *Universal Studios*. "Don't tell my wife about it," Arthur says, smiling, before getting in line again.

My visit continues with a visit to the UCLA campus, the planetarium at *Griffith Observatory*, and a shopping trip with Trudie. Yet my favorite memory of all is snuggling up on the sofa in the afternoon to watch TV. Just like one would with one's grandparents. "This is our *Austrian granddaughter*," Arthur says, introducing me to various people during our many ventures.

Trudie and Arthur have been living in their one-story family home on Liggett Street for fifty years. Some of the walls of the spacious, typically American bungalow are covered with large natural stones, and the house is surrounded by a well-kept garden that Arthur has created himself. In the living room, I admire knick-knacks and dozens of souvenirs that the two retirees have brought back from their numerous journeys across the continents. Paintings by Anne Kellogg hang on the walls. I sleep in the guest room on the left side of the house, which used to be one of the children's rooms once. In the large garage adjacent to the house, I come across two conspicuous cardboard boxes labeled *"Future Home."* "There are our urns inside!" Arthur explains laughing.

St. Patrick's Day falls in the middle of the week and in typical American fashion, green-colored bagels are served for breakfast. Afterward, Arthur's granddaughter, Sami, and some of her friends take me to the *Six Flags Magic Mountain* amusement park – it is the first time I meet a younger member of the Kerns. And just like when I first met Trudie and Arthur, I feel warmly welcomed at once.

Sami (actually Samantha) is three years older than me and a student at a local university. Her mother was born in Mexico and Sami's circle of friends speaks a wild mix of English and Spanish, my two years of school Spanish barely enabling me to follow their conversation. Her friends burst out laughing when Sami introduces me to them, saying "This is a friend of my grandparents. But she is younger than me."

In the next few days, I also get to know Arthur's three sons and his best friend, Aaron Low. They have all heard a lot about me already and there is hardly anything new I can tell them about myself. They give me a warm hug before they start joking. No matter the nature of said jokes, there is always a lot of laughter at the Kerns. Sarcasm is on the agenda, woe to the weak and faint-hearted who cannot keep up! Luckily for me, though, I am a fast learner. "You perfectly fit in with our family," Arthur's eldest son, Aaron, declares.

* * *

It was June 1952, seven years after the end of the war. Arthur and Trudie were young and engineers in America were much sought after.

"As long as you were breathing, you got several job offers from companies across the country," Arthur told me later. The young couple had chosen to work for *Lockheed Aircraft*, an aerospace company in Burbank, California. Eddie, a fellow classmate from New York, who had also got a job at *Lockheed*, possessed a car, which turned the move to the west coast into a road trip across America. The 2,500 mile drive became Trudie's and Arthur's first real holiday. "We traveled through the Badlands, with their magnificent landscapes, through stretches of prairie lands with roaming cattle, enjoying the aroma of wind-swept wheat and flower fields," Arthur recalled. "All things we had never seen living over ten years in New York."

Once in Burbank, a suburb of Los Angeles, Arthur, and Trudie rented an apartment within walking distance of *Lockheed*. For the first time in a very long time, Arthur no longer lived in the same city as his best friend. Aaron Low would have loved to come along to California – but he was drafted into the military.

In 1952, the United States had been in the Korean War for two years. As students Arthur and Aaron had escaped the draft, but now they had to register with the draft board. Arthur was lucky: As an engineer in the aerospace company *Lockheed*, he was considered an "essential" worker and therefore did not have to go to war. Aaron, on the other hand, was an accountant and was thus drafted.

For the next year and a half, Trudie and Arthur worked for *Lockheed*, Arthur at the aircraft seats division, and Trudie at the department of control engineering. Arthur did not really like his work but feared he would be drafted into the army if he quit. It was not until Trudie became pregnant that the young engineer could safely look for a new job, young fathers being exempted from conscription.

In 1953, both Kerns quit their jobs at *Lockheed*, Arthur starting to work in an air conditioning company, while Trudie spent the next years at home with the kids, occasionally working part-time. After the air conditioning company, Arthur had two more jobs before starting at *Rocketdyne* in 1956, in the field of rocket engine development. "I was very lucky," Arthur told me. "I came to a very new industry that was just beginning to emerge. I really enjoyed the work. And I stayed with this company most of my life." Except for a brief three-year pause, Arthur worked at *Rocketdyne* until his retirement in 1994.

When Arthur started working at *Rocketdyne*, the company was part of *North American Aviation,* a major aircraft and missile manufacturer, owned by *Boeing* today. In its heyday, *Rocketdyne* designed and built rockets for the Army, the Navy, the Air Force, and NASA. Arthur worked as a test engineer, vetting single components at first and later conducting missile tests. The latter took place in the Santa Susana Mountains, in San Fernando Valley, a valley on the outskirts of Los Angeles, not far from the house on Liggett Street, which the Kerns purchased in 1959. "When they tested the rockets up in Santa Susana, the whole valley was shaking," Arthur's eldest son, Aaron, told me. "You could not miss it."

Arthur conducted rocket tests as a rocket engineer here.

Over the course of a few years, Arthur worked his way up to senior engineer. In the spring of 1959, a photo of him was published in the company's internal newspaper, *Valley Skywriter*, with the caption: "An unprecedented 109 consecutive engine tests without a facility malfunction was the new test performance record attained this week at the *Propulsion Field Laboratory*."[1]

During one of these tests, the rocket engine was kept at 160 °F for five days, before being frozen for three days and then ignited – the change from extreme cold to extreme heat was supposed to simulate different environmental scenarios.

Dale Carpenter, Arthur's supervisor at *Rocketdyne*, was also a friend of the Kerns. These days, one hundred-year-old Carpenter, who has also become blind, does not leave his house anymore, which is why his wife Dell interviewed him for me in the summer of 2016, emailing me his recollections. "Dale has told me that Art was always joking, very sociable, smart, so qualified and detailed," she wrote to me. "When he asked him to get something done, Dale knew Art would accomplish his tasks with never any problem. Dale never asked how it was done. Art had it recorded."

"Art was in charge of three test stands and over three hundred employees in three shifts," continued Dell Carpenter. "Most of the engines tested in these areas were the *Atlas, Thor,* and the *J-2*. Some of the Intercontinental Ballistic missiles were used for space exploration, putting satellites in space and offensive and defensive weapons."

In the early 1990s, at the height of his career, Arthur was responsible for over 400 employees, yet the 1960s remain the most exciting time in his professional life – at this time, he switched to the *Downey Space Division*, where the Apollo space capsules were being built.

"That's one small step for a man, one giant leap for mankind," Neil Armstrong said on July 20, 1969, as the first person to ever set foot on the moon. The Apollo 11 Mission fulfilled President John F. Kennedy's goal to bring a man to the moon before the end of the decade. To meet this Herculean task, the Apollo program employed

400,000 Americans and worked with 20,000 companies and universities.² The engineers at *Rocketdyne* (now *Rockwell)* built and tested the Apollo space capsules for NASA. "I headed the department of engineers that ran the tests during the final inspection of the space capsule," explained Arthur. The little boy from *Gussenbauergasse* in Vienna, Austria, whose parents had sent away all by himself, had come a long way – almost to the moon.

"It was a very exciting time for Bob and Art," Janet Taylor, whose husband Bob had worked with Arthur for the space program, told me. "It was something they were both very proud of and excited about. It was a good time for them to be there, on the threshold of something new."

For Arthur's three sons, their father being involved in the construction of the Apollo space capsules was more than exciting, not least because they got to know real astronauts! "There were family nights when you not only got to watch the engines test-fire, but you'd got to meet the astronauts," Arthur's son, David, told me enthusiastically. "The reason for doing that was to create a positive scenario. You got all these engineers building stuff. Then you'd have these astronauts, two or three people in very tight quarters and their life is dependent on the quality of what the engineers did. So they created a positive atmosphere by having everyone meet. The astronauts saw that real humans had built their space capsule. And the engineers saw who would fly their creation. Yes, and so we met real astronauts," David finished his story. "And it was pretty cool to go to school and say, 'I met an astronaut today.'"

Decades later, I come across a large certificate from NASA in Arthur's papers: the *Apollo Achievement Award*. Arthur was honored "in appreciation of dedicated service to the nation, as member of the team which has advanced the nation's capabilities in aeronautics and space and demonstrated them in many outstanding accomplishments, culminating in Apollo's 11 successful achievement of man's first landing on the moon." I also find a photo of the ceremony:

Arthur smiles broadly into the camera, already wearing the big round glasses that would still be his trademark thirty years later, and carries – quite the engineer – a small screwdriver in his breast pocket.

The National Aeronautics and Space Administration
presents the
Apollo Achievement Award
to

A.O. KERN

In appreciation of dedicated service to the nation as a member of the team which has advanced the nation's capabilities in aeronautics and space and demonstrated them in many outstanding accomplishments culminating in Apollo 11's successful achievement of man's first landing on the moon, July 20, 1969.

Signed at Washington, D.C.

ADMINISTRATOR, NASA

Arthur took part in the tests on the Apollo space capsule,
which earned him the *Apollo Achievement Award.*

After his work on the Apollo space capsule, Arthur went on working in various departments of *Rocketdyne*, before retiring in 1994, after 35 years at the company. Yet as a matter of fact, his career would not have been possible without the help of one person: Trudie. "I was fortunate to have a very supportive wife who took care of the household and our three children," Arthur told me.

In 1952, Trudie had started as an engineer at *Lockheed*, together with her husband, before quitting in 1953, when she became pregnant with her first son. For the next 16 years, Trudie stayed at home, occasionally working part-time. When Danny, the youngest Kern, turned thirteen, she resumed working full-time again, not as an engineer, though, but in finance. The gifted mathematician eventually became vice-director of a large banking company, managing 200 employees.

"I've never regretted staying home so long," Trudie declared. "I had the best of both worlds: I had a career and I was with my kids."

* * *

All Kern boys were born in May: Aaron on May 11, 1953, David on May 20, 1956, and Daniel (Danny) on May 6, 1958. Arthur named his eldest son after his best friend. "I always tell Aaron he should be happy that he was born after I was naturalized," Aaron Low told me, laughing. "Otherwise his name would have been Adolf!"

After his release from the army, in 1954, Aaron Low followed Arthur and Trudie to California. The trio was reunited at last, Aaron even living with his friends in the first months. Then he got married the following year and started his own family. After the two-year war break, Arthur and Aaron lived close to each other for the rest of their lives, meeting at least once a week. To tell the adult from the child, Aaron Low was from now on "Big Aaron" while Arthur's son was "Little Aaron."

"I loved being a father," Arthur declared proudly. Especially on Sundays, which always started with a special ritual: the torture hour. "My oldest memory is torture hour on Sunday morning," Little Aaron – now grown-up – told me. "We would all jump into bed with Dad, and while Mom was making breakfast, he played all sorts of games with us." – "He pretended to be asleep," Danny added. "He would lie on his back, his eyes closed. Then one of us touched his forehead with a finger. And: AARGH!! Suddenly he turned into a monster and tickled and chased us. Then someone touched his forehead again and it would put him back to sleep."

Trudie and Arthur with their two eldest sons, Aaron
and David, in their garden in California, 1957.

Lying in bed snorting and out of breath, the three young Kerns liked to
ask their father how he got the scar on his leg. "He would have a different
story every Sunday, for 18 years," Danny recalled. "Once it was a motor-
cycle accident, once a shark fight. We never really found out the truth."

Just like he used to as a boy, Arthur played clever pranks on
his sons. When he discovered that David secretly read *Playboy* as
a teenager, Arthur bought a card set with a scantily clad lady on
the packaging and left it half in sight in the living room. As he had
expected, David could not resist and opened the package, promptly
receiving an electric shock! Arthur had hidden two electrodes inside.

As soon as Aaron, David, and Danny were old enough, their father
gladly joined forces with them to tease Trudie. "They did so much
mischief," Trudie told me, half laughing, half sighing. "The boys
came 100 percent after their father. But that's a good thing: I never
wanted a girl. I was a *tomboy* myself. I wouldn't have known what to
do with a little girl."

In a house full of half-grown boys, there were often smaller and larger tragedies – especially when the three Kerns rode their bikes. Broken teeth, broken arms, blood poisoning. "In the emergency room, they knew me by name!" Trudie explained with resignation.

The numerous camping and water-skiing family trips proved just as eventful. Most of the time, the Kerns would go to a national park for a weekend, but in 1968, Trudie and Arthur packed their three sons into the car for a six-week trip along the west coast, from Oregon and Washington to Canada. In San Francisco, they celebrated Trudie's 38th birthday in a fancy restaurant, but most of the time stayed in motels or cooked on campsites.

On the second week, they stopped at a supermarket in the city of Astoria, Oregon, to replenish their supplies. Trudie was just standing in front of the bread shelf, wondering which brand to choose, when a woman suddenly addressed her, saying: "Excuse me, but your four sons are terrible!"

"That cannot be. I only have three sons," Trudie answered.

"So those are not yours?" the woman asked, pointing to the fruit counter where Aaron, David, Danny – and Arthur – were fooling around, juggling with bananas. "I did not know if I should be more ashamed of how they acted, or because the lady thought me old enough to be Arthur's mother," a resigned Trudie told me, years later.

Nonsense was always on the agenda in the Kern family. And although she was sure all that tomfoolery would turn her hair white – in truth, Trudie loved her family for it. "We used to laugh a lot," Trudie said to me. "I never met my father-in-law, but Artie told me his father was just like him. Always playing jokes."

In one respect, however, Arthur came completely after his mother, namely in the raising of his sons.

With all the tricks and pranks, the family father did not give his sons a lax education. "Dad was very authoritarian," Aaron told me. "His credo was 'my house, my rules' and if you wondered why you could do or not do something, it was usually, 'Because I said it.'"

His brother Danny put it like this: "My dad was so strict that the other parents in our neighborhood warned their children, 'If you don't behave, we're gonna make you spend the afternoon at the Kern house.'"

Aaron was considered the sensible one, but the younger brothers David and Danny were in constant trouble. "The daily routine from my Mum was, especially for me and Danny, 'you just wait till your dad gets home,'" David recalled. "From the age of sixteen to eighteen, I was probably grounded one out of every three weeks," Danny added.

My house, my rules. As it turned out, there really were rules for everything: Eat what is on your plate. Clean up your room. Make your bed. You are not allowed to play unless your homework is done. If you use tools from the garage, you have to put them back in exactly the same spot. You have to be home at midnight – not one minute later. If your friends swear in our house, they are not allowed to visit anymore. If you are not satisfied with your pocket money, you can look for a side job. If you want a car, we will buy you one, but you will have to pay for petrol and repairs yourself. If you have problems at school, you have to tell us. If you have a worse grade than a B, you have to answer to me. As long as you live under my roof, you follow my rules.

The penalty for even the smallest violation of said rules was invariably the same: house arrest. Quite frequently, however, the victims were not the boys themselves, but Trudie.

"The only thing Artie did that I did not like was when he punished the children," Trudie confessed. "I always felt it was important for a wife and a mother – whether you agreed or not – to follow through. So I said to him, 'If you really believe that, I will make sure that they are grounded.' But I was the one who was grounded when they were! I had to stay home to be sure they were there."

Arthur took his rules extremely seriously, yet whenever something really bad happened, he remained surprisingly calm. "If there was some catastrophe, then that was not an issue," Aaron told me. "For example, one time Danny was teasing me and giving me a real hard time. I asked him to stop, but he just kept persisting. So I threw a little wooden bowling ball in his direction. It went over his head and broke the glass window in the sliding door. I was in an absolute panic about how Dad would react. But he didn't get angry about it. He was just worried that I could have hurt Danny. Whereas if I got home late, oh my God, you did not want to be there."

* * *

Every adventure and prank on Arthur's and his three wildlings' part formed a new chapter in the family chronicles of the Kerns. But that did not mean the past was forgotten. Much to his delight, more family members had survived the Holocaust than Arthur had originally believed.

There was Aunt Erna of course, her husband Sigmund, since then deceased, and their daughter Gina. Frieda's brother David, his wife Helen, and their daughter Renee had already attended Arthur's wedding in New York. Then there were also two cousins: Detta, who like Gina, had been on a *Kindertransport* to England, and her brother Albert, who was fifteen years older than Arthur and who had lived in Italy before the war began. Both emigrated to New York in the early 1950s. Yet, even ten years after the end of the war, there was no trace of some other family members: Arthur's "modern" Aunt Paula, Uncle Leo, and Otto, his favorite playmate from childhood.

"We are now in Genoa and traveling, so God wants, to Chile on Dec., 2," says a postcard that Arthur received in France in late 1939 and that he had kept all these years. There was thus every reason to believe that Hermann Kernberg's brother and his family were living in South America. Yet how – before the invention of the Internet – does one find a person in a country 5,500 miles away whose language one does not speak?

By chance, as it was: "We had a relative of my mother, a distant cousin, who had business in Chile," Arthur told me. "I met him one time and told him about an uncle I had there and the person that that particular man went to see in Chile turns out to be a friend of my uncle's, and that's how we found each other."

In November 1958, Arthur finally received a letter from Santiago de Chile: "For a long time we tried to get in touch with you," Leo Kernberg wrote. And Paula added: "Pleasantly surprised and late, yet not too late, we finally got a sign of life from you. ... It was not so easy, all these things one went through, and such events cannot be expressed with a few dry words. That you, dear Ossi, made your way through life alone, and now are a married man and the father of 3 children, makes me feel very proud. I have always remembered you as a capable, intelligent boy, who proved himself accordingly in life."

Arthur was overjoyed to have found that long-lost part of his family, but it would be a few more years before they would actually meet face to face. "Little Otto" was the first to visit in 1962. Otto Kernberg had studied medicine in Chile and then trained as a psychoanalyst. In 1961, he emigrated to America with his wife Paulina, a child psychoanalyst, and their two children. The following year, Otto and his family visited the Kerns in California.

"Ossi was still his old self," Dr. Kernberg told me during our conversation in his practice in New York. "I could recognize the same personality. Open, direct, warm, intelligent, and very thoughtful. If we had lived in the same city, we would have been close friends again. I have not the slightest doubt about that."

In 1964, Paula and Leo Kernberg also came to America from Chile to visit Arthur. A quarter of a century had passed since he had last seen his "modern" aunt and uncle. "My mother was overjoyed!" Dr. Otto Kernberg said. "Both my parents loved Ossi very much."

* * *

Paula and Leo visited the Kerns several times over the following years. Yet someone else played an even more important role in Arthur's and Trudie's family life: Anne Kellogg. Trudie's father Geza had already died in 1961, in New York. In 1972, Anna moved to California to be closer to her youngest daughter. Anna, whom even her English-speaking grandchildren called *Mutti*, rented a small apartment a stone's throw away from the Kerns' house on Liggett Street, where she would often have dinner. She continued painting and exhibiting her work regularly – today many of her paintings hang in the houses of the Kern sons. Anna was quite the artist, considered a hippie even in liberal California.

"*Mutti* was a riot. She was really funny. Her personality was uber-liberal, like to the left of the left. She was really progressive," Danny told me. As far as politics and raising children were concerned, Anna and her son-in-law, Arthur, often disagreed; *Mutti* would have raised her grandchildren in a much more free-spirited way. This being said the spry retiree fit perfectly into the family: on David's 13th birthday, for instance, she – anonymously – offered him a *Playboy* subscription, for which the teenager then had to explain himself to his parents, stammering with embarrassment.

"We all loved *Mutti*," Arthur wrote years after his mother-in-law's death in a short story. "We think of her every Halloween, flying somewhere out there, still guiding us on her broomstick."

Trudie and Arthur had been living in California for twenty years before *Mutti* moved to the West Coast. Until then, they had only seen her every few years. All their remaining relatives lived far away too, in New York or in Chile. But that does not mean the Kerns did not have a busy family life, quite the contrary!

Almost every weekend, Trudie and Arthur did something with "their" family – the fact none of them shared the same genes was of no significance. First of all, there was Aaron Low, of course, who had been like a brother to Arthur for a long time, and his wife, Ellie. Eric Green – formerly Erich Grünebaum – too had moved to California in the early 1950s. In 1958, Arthur was the best man at the wedding of his former blood brother and best friend from Eaubonner days. Norbert Rosenblum and his wife Marion also lived close to Trudie and Arthur, as well as Renee Eisenberg, a former Viennese who had been in Montmorency like the "boys," and her husband Morris.

"We always saw our OSE family over the weekend or on holidays," Danny told me. "They were our uncles and our aunts."

The close family ties Arthur (then Oswald) and his OSE friends had created in France had lasted for decades. "We consider ourselves as a family. We are more than friends," Norbert Rosenblum said to me. "We are a family."

They played cards together, went on camping trips, and taught the children absurd songs – like the one about the Chinese man that Arthur and Aaron used to sing all the time before it became the official *Kern Family Song*. Trudie and Arthur also quite frequently hosted cocktail parties or summer festivals at their house. "Mom always did all the preparations," Little Aaron recalled. "Except for food tasting. That was Dad's job. Which usually meant you had to make a second batch."

The Kerns also celebrated birthdays, the traditional American Thanksgiving and Jewish holidays like Passover or Hanukkah, with "their" family.

"The bond that Artie shared with my dad was beyond words," Steve Low wrote to Trudie, in a letter I find in Arthur's papers. "I loved our multiple decades of family Seders together, especially the way Artie and my Dad harmonized. When they sang together, it was as if you could tell from the sounds of their voices that they had shared so many life experiences and had been such wonderful friends for so many years!"

"I also enjoyed the tradition of introducing my various girlfriends over the years to Artie for the first time," Steve went on in his letter. "That was actually a test of potential girlfriends. If they couldn't at least try to make Artie laugh, they were probably not worth keeping around anyway."

Arthur's and Trudie's OSE family made for the best part of their circle of friends. Then there were also some work colleagues, such as Bob and Janet Taylor of *Rocketdyne*, or acquaintances from the synagogue. When their children were small, Trudie and Arthur took them to the synagogue every week; it was important to them that their sons should know about Judaism. They would be able to decide for themselves, later, just how religious they wanted to be.

"We raised them to be very culturally Jewish," Trudie told me. "But we were not what you would call very religious." Aaron, David, and Danny went to Jewish camps and attended Hebrew School on Sundays to prepare for their bar mitzvahs. But the Kerns did not observe religious or dietary laws and synagogue visits were more about socializing than religion. "We would all sit there and you'd sing the prayer together, even though you didn't really know what they meant," recalled Danny. "People were laughing and smiling, and after the service, there were all kinds of desserts and coffee in the back of the synagogue."

The Kerns became friends with Fred and Barbara Weiss during the cozy get-togethers in the synagogue. The children also got along well: As a teenager, Aaron went out with their daughter Dana for a while.

* * *

In the summer of 2016, I meet Fred Weiss and his second wife, Ileene, at their home in Porter Ranch, a Los Angeles neighborhood just fifteen-minute drive away from Arthur's and Trudie's home. Fred and Ileene's house is entirely decorated in a Japanese style, with pictures of geishas, small statuettes, Japanese characters, shiny draperies, and a perfectly designed Japanese garden.

Two paintings, hanging above the green couch in the living room – and quite strikingly non-Japanese – seem oddly familiar to me. Yet before I can remember what the pictures remind me of, Fred informs me: "They're from Anna Kellogg! Trudie's mother."

"How would you describe Arthur to someone who does not know him?" I ask the Weiss' after we have made ourselves comfortable.

"He was very an extrovert," Ileene begins. "Always with a smile. Always with a joke."

"A prankster," Fred adds. "He and Trudie were always playing tricks on each other, Trudie would always try to get even with him. But she never could. And he kept saying, 'I won another one, I won another one!'"

"I thought that was so adorable for having been married for so many years," comments Ileene with a big smile on her face. The retired family therapist received many recipes from Trudie over the years. "She was a marvelous cook. She made the most wonderful lunch and dinner invitations."

"And Arthur," Ileene goes on, "Arthur always made everybody happy."

* * *

No matter whom I talk to in the summer of 2016, whether friends, acquaintances, or work colleagues, everyone describes Arthur in a similar way. "Artie was just a wonderful human being," Susie Katz, a friend of the family, says. "He was the happiest person ever. Everybody just loved him."

Dell Carpenter, the wife of Arthur's supervisor, Dale, also knew him quite well. "I felt Art used humor to get through. I knew underneath there was something. He was a great writer and I always felt his soul came to the surface when he wrote. Some of the other survivors were angry, some lost their ability to see good things ahead, and some were eternally depressed. But even in the face of death, Artie saw the bright side."

In his neighborhood and among his circle of friends, Arthur

was known as *Mr. Fix It*. A car that would not start, a toaster that no longer toasted, or a wobbly fence – Arthur fixed it all. After his retirement, Arthur devoted himself to one of his youthful passions, becoming a volunteer dance teacher in a Jewish retirement home and conjuring a smile on more than one elderly lady's face.

Arthur and Trudie in later years.

Janet Taylor, whose husband Bob worked at *Rocketdyne*, knew Arthur and Trudie from their monthly bridge rounds. "They are both super wonderful people," Janet explained. "It was fun for Bob and me to watch them. They had a super wonderful marriage."

Janet was particularly impressed by Arthur's attitude to life. "The things that he went through are incredibly impossible to imagine yourself going through. And especially coming out with his attitude toward life. I think he was absolutely an incredibly amazing person. He was one of those people you never forget."

And what does Trudie say? "I could not have wished for a better husband. There is not a man among our friends who compares to Artie. Not even close."

* * *

On June 1, 1980, the first wedding in the Kern household was upon us: medical student Aaron married a young, ambitious nurse named Leslie. In the same year, Aaron graduated from UCLA, working from then on as a Doctor of Internal Medicine. Leslie also made a career: She has a doctorate in nursing.

In 1987, it was the turn of the second oldest Kern son. Insurance broker David married Nena, a Latina. "Before I met David's parents, I was nervous as can be," the observant Catholic confessed to me. "I was afraid that they would not accept me because I'm not Jewish. And David had told me all sorts of stories about his crazy family and their pranks. But I need not have worried: they just accepted me as part of the family since day one."

Danny followed his parents' example and studied mechanical engineering at the prestigious *Stanford University*. But there would not be another Kern engineer: Danny continued to study and became a lawyer. Yet he took his time with marriage, celebrating a Hawaii-theme wedding with his longtime girlfriend Elise, a lawyer herself, in 2009.

In the family photo album Trudie lovingly designed, I count seven Kerns in the mid-1980s. By 2012, there were already 14 of them.

* * *

In the summer of 2017, I find myself visiting Los Angeles once again. This time I am staying with Arthur's son, Aaron – Trudie and Arthur reluctantly sold their home in early 2014 to move to a so-called *Senior Living Community*. In the luxurious housing complex for pensioners, all residents have their own apartments, all the while being able to fall back on any kind of support – whether domestic or medical.

Each time we stop by for brunch, Trudie reserves a large table in the middle of the adjoining restaurant – so everyone can see us. Luxury or not: Only very few inhabitants receive regular visitors here. And certainly not from so many people at once.

Because I am not often there, I am allowed to sit next to *Grandma* Trudie. Left and right of us are Arthur's granddaughters Shira, Sami, and Rachel. At the far end of the table, great-grandchildren AJ and Cash prove quite adeptly that they are just as boisterous as the rest of the Kern men, but their father Alex, and their grandmother Nena manage to pacify them with cocoa and toast. Aaron, Leslie, David, Danny, Elise – wherever one looks: laughing Kerns everywhere.

Trudie's plan works: For weeks, her big family will be the number one topic of conversation in the *Senior Living Community*. At least until our next visit.

23. THE GREAT REUNION

"72 people who survived the Holocaust as children met for their first reunion in almost 50 years," the host of a Californian local TV station announced, welcoming her viewers on March 25, 1989, a purplish Los Angeles skyline gleaming behind her in the setting sun. Then the image switched to dozens of men and women – among whom Arthur and Aaron Low – eating hors d'oeuvres and talking animatedly. The camera zoomed in on large-format pictures of Montmorency, *Montintin,* and Eaubonne, while the moderator went on talking in voiceover: "At first glance, this could be any group getting together with family and friends after a long separation, but for this group, the pictures tell the story. The story of children sent to France to escape the oncoming Holocaust. The friends were scattered again not to meet again until tonight."[1]

March 25, 1989: fifty years ago almost to the day, the Jewish refugee children left their German or Austrian home and sought refuge in France. Reason enough to celebrate a big party: the *50th OSE Reunion.*

* * *

Seventy former OSE protégés took part in the *Reunion*, about one-third of the 250 refugee children from the OSE homes who could be rescued to America. Quite a considerable number: after all, the American welfare organizations – and most notably, Lotte Marcuse – had gone a great length to prevent any contact between the children. Yet in the long run, no one could keep the former friends away from each other. Many of them had found one another again over the years and had also been able to contact Ernst Papanek.

Once again, an element of chance was involved: Renee Eisenberg, for instance, belonged to the same book club as Arthur and Trudie. During their monthly meetings, Arthur noticed her strong German accent and when he addressed her, it turned out Vienna-born Renee had lived once in a home in Montmorency.

Another time, Trudie made friends with an African American woman in a coffee shop. The two of them agreed to meet for weekly donuts and went for regular walks when one day the woman suddenly mentioned her husband had been born in Czechoslovakia. Trudie paused and asked how long the man had lived in America. "She told me the date, the exact date that he came," Trudie recalled. "And I said, 'That sounds very familiar.'"

Soon it was clear Tom Mertens had come to America on the same ship as Arthur and had been living for years close to the Kerns without them knowing about each other. In Eric Greene's case, it was Aaron Low who recognized a waiter, as he was having lunch at a Jewish Deli somewhere in the Midwest during his military training. The waiter in question was Eric's cousin, Ernie Marx, who readily passed on his cousin's address. Eric was so overjoyed to have found his former best friend Arthur again that he looked for a job in California and from then on also lived close to the Kerns.

"Slowly but surely we were finding people," Arthur told me. "Every time you meet some of these people, it's a shock to them."

The need to find each other again is something all former *Kindertransport* children have in common, quite noticeably and regardless of the country that welcomed them. In the case of the OSE children, this quest started quite early, while the British children, on the other hand, first began looking for each other in the early 1990s.

In 1979, a small OSE group held a private party to celebrate the 40th anniversary of their rescue. Three "mini-reunions" followed in quick succession: one at the Kerns' home, one at the Lows', and one at Henry and Anita Schuster's, whom Arthur met there for the first time. Ernst Valfer – the former home speaker at Eaubonne – also attended these small parties and was now part of Arthur's and Trudie's larger group of friends.

The OSE family grew, people meeting for barbecues, to play cards or simply to talk. In February 1988, Norbert Rosenblum invited five OSE couples to his home. Arthur remembered that meeting quite vividly: "Henry Schuster said suddenly, 'Really we should get going on a 50-year reunion.' And everybody cheered. And then Henry pointed at me and said, 'And I think Art Kern ought to be the chairman.'"

Arthur was very enthusiastic about the project and took over the chief part of the organization of the *Reunion*. Trudie, who was already retired at that time, actively managed the whole organization. There were only thirteen months left to locate as many former OSE children as possible.

As a first point of reference, Arthur inquired of the Quakers about the transport lists of the *Kindertransports* that reached America, but the names alone were not very significant, unfortunately. After all, Arthur himself was no longer called Oswald, Aaron was no longer Adolf and married women no longer bore their maiden names. Not what one would call a simple task. Today a quick browse on Google would solve that problem quite easily, but the search engine would not be invented until nearly a decade later. Arthur had no other choice but to set to work the old-fashioned way.

"Montmorency! Tourelles! Eaubonne! The Ship *Saint Louis*! Montintin/Chevrette! Broût-Vernet! Masgelier! If these places in France have meaning to you, you are one of us," Arthur wrote in a letter he sent to dozens of people in the summer of 1988, asking them to forward it to other OSE protégés. At the same time, the *Simon Wiesenthal Center* in Los Angeles published over fifty search ads in local and Jewish newspapers worldwide. The children of Ernst Papanek – who was already deceased at that time – were also of great help, their father having searched actively for his former protégés. Little by little, Arthur and his comrades found a great number of their former friends. "When the responses for the reunion started arriving, I was so excited I couldn't eat or concentrate," Henry Schuster said, describing his feelings. "I had been yearning to find my past – now I didn't have to remember alone."[2]

Letters began to trickle in from Germany, France, Austria, Switzerland, England, Canada, Australia, South Africa, Israel, Mexico, Ecuador, and every corner of America. "119 people responded!" Arthur remembered. "The enthusiasm in these responses that we received! They were awesome."

* * *

"It is a real pleasure for me to welcome you here tonight, in beautiful southern California, to our 50-Year Reunion for OSE children," Aaron Low said, opening the *50th OSE Reunion*. Standing on a wood-paneled stage in a meeting room of the B'nai David-Judea synagogue in Los Angeles, the sixty-year-old let his gaze wander around the room: "It is just wonderful to see so many of you. It exceeds any and all of our previous expectations." Over 150 people had come: seventy former OSE protégés, two former OSE members, as well as spouses, children, and grandchildren. The room was as large as a ballroom, with seven to ten people sitting around circular tables, decorated with tiny children figurines on board ships, golden fifties, and the OSE logo. The tables were named after the different OSE homes, allowing people who had lived together during the war to sit next to each other.

"I've been watching you a bit earlier," Aaron went on. "And there's one sentence I've kept hearing again and again: 'You look familiar, but who are you?'" Aaron presented the program of the evening, before introducing Arthur as the next speaker.

Just like everyone else in the room, Arthur wore a name tag bearing two names: his old name and his new one. "Aaron and I have been very fortunate that we kept in touch ever since we arrived on the second transport to New York," he began. "And slowly, over the years, we have been finding other people, which I call my family."

Every "child" stepped on the stage in turn, introducing themselves briefly. Some had brought their Quaker cardboard number cards, others showed yellowed photographs or poetry albums, holding them up high. "*Le plus grand directeur de cirque*," Ernst Valfer suddenly sang in accent-free French, as he stepped on the stage, "The greatest circus director." It was one of the songs the young refugees had composed on the occasion of the great circus in Montmorency. When he was finished, Valfer pointed at the audience: "I see some bears around here, some dancers. And naturally lots of us who were in the orchestra." After the laughter had died down, the psychologist became more serious: "*Le plus grand directeur* – that was Ernst Papanek. I believe that without Ernst Papanek, very few of us would be alive. And those of us who would be alive, would probably mentally be in much worse shape than we are. There is one more party that I want to recognize today for helping us keep our sanity. And that party is all of you. We kept up the spirit and we kept each other up and we encouraged each other. And we didn't let us despair. And that is what saved us, I think. And for that, I think, all of us, all of you" – he pointed to the room once again – "need a big hand."

During the pauses between the speeches, people crowded around the photo panels propped against three walls in the room. The organization committee around Arthur had gathered dozens of pictures from their time in France and now everyone was trying to discover themselves on one of the pictures. Pinned to one of the panels, one photo showed a three-year-old child during the journey to America, with the following question written in capital letters above it: "Do you know this little girl?" What looked at first glance like the search for an old friend turned out to be a much more important and emotional request from the adult girl herself, who knew nothing about herself, except for the fact she had come to America with other OSE children as a toddler.

People kept pointing at a picture, believing they had just recognized someone. And then when they turned around, that very person stood right before them! The presence of the cook and *topinambour* (Jerusalem artichoke) virtuosa, Amalia Kanner, was a very special surprise for many former OSE protégés. After Arthur had helped the frail 84-year-old on the stage, she went on reading a brief message with a strong German accent. "I know you all as you were children. When you left for America, no one knew what the future would be. And I see you now, the little children I once knew became happy and successful. And you did it all on your own. But today you are all my children," Kanner read under thunderous applause, "and I love you all very much."

Amalia and her husband Salomon – the 91-year-old man had also worked for OSE during the war – stayed at Arthur's and Trudie's during the *Reunion*. Arthur had developed a close relationship with Amalia in France and during the reunion dinner, he happily declared: "When I saw them, I thought I had found my parents again."

Rabbi Abraham Cooper, the deputy director of the *Simon Wiesenthal Center* also addressed the assembly: "This evening is a testimony to the triumph and power of love and of hope," he said. "Everyone sitting here tonight is a miracle."

At the end of the evening, all seventy "miracles" gathered on the stage for a group picture. Holding hands, they sang a well-known Hebrew canon – "*Hineh mah-tov u'mah-nayim shevet achim gam yachad,* how pleasant it is for brethren to dwell together in unity" – ending the song with a loud "whoopee!" And for just one moment, everything was just like before. For just one moment, they were five, or ten, or eleven-year-old boys and girls again, sitting on the great staircase of the veranda and singing together. For just one moment, they were children again.

The Hirsch brothers, Jakob and Anselm, with
Oswald (right), in Eaubonne, in 1939.

At the OSE-Reunion in 1989, the three friends recreated the same picture.

* * *

"It was a very joyous thing. I mean people really hugged and told their stories and they were so happy to see all of them. Lots of friendships came because of that," Arthur told me years later. "It was probably one of the highlights of my life."

The family feeling that united Arthur, Aaron, and a few of their closest friends for many years was now spreading to many people. "It was like old times," Siegfried "Siggy" Knop explained to me. "When all your family were killed in the Holocaust, you try to attach yourself to something that is of memory and that takes you back to your younger years. Some of the kids that I know were with me – it's like family."

Even people who no longer had any recollection of their time in France experienced this feeling of belonging together: "The 1989 reunion of OSE children in Los Angeles was an overpowering emotional experience for every one of us," Eve Kugler, Amalia Kanner's daughter, wrote in her autobiography. "I felt enveloped in friendship and love, perfectly at ease with people I did not remember or had never met."[3]

Now so many of them had found each other again, they made sure never to lose touch again. As always, Arthur and Trudie played a key role, organizing every summer an OSE garden party for seventy people. Trudie did all the cooking, Arthur nibbled at the food and set up loads of chairs. "And then we talked about Europe," Trudie recalled. "It was always Europe."

Gerry Watkins was an annual guest, his birth name, Gerhard Herbert Mahler, betraying his distant kinship to the composer Gustav Mahler. "Artie used to say, 'Aren't we lucky?' and 'Isn't it wonderful that we have this big family?'" Watkins told me. Without Arthur, this "family" would not have been possible, Watkins feels sure of it: "Artie became sort of the historian of the group and the record keeper. Artie knew everybody's profile and everybody's birthday and where they had been in France."

This is also why Arthur received the visit of many historians over the years, who researched the *Kindertransports*, or of Holocaust groups wishing to organize *Reunions* of their own. Shortly after the 1989 *Reunion*, some participants created the *Friends and Alumni of OSE-USA* association of which Arthur became a member. Money, collected during the annual garden parties, was then sent to OSE in France, so the association could support other children, just like it had helped and supported them all these years ago.[4]

* * *

Arthur did not stop looking for former OSE children – or coming across them by chance – even after the *Reunion*. Gunther Katz, an acquaintance of Fred and Barbara Weiss, is one of them. In August 2016, I meet Gunther's widow, Susie, in their Los Angeles home.

"Gunther's birthday would have been yesterday," Susie begins. Then she gets up to fetch a photo of him and puts it on the table. "I think Gunther has to be here with us."

Susie insisted on my interviewing her for this book because according to her, Arthur had changed her husband's life. "Meeting someone like Artie was transformative in Gunther's life. He did finally start talking about his past!"

In 1940, Gunther had been deported, together with his parents, to the French internment camp *Gurs*, from which he was rescued by OSE and sent to the *Château de Montintin*. After his emigration to America, Gunther remained silent for decades, never speaking about his childhood, even to his wife. Yet this all changed when he met Arthur – and through him, other OSE children. In 2000, Gunther even began speaking in public about his past, as a lecturer at the Simon Wiesenthal Center's *Museum of Tolerance* in Los Angeles and at schools.

Like so many before him, Gunther became part of the OSE family. For many years, he regularly met with the Kerns and of course, attended the great garden parties in the summer. "Trudie and Artie were the glue," Susie Katz says to me. "That's the word I've always used. They were the glue that kept the whole group together."

With advancing age, hosting so many people at once became too much for Trudie. The last OSE garden party took place in 2003, after more than twenty years. The former OSE protégés have met less frequently since then, but the core of Arthur's family has remained.

24. LIFE AFTER THE *KINDERTRANSPORT*

In December 2013, I find myself in a house in Hicksville on Long Island, a little outside New York City, waiting for snow. It is the first time in my life that I do not spend Christmas together with my parents. I have just completed an exchange semester at *American University* in Washington, D.C. a few days before, and now I plan to travel the country for the next couple of months, to interview former *Kindertransport* children for my undergrad thesis.

The house in Hicksville belongs to Margaret and Kurt Goldberger, two Holocaust survivors I met when I first came to New York with the *A Letter To The Stars* group of students. In the meantime, we have become great friends and when Margaret heard, a few months ago, that I would spend Christmas in America, she invited me over at once, along with a few other friends. And so it happened that nine eighty- and ninety-year-old Jews throw a Christmas party for me, although they do not celebrate Christmas themselves, of course.

Even though I am denied a white Christmas, the party turns out to be unforgettable, as we listen to German Christmas songs, a red sock crammed with chocolate hanging on the fireplace. "That one's from Santa Claus," Kurt tells me, winking. 92-year-old Vienna-born Anita

Weisbord, who still wears high heels and has just purchased a new car, has even brought homemade cookies. "*Austrian style,*" she says with shining eyes. "The secret with the American recipes is simply to reduce by half the sugar amount." Anita and the others take great pleasure in celebrating Christmas this once. Margaret serves bagels with *schmear* (Yiddish for "cream cheese") along with the cookies: "It won't do without a little something Jewish," she declares.

Almost all those present have come to England on a *Kindertransport*, later emigrating to America as adults, with the exception of one of the "younger" guests, who presents me with a self-made piece of jewelry shaped as a Christmas tree. Having no *Kindertransport*-past herself, she asks many questions as to my research. "Why didn't people know about the *Kindertransport* for so long?" she wants to know first.

* * *

The *Kindertransport* went unnoticed for a long time as far as historical research was concerned. Generally speaking, the history of exile and refugees aroused the interest of Holocaust research very late, and even then the main focus was at first on the adult generation.[1] For decades, almost no one knew about the extraordinary rescue of thousands of children thanks to the *Kindertransports*. In fact, many of the young refugees were not aware of their being part of a bigger story, even more so since postwar society was not interested in talking about the Holocaust and the Second World War. It was only with the American TV series *Holocaust*, featuring Meryl Streep, that the Holocaust moved to the center of attention in the late 1970s, and that concentration camp survivors began to talk about their ordeal for the first time. Yet for most of the *Kindertransport* children, it would be another ten years before they too were ready to speak about their experience in public. By the end of the 1980s, most of the former concentration camps inmates had already died, which made it easier for the *Kindertransport* children to break their silence. German historian Rebecca Göpfert very accurately describes this as the "stepping out of the shadow of the Auschwitz survivors."[2]

In the same year the *50th OSE Reunion* was organized, the first *Reunion of the Kindertransport* was held in London, though on a much bigger scale than in Los Angeles, with over 1,200 people attending the meeting for children who had been rescued to England. Virtually overnight, the *Kindertransport* became the focus of attention of the media, the Holocaust research, and the survivors themselves.

The high number of children rescued on British *Kindertransports* led to the creation of survivor organizations on several continents, namely in America, Israel, and England. Unlike Arthur's and Trudie's informal OSE garden parties, these were actual associations, with clear structures and elected offices. I had already been in touch with the North American branch quite often over the years: Kurt Goldberger was the president of the *Kindertransport Association* (KTA) for several decades, and his wife Margaret, as well as Anita Weisbord, were both active members of the board. Today, the KTA counts hundreds of members, runs several local sections, and organizes regular events. As mentioned previously, I spoke at one of their conferences in Detroit, in 2015.

Apart from the larger number of participants, there is yet another significant difference between the British *Kindertransport* children and the former OSE protégés: the Holocaust survivors who were saved by the British *Kindertransports* still refer to themselves as *Kinder*, using the German word for children even when speaking English, saying for instance "I am a *Kind*" or "We are the *Kinder*." Arthur and his friends, on the other hand, have never called themselves that. "We called ourselves the French Connection," Arthur confessed to me once, laughing. "After a gangster movie with drugs and everything. A very successful movie. We liked that."

Several comprehensive studies have been published about the British *Kindertransport*, yet the smaller *Kindertransport* to France remains largely unknown, even today. "Forgetfulness leads to exile

while remembrance is the secret of redemption," says a much-quoted
Jewish saying. After the *Reunion* in 1989, Arthur too began to look
actively into his past, first contacting the OSE archive in Paris, which
sent him a copy of his file. But it was mostly Trudie who made inquiries. As a newly retired, she could devote quite a lot of time to her new
hobby, genealogy. "I wanted to find out as much as possible about our
families," she said to me. With the help of the Jewish community in
Vienna and the genealogical databank of the Mormons – who run
family archives worldwide for religious reasons – Trudie managed to
trace the Kernbergs' history back to the year 1780.

* * *

Two months after the Jewish-tinged Christmas celebration, I fly back
to Munich to pursue my studies in history at the *Ludwig-Maximilians*-
University. I now need to analyze and go through all the interviews
and archival research I conducted, and begin to write my undergrad
thesis. My subject, entitled "Life after the Kindertransport," considers the impact of the rescue on a *Kindertransport* on the adult lives
of the *Kinder*.

Indeed, the end of the Second World War was not the end of the
story for Arthur, Aaron, Margaret, and Kurt! The rescue of the refugee children was not without consequences. Interestingly, the adult
lives of the *Kinder* bear some striking similarities, starting with their
great professional success up to their sense of social commitment.

"It's just amazing. We have doctors, we have lawyers, we have
accountants. There are several business people. There are at least
three or four millionaires. It's a very success-oriented group," Arthur
told me more than once, himself a successful rocket engineer. "It
really amazes me how kids who started with absolutely nothing
made something of their lives."

Eric Greene gave a similar description, saying: "An interesting
pattern is emerging in our lifestyles. We're all in the above-average

income bracket. We are all sending our children to higher education, e.g. universities. No one with our background that we have been able to find is either destitute or on public welfare."[3]

No one expected such a development when the European refugee children first set foot in America. Yet against all odds, not only did almost all of them manage to overcome their traumatic experiences, but they also became extremely successful. Among the approximately 2,500 people who were saved on a British, French or American *Kindertransport*, and who lived as adults in the United States, there are for instance three Nobel Prize winners: Walter Kohn (Chemistry), Arno Penzias and Jack Steinberger (both in Physics).

* * *

"They were tremendously successful," sociologist Gerhard Sonnert confirms during an interview in the winter of 2017. "Given their situation on arrival, this collective effort is just amazing."

Sonnert and his colleague Gerald Holton are scientists at the renowned *Harvard University*. In 2006, they presented the results of a five-year study, for which they evaluated tens of thousands of census records, in order to prove statistically the professional success of the former refugee children.[4]

"The basic concept here is resilience, the amazing ability of the human spirit to rise from disaster," Gerhard Sonnert explains to me during our conversation. Like a phoenix reborn from the ashes, Arthur and the other young refugees managed to build a successful life after the Holocaust.

The Harvard study shows that almost half of the male survivors went to college and studied – compared with only 15.3 percent of the average American population of the same age group. What is more, the former refugee children earned almost twice as much (185 percent more) on average than their American-born peers.

It also shows, as mentioned earlier, an above-average high chance for German and Austrian refugee children to win a Nobel Prize. According to Sonnert and Holton, the probability is 1 to 5,500 compared to 1 to 650,000 for the American-born population.

Also worthy of note is the fact that the former *Kindertransport* children as a group were not only much more educated and successful than the average American but also than the Jewish-American population. "Jewish ancestry alone is not enough to explain their achievements," the Harvard scientist maintains.

* * *

A variety of reasons contributed to this extraordinary success story. Many of the *Kindertransport* children had promised their parents, on parting with them, that they would be studious and hard-working and make something of their life. Additionally, they often felt a sense of responsibility to build successful lives, because they had survived.

Quite conceivably, the refugee children could have broken under such emotional pressure, yet in most cases, the exact opposite happened. The survivors had had a short, carefree, and untroubled childhood before becoming prematurely adults and being forced to take responsibility for things they were much too young for. And yet: as traumatic as their experiences might have been, the fact that they had to take responsibility early on is exactly what often gave them an advantage later on, in their professional lives.

The combination of their European upbringing and the opportunities America provided was yet another reason for their success. Before the beginning of the Second World War, most schools in Europe were far superior to American schools, especially in the field of natural sciences. One glance at the variety of subjects taught illustrates this: if at the time, most American high schools did teach math and science, in Austria and Germany these subjects were subdivided into arithmetic, geometrical drawing, physics, biology, and chemistry classes. So it happened that upon their arrival in the US, the young refugees soon became best in class, despite the language barrier, and received university scholarships. "Several former refugees in our study noted that in an ironically cruel way, Hitler did them a favor by expelling them," Sonnert explained to me.

The survivors' childhood was marked by numerous traumatic experiences and deprivations, which they tried to compensate for, as adults, with ambition and hard work. "They became workaholics and were very successful," psychologist Ruth Barnett summarizes.[5]

However, the extraordinary professional success of the adult *Kindertransport* children does not mean that they survived the Holocaust psychologically unscathed. Indeed the pursuit of success is a well-known psychological coping strategy to avoid having to face one's traumas. "It is thus not an entirely positive story, but it shows how, under the right conditions, human beings can rise above horrendous tragedies," Sonnert and Holton write in the closing words of their large-scale study.[6]

* * *

The picture is quite similar in the case of the OSE children in America, as I notice, leafing through a *50th OSE Reunion* remembrance book Trudie and Arthur have made, and that includes short biographies of 89 people.[7]

50 among these 89 people have a university degree, which is an even higher average than in the Harvard study. As I browse through the yellowed pages, I discover seven university professors – among which three women – five engineers, several lawyers, doctors, psychologists, architects, and one rabbi. 17 people owned their own business, among which a carpenter, who had put into practice the skills acquired in the OSE homes.

In addition to their extraordinary professional success, the lives of the adult *Kindertransport* children reveal yet another remarkable similarity: a strikingly high percentage of them worked in the social sector.[8]

Knowing they had been rescued themselves, many of them felt the need to help in turn – exactly like they had been helped as children.

Anita Weisbord for instance, the cookie-baker at the Hicksville Christmas party, took care of disabled children for a decade. "I said to myself: 'How come one-and-a-half million children perished and I am alive?' There must be a reason. I felt that I have to give something back to society," she said to me, explaining her commitment. Esther Starobin, whose brother came to America on board the same ship as Arthur, used her *Kindertransport* experience in her daily work as a schoolteacher. "I was much better with the kids who were not the 'in-group.' I was much better with the kids who had a different background," she declares today.

Since their retirement, many survivors have even increased their social commitment, with quite a number of them working as volunteers, just like Arthur. For almost twenty years, from 1995 to 2014, he helped out twice a week at the *Jewish Home for the Aging*, a Jewish retirement home in Los Angeles. "I started there when I was 65. Most of the residents were around 90 years old," Arthur told me. "For them, I was only ever the '*Kind*.'" Every Tuesday morning, from nine o'clock to twelve, he would take the ladies to the doctor, the beauty salon, or shopping. Every Thursday, he volunteered as a dance partner, at the retirement home suffering a flagrant shortage of men. Arthur love to dance with these "small, old ladies" as he called them, despite some of them clearly having two left feet.

* * *

The many interviews I have conducted with survivors over the years show a recurring issue, namely whether the *Kindertransport* children consider themselves Holocaust survivors or not. To better comprehend this debate, one must know that it was decades after the end of the Second World War, before research acknowledged that children could suffer from traumatic experiences their entire life. For a very long time, it was commonly believed that they had been too young to consciously perceive suffering and pain. As late as the 1960s, West German courts dismissed compensation applications on the grounds that the persons concerned could no longer remember the wrongs that had been done to them, having been children during the Nazi period. It was not before the 1980s that this all changed when the term *Child Survivors* was first used in Holocaust research.[9]

Exactly like it had been collectively assumed that *Child Survivors* had no recollection of any pain, the *Kindertransport* children would not be recognized as "full-fledged" Holocaust survivors for a very long time. As terrible as it sounds, for a while historians talked about a kind of "hierarchy" among survivors, comparing the pain and suffering people had experienced. According to that logic, a concentration camp survivor was "worth more" than a *Kindertransport* child, because he had suffered more. "During our *Reunion*, one of the guys was absolutely furious that we called ourselves survivors," Arthur told me. The man had been arrested by the French police in one of the OSE homes and had been deported. He survived Auschwitz and considered himself a Holocaust survivor, but he did not see the rest of the children as such.

Since the 1990s, it is generally accepted that it is not possible to compare people's suffering. Internationally recognized institutions, such as *Yad Vashem* in Israel or the *United States Holocaust Memorial Museum* in Washington, D.C., nowadays consider a Holocaust survivor any person who lived between 1933 and 1945 under Nazi rule, was persecuted and survived – regardless of whether they lived through Auschwitz or managed to escape to America in 1933 on the *Queen Mary*.[10]

Yet the fact this debate took place led many former refugee children to experience some difficulty considering themselves as Holocaust survivors. Before the *Reunion* in 1989, Arthur himself had not given the term a lot of thought, but he never hesitated to apply it to himself. "I keep saying, 'We're all Holocaust survivors,'" he explained to me.

After Steven Spielberg made the Oscar-winning movie *Schindler's List*, he created the *USC Shoah Foundation* in 1994, which conducted 55,000 video interviews with Holocaust survivors worldwide to keep and preserve their stories for the next generations. That interview was a particularly decisive moment for many survivors. "Gunther never thought of himself as a survivor," Susie Katz, Gunther's widow, told me during my visit. "It wasn't until the *Spielberg Shoah Foundation* started talking about whom they wanted to talk about, that all of a sudden it went 'click,' I guess, 'I am a survivor.'"

Arthur was interviewed in 1995, Trudie on the other hand never agreed to speak with the *Shoah Foundation*. "I don't think I'm a survivor," she would insist.

Only half of the *Kindertransport* children I have interviewed answered the question of whether they consider themselves Holocaust survivors or not with an unreserved yes. The others, while calling themselves survivors, have obvious reservations and do not feel quite comfortable with the term. Many children "tend to relativize their suffering," Viennese psychotherapist Anna Wexberg-Kubesch explains. "They don't believe having gone through anything 'that horrible,' their own experience appearing 'less terrible' compared with the death camps."[11]

In many cases, the *Kinder* refuse to consider themselves as survivors, because they feel guilty. Not only do they feel concentration camp survivors suffered much more than themselves, but they also feel guilty because they survived, unlike the millions of people murdered during the Holocaust. The feeling others would have been more worthy of surviving than themselves is a crucial aspect of the so-called survivor guilt.[12]

* * *

Early December 2014, almost one year after my Christmas in Hicksville, the University of Munich awards my undergrad thesis their Research Prize for Excellent Students. It is the first time the history department has won this prize. For Arthur and the other twelve survivors I have interviewed for "A Life after the Kindertransport," this distinction has a very special value. "It means so much to me that Munich, the center of the beginning of Nazism, is honoring a work on the *Kindertransport*," Freddie Traum writes to me from Maryland.

25. ARTHUR AND HIS FAMILY

At six o'clock in the morning, I get into the car with Aaron. We are invited for brunch at Trudie's and want to avoid morning rush hour – that means an early rise. It is a fifty-five miles drive from Seal Beach, where the Kerns' oldest son lives with his family, to Trudie's, yet even in the early hours, entirely avoiding traffic jams in and around Los Angeles is close to impossible. It is an hour and a half before we finally reach our destination. But then at least I can use the time to interview Aaron for this book.

"Would you say you take after your father?" I ask as we drive through West LA.

"Oh yes, absolutely." Aaron cannot quite suppress a laugh. "In general, I hold the values system that he had very high. Moral and ethical standards. I believe in treating people correctly. Playing jokes on people, that's definitely something I get from him." As a matter of fact, it suddenly occurs to me as we speak that I have fallen for the exact same kind of jokes from father and son over the years.

"My sense of obligation to volunteer my time for philanthropic endeavors I also get from Dad."

"What influence would you say your parents' past has had on your present life?" I ask, the surface of the ocean in the distance glistening in the rising sun.

"I think it shaped me to be who I am. My drive to learn to be successful, I think it comes from that. If my parents had not encouraged and supported me, I wouldn't be a medical doctor today. Both my parents worked very hard to make us successful. And I felt, as a child, that they gave their all and they encouraged me to work hard to get to where *I* am. When you grow up in an environment where you don't know if you'll ever eat again, you eat when food's available. And then even after food was readily available, that behavior didn't change. So for example, when my dad would eat an apple, he ate the entire apple to the core. So that gets passed on, and you begin to appreciate what you have, be satisfied with what you have."

* * *

Their family was extremely important to Arthur and Trudie. They are no exception: many of the adult *Kindertransport* children consider their founding a family as their greatest achievement in life.[1] "For many, the most fundamental response [to the Holocaust] was to marry and have a family, thereby creating a home to replace that which was destroyed," psychologist Sarah Moskovitz writes in her essay "Making Sense of Survival."[2]

According to various surveys of survivor associations, 84 to 93 percent of the *Kinder* had children themselves.[3] My favorite statistic also confirms this: If one takes into account all the children, grandchildren, and great-grandchildren, today well over 60,000 people owe their lives to the British *Kindertransport*.[4]

Being a parent was a mission of utmost importance to the survivors associated with a great sense of success. And yet at the same time, there was also "the possibility that their ability to raise children could have been affected by their separation from their own parents," psychotherapist Ruth Barnett explains. Even though the *Kinder* did not want to admit it: their experience during the *Kindertransport* did affect the second generation.[5]

Many survivors went through a very emotional time when their own children reached the age they had been when they were forced to leave their homes to join a *Kindertransport*. For the first time, they truly understood the tremendous sacrifice their own parents had made. "When my kids got to be ten, it was a very emotional time for me," Arthur confessed to me. "Especially with the oldest, Aaron. I thought, 'God, how could I send my kids away? And what would have happened to them, how could they survive?'"

I gave my first lecture on the *Kindertransport* and its subsequent impact in early 2015. Since then, I have spoken about that subject at many universities, schools, churches, and Jewish museums in Germany, Austria, and America. The chief part of my audience is usually in their fifties and sixties, the age of Arthur's sons. Accordingly, they show great interest when I speak about the impact on the second generation.

The second generation very often experienced a highly emotional transgenerational trauma many parents were not even aware of. Out of the desire to protect their children, many survivors did not speak about their past experiences. Ruth Barnett calls this the "Wall of Silence." When such a crucial aspect of life is kept secret, it renders "the normal conversation flow between the two generations" all the more difficult.[6]

Of all the survivors I know, very few talked about their past to their children early on. Arthur was one of them. Many others kept silent. Yet the fact their parents did not speak about their story did not mean the children were not aware something tragic had occurred in their parents' past.

During the *OSE Reunion*, a representative of the second generation also gave a speech. "Having known a group of these OSE children all my life, in my mind they are all heroes," Sharon Mullowney, the daughter of Renee and Morris Eisenberg, began. "And growing up with all these heroes has in some ways been a challenge. No matter how much my mother has ever reassured me that my personal dreams, choices, and visions are my own to make, it's hard not to feel a measure of expectation and comparison to her and the world she so magnanimously emerged from. The difficulties and hardships of my life seem often pale, compared to the Holocaust experience. The feelings of needing to do something extraordinary with my life, to imbue meaning into my mother's survival are sometimes hard to avoid. There is a very important and positive by-product of all this – and that is the belief that if I have the desire and determination that I can do anything with my life."

Just like Sharon Mullowney declares at the end of her speech, the childhood experiences of the survivors also had a positive influence on the second generation. "The values Mom and Dad gave me, I consider them a gift that will always keep giving and I'm immensely thankful for it," Danny confirmed to me. "Dad always was trying to teach us how to take care of ourselves," his brother David added. "You gotta work for what you want and you have to give back to society. Those are the two things that he taught me that I do, to this day."

The extraordinary success of the *Kinder* did continue in the second generation, the latter even surpassing their parents as regards education and professional success, as Sonnert and Holton discovered in their Harvard study.[7] Only in the third generation is there no longer any noticeable difference to Americans of the same age, the grandchildren being completely Americanized.

During all the conversations I have had over the years with members of the second generation, one circumstance, in particular, was especially striking: the more the children knew as they grew up and the more their parents told them about their past, the sooner they were able to detach themselves from it. Aaron, David, and Danny, for instance, already knew about their parents' story as children and even though they are still interested in it, it no longer burdens them and they are also not active in survivor organizations.

Things are very different, however, for children who only learned about their parents' war and escape experiences as adults, many of them developing an almost manic need to come to terms with their family history and learn about the Holocaust. The first films about the *Kindertransport* for instance – such as *My Knees Were Jumping* and the Oscar-winning documentary *Into the Arms of Strangers* – were produced by women, whose parents had only talked about their past very late, or not at all.[8]

As much as Arthur's sons know about their family history, his daughters-in-law know even more. "We sat for hours talking, and Dad told me a lot of his stories," Nena recalled. (Trudie and Arthur made all three of their daughters-in-law call them "Mom" and "Dad.") "So I knew a lot, things that my husband David didn't even know. Because when you grow up with someone and that's their history, you don't really talk to your family about it. But when you come from the outside, you ask questions. Just like you, Lilly. We both come from the outside, so we ask questions."

Arthur and Trudie treated their daughters-in-law like their own daughters. "Whenever we saw each other, Arthur would call me the next day to say thank you," Nena said. "'*Sweetheart*, I wanna thank you so much for coming over, it was so great seeing you.' To him, thanking us for being part of the family was important. It was important for him that you knew how much he loved you."

Even though they might know a little less about their story than their wives, all three Kern sons consider being second-generation Holocaust survivors as a responsibility. "It is actually miraculous that I exist," Aaron told me. "I think that influences my view of life, my interest in perpetuating Judaism, and being active in the Temple. The Holocaust is a part of history I cannot remove from myself. I am a part of it or it's a part of me." Aaron told me.

David sees things the same way: "I am only here because America opened its doors to accept a group of people who would have been annihilated. If they hadn't, I wouldn't be here."

Together with their wives, Aaron and Danny visited *Villa La Chesnaie* in Eaubonne, about which they had heard so much as children. Until very recently, their brother David was the only one of the three Kern sons who ever went to Austria, though. In 1975, the nineteen-year-old traveled through Europe and tried to visit Arthur's old apartment in Vienna. "So I went to the address, knocked on the door of the apartment, and had no clue what I was going to say," he recalled. "But nobody opened the door anyway."

David's tour also brought him to Munich, where he visited the nearby Dachau Concentration Camp Memorial. "Before I went to Europe, I had read the letter my grandfather had sent Dad for his bar mitzvah," he told me. "I thought it was a nice letter, you know, but nothing more. And then I went to Europe and then I went to Dachau. I felt like – I don't know how to describe it, but as if there was an evil spirit hanging in the air. It was just mind-boggling to look at the place. When I got home from Europe, I reread the letter. This time I was in absolute tears. Because it was at that point that I realized – to the extent that you actually can – under what conditions my grandfather actually wrote that letter. He was being tortured, humiliated, starved to death; and it still blows me away, how he would have had the ability to write a letter under such situations to encourage his son to survive."

* * *

Twenty years later, David's son Alex also had a moving experience with his grandfather's past. When he was fourteen years old, he visited the *Museum of Tolerance* in Los Angeles with his class. Inside the Holocaust museum, every visitor is given a card with the photograph and the name of a Jewish child. There are thousands and thousands of different cards – whichever one gets is completely random. Yet once again, against all odds, Alex picked his grandfather's card!

"It was kind of crazy," the now thirty-six-year-old Alex tells me. "No one wanted to believe me that it was actually my Grandpa." His classmates' reaction was actually quite understandable, though: who would expect a fourteen-year-old Latino, who goes to church every Sunday, to be the grandson of a Jewish Holocaust survivor? "It was a very special feeling, going through the museum 'with' my Grandpa and seeing what my great-grandparents and my great-uncle had to go through," Alex tells me, as we sit and talk in Trudie's study.

As a soldier, Alex was sent to Iraq twice, which makes him the only member of the Kern family who has experienced war, apart from Arthur. "It was something he and I talked about," Alex confides in me. "No one in our family knows what it's like to be in war. I got to see war as a Marine, fighting the war. And he got to see it as a young child, escaping the war. And that was something only he and I talked about. I haven't even really talked about it with my father. It was a bond that only Grandpa and I had. But at the same time, you start to think about how no child should ever have to go through something like that."

Alex sits back and gazes thoughtfully into the distance. Then his four-year-old son pokes his head around the door, giggling, and Alex smiles.

* * *

Arthur's grand daughters, including Lilly.

All of Arthur's grandchildren – apart from Alex, there are also his sister Sami and his cousins Rachel and Shira – have faced their grandparents' past in one way or another. As a ten-year-old, Sami gave a presentation about her grandmother in her English class. "Hello, my name is Samantha Kern and I will be telling you about my Granny Trudie," she began reading the presentation Trudie has since then pasted inside the family photo album. Even today, the marketing manager still thinks quite often about her family history. "Every time I watch a movie or every time I read something, it always hits close to home when I think about what my Grandpa and my Grandma went through," she told me during one of my visits.

Shira, another of Arthur's granddaughters, earned a Ph.D. in clinical psychology. "Knowing my Grandpa's story definitely had an impact when I was growing up," she said to me. "It helped me have a bigger appreciation for Jewish culture and history. When I think about how he escaped that situation early on, came to America, got a job and went to school, and started a family. Every time things get tough, I think, 'You know what? If he survived all that and everything turned out alright in the end, I will be just fine."

Shira's older sister Rachel, for her part, has taken a very practical approach to her family history, namely through her art.

Lilly during one of her numerous visits to Los Angeles, here with Shira.

* * *

Graphic designer Rachel has studied at the *California College of the Arts*, in San Francisco, where she lives until today. Her apartment is quite unmistakably that of an artist, with prints hanging on the walls, an old typewriter resting on the coffee table, and a whole shelf crammed with papers, colors, and stamps waiting to be used.

After her great-grandmother, Anne Kellogg, Rachel is the second artist in the family. "*Mutti*'s art was always a great source of inspiration for me," the thirty-year-old reveals, when I visit her in the fall of 2016. We have made ourselves comfortable on her large bed, Rachel sitting cross-legged as I stretch out my legs, a tiny white cat nestling between us.

"Grandpa was always so appreciative and thankful for the family he had," Rachel begins. "I remember him always saying how blessed he felt for having such a wonderful family. And that is something that I think made me realize what a blessing our family was and how easy it was to take it for granted."

In her first year at art school, Rachel dealt with Arthur's past very intensively. "I felt like there's still people denying the Holocaust and there's still people who don't know this story," she declares. "It was important for me to tell that story."

Leaning over to reach under her bed, Rachel pulls out a large box. She sets aside a few paper pads and folders and finally finds what she is looking for: a book with five woodcuts, each representing a turning point in Arthur's life.

The first woodcut shows a factory, of which only a few details can be seen, like a memory, faded over the years. "The project was a way to find out more about Grandpa. I asked him a lot of questions and spent a lot of time investigating that," Rachel explains to me. The second woodcut shows a shattered windowpane, as a symbol for "*Kristallnacht.*" On the third one, Arthur is surrounded by his parents' and brother's faces, fading into darkness. "It stands for him sort of being separated from his family," Rachel says, leafing through the book. The second last picture is the carved copy of one of Hermann Kernberg's letters, sent from the Opole ghetto, and the last woodcut finally shows a ship just reaching America: Arthur's rescue.

"Then I made another piece, a zinc plate etching. I found a picture of my grandfather as a boy and his face is sort of floating in the middle. On his left, there is this star patch, and also barbed wire and fire to stand for everything he had to go through. But then there's also hope and a peace dove breaking through the barbed wire. I wanted to show that while he had this very rough and difficult past, he still had these blessings in his life and the more he moved forward the more he could embrace and appreciate them."

Arthur had the print framed. It still hangs in his and Trudie's bedroom.

Zinc plate etching by Rachel Kern.

* * *

There are now four generations of Kerns. In 2010 and 2012, AJ and Cash, Arthur and Trudie's first great-grandchildren were born. The boys call their great-grandparents *Oma* and *Opa*, in German, to distinguish them from Grandma and Grandpa. When Cash was born, Alex thought of a special surprise for Arthur.

"We gave Grandpa a sealed envelope with the birth certificate," Alex told me. "And when he opened it up, it said, 'Cash-James *Fritz* Kern.' His brother's name. Grandpa became very emotional, looked at Cash, and said, 'Now he's a real Kern.'"

26. A PARCEL FROM THE PAST

"I had a wonderful life," Arthur told me more than once. "I mean there were some rough spots, but everybody has rough spots in their lives and I was fortunate enough that I had my rough spots early. Today Trudie and I have three children, three daughters-in-law, four grandchildren, two great-grandchildren, and my entire OSE family. We're truly blessed."

Arthur's fundamentally positive attitude to life was a matter of surprise to many. "When you think about the fact of what he survived, in terms of the Holocaust and losing his family, you'd think he'd have a right to be very angry and bitter and depressed," Arthur's daughter-in-law, Leslie, told me. "But he was none of those things. Dad always had a positive attitude about everything. Always. I find that pretty amazing."

Already as a young man, Arthur had very deliberately chosen to make peace with his dreadful past. "You have to fight the hate in your heart," he said to me, when we got to know each other. "I recognized early on that hate doesn't help you. If you're gonna keep hating, you're only gonna destroy your *own* life."

For Arthur, making peace with his past also meant forgiving

Austria and the Austrians. His mindset is quite similar to Auschwitz survivor Eva Mozes Kor's. A few years ago, Mozes Kor made headlines all around the world, when she hugged former SS-guard Oskar Gröning, charged with aiding and abetting mass murder, during his trial. As I read her book, *The Power of Forgiveness*, I am often reminded of Arthur.

"The major victim of hate is the one who carries it inside him," Mozes Kor writes. "A victim has the right to be free, but one cannot be truly free without first shaking that daily burden of suffering and rage." Mozes Kor survived Josef Mengele's experiments on twins in Auschwitz as an eleven-year-old. When she managed to forgive him decades later, she called it "a gift to herself": "The idea that I could somehow gain the upper hand over Josef Mengele was an incredible experience for me. I was no longer a victim, passive and helpless, but the active person. That made me feel powerful. I realized that forgiveness was freeing – not for the offender, but for the victim," she writes.[1]

Mozes Kor suffered a great deal of criticism on the part of other survivors for her position. Arthur too was definitely an exception within the group of former OSE children. "You could find maybe three or four who were like Artie," Trudie confided in me once. "Artie was one of the few who did not hate."

* * *

Instead of clinging to the horrors of his past, Arthur enjoyed his life. When the children left the house, Trudie and he began to travel the world in style. Leafing through their photo albums, I come across countless pictures from all around the world, starting in the 1970s: Puerto Rico, the Panama Canal, Hawaii, New Zealand, Israel, Egypt, and Alaska were just some of their many travel destinations. In 1979, the Kerns decided they would travel to Europe for the first time since their escape. Trudie had not set foot in the "old continent" for forty years, Arthur for 38 years. "It was a nostalgic trip," Arthur remembered. "To visit places in which I had resided during my childhood."

They first went to France, where a huge surprise awaited Trudie. "We had been married for 28 years and it was the first time I found out that Artie spoke French! After all this time!" Trudie told me.

Arthur's astonishingly reemerged language skills turned out to be quite useful indeed: the couple was almost arrested in Montmorency for taking pictures of *Villa Helvetia*, now housing a police station. The policemen did not speak a word of English, but Arthur managed to explain to them in French why he was so interested in the station. In the end, Trudie and he spent almost one hour with the police officers, who showed great interest in Arthur's childhood and asked him all manner of questions about the former children's home.

On their journey into the past, Arthur and Trudie followed the same route I took decades later while doing research for this book. After the Montmorency police station, they went on to visit *Villa La Chesnaie* in Eaubonne, still in possession of its former owners at that time. On the following day, they boarded a train to the south of France. "We rented a car in Limoges and drove to *Château de Montintin* on a dirt road," Trudie recalled. "And all of a sudden, it was like being back in the 1700s. The ladies were wearing these long black skirts and carrying baskets on their heads… It was totally out of our time period."

Another curve, and they halted in front of *Montintin* with its stone walls and high turrets. At that time, the chateau was used as a summer camp for Jewish children, standing empty the rest of the year. Arthur knocked on the door of a neighboring building. "*Que voulez-vous?*" snapped a grim-looking farmer's wife. "What do you want?" Arthur began to explain and after a few words, the woman's face lit up. As it turned out, she had worked for OSE as an eighteen-year-old and was now taking care of the *Château de Montintin*. The peasant woman promptly showed Arthur and Trudie around the entire chateau, including the small room in *La Chevrette*, which Arthur had once shared with Eric Greene and Norbert Rosenblum. On their way back, Arthur "nicked" an apple from one of the trees, just as he had used to when he was a little boy. The then 51-year-old felt like he had traveled back in time. "Nowhere else in the world do the apples taste like they do in *Montintin*," he told me dreamily. "The whole visit was very cathartic. I was finally able to close a chapter of my life I had lived 33 years ago."

But still, another chapter awaited him, though: Vienna.

* * *

The first time adult *Kindertransport* children return to their place of birth represents a major step in their coming-to-terms with their past. It often took several decades before they not only wished to visit their hometown but also felt emotionally strong enough to actually do so. David Kern believes his visiting Vienna was the trigger for his father's travel to Austria in 1979: "When I went to Europe and took a picture of his parents' old apartment, it opened a door. It opened a door for him to change his mind."

Trudie later briefly summarized their first return to Vienna: "Artie remembered everything and I couldn't remember anything at all. But it was still a nice trip."

The Kerns arrived in Vienna around ten o'clock in the evening, but Arthur was far too excited to go to sleep. He left Trudie at the hotel and set out on his way. "Do you know your way, honey?" Trudie called, as he had already gone out the door. But Arthur found the way to his former house almost intuitively. Coming from the Danube Canal, he turned into the *Gussenbauergasse*. A large public housing block stood on the right, – in the dim light of the street lamps, he managed to make out the inscription, *Sigmund-Freud-Hof* – another small cross street, and there he was. Forty years after his escape, Arthur stood once again in front of *Gussenbauergasse* 1. His parents' home had not been bombed out during the war and still looked exactly like he remembered it: the stone ornaments, the women's faces above each of the high windows, and the wrought iron entrance door. It all just seemed smaller to him than it had before. But then he had grown a lot since he had left Vienna as a ten-year-old, in 1939. Arthur did not try to enter the house – after all, it was the middle of the night – but he looked up to the window of his old room for a long time. Then he roused himself and walked on. He could not find his old elementary school anymore, but he did find the house in the *Döbling* area that had once housed the knitting factory Goldfeld & Kernberg.

"He was so excited when he came back!" Trudie told me. "He must have talked for three hours straight. Telling me all the places that he saw and everything. I was very excited for him." On the following morning, Arthur tried to visit his old apartment. "I rang the doorbell. And somebody answered and I said that I used to live here a long time ago. But they said they were no interested, period," Arthur explained to me later, describing the frustrating situation of not being allowed inside.

Together with Trudie, Arthur then took the eight-minute walk to *Nußdorfer Straße 4A*. Visiting her former home did not shake Trudie's repressed childhood memories: even as she stood right in front of her parents' house, she could not recognize it! "It was also the first time I realized how near Artie and I had lived to each other as children," Trudie said to me.

The Kerns spent the next few days sightseeing and rediscovering Vienna, eating *Schnitzel* and *Apfelstrudel,* and riding the Ferris wheel. Arthur bought a copy of the famous 1845 illustrated children's book, *Struwwelpeter* ("*Shockheaded Peter*"). "When we came back home, all my Austrian and German friends wanted to borrow the *Struwwelpeter,*" Arthur told me. "I don't know why we are all so moved by this book; probably because it reminds us of our childhood."

"The only thing that was strange about that trip," Trudie confessed to me, "was that Arthur had a problem with younger people." Almost all survivors I know have a huge problem talking to older people in Austria and Germany today. Survivors quite commonly fear people from a certain age group might have been Nazis back then. Yet in Arthur's case, it was the exact opposite. "When I went to Austria, I sort of displaced myself to the age when I was a child," he explained to me years later. "I would look at people who were in their twenties and think, 'they must have been a Nazi,' But they couldn't have been, of course, because they were much too young. But when I looked at their grandparents, who would have been the Nazi generation, they looked like my grandparents used to look! And I couldn't have any ill feelings toward them. Later I realized it didn't make any sense. But that was how I felt at the time. But it was only uncomfortable at first, from then on, I always was very comfortable in Austria."

* * *

After their return from France and Austria, the Kerns' trip into their past became a major topic of conversation among their circle of friends. Time and again, Arthur was asked to recount what it felt like finding himself at *Château de Montintin* or wandering the streets of Vienna. He often missed his copy of *Struwwelpeter* for weeks, because Aaron, Norbert, and Eric could not bring themselves to return the children's book to him. (Today, Arthur's *Struwwelpeter* stands on my bookshelf; Aaron has given it to me after his father's death.) There was one thing Arthur regretted a great deal, though: that he was not able to see his old apartment again.

Twenty years later, he moved considerably closer to realizing this most ardent wish. In 1999, the Kerns took a longer journey, this time to Turkey. As they sat by a pool in the Anatolian mountains, they met by chance a Viennese couple, Brigitte and Fritz Kodras.

"Arthur was always very happy to have the opportunity to speak German," Fritz Kodras remembered, when I visit him in his attic apartment in Vienna, in the fall of 2017. "That's how I met him and that's how a friendship developed." The retired civil engineer is the only person I know who pronounces Arthur's name in German and not in English.

Three years after their holiday in Turkey, Brigitte, and Fritz visited their new friends in Los Angeles. During a conversation, the Kerns mentioned planning a trip to Vienna. "Then I said to him: 'Listen, Arthur, I'm going to help you visit your apartment this time,'" Fritz Kodras told me.

And so it happened that in the fall of 2002, Mr. and Mrs. Kodras knocked on our door on *Gussenbauergasse*. I was ten at the time and had just started my first year at high school. My mother Sabine, a journalist, and I had been living for three years in the spacious old apartment in the mezzanine on *Gussenbauergasse*. What had started as an ordinary and peaceful autumn night turned into the very evening I first heard the name of Arthur Kern.

"We had just been cooking, remember?" my mother recalled, when we talked about the visit later. "And then this older couple suddenly appeared on our doorstep, all fidgety and nervous. When they wouldn't answer my repeated questions, I began to think they might be Jehovah's Witnesses and wanted to get rid of them. They just would not say what they wanted!"

In the end, the couple managed to present Arthur's request. "'This is out of the question'; that's the kind of answer I would have expected from people who would have no understanding for it," Fritz Kodras confessed to me. "But your mother understood, fortunately, and simply said: 'That's quite possible.'"

"I didn't need to give it a lot of thought," my mother confirmed when I asked her about it recently. "Of course, I knew right away I would grant their wish. Besides, being a journalist, I am also notoriously curious. I found all this extremely exciting." One thing worried her, though: "We now knew that all the inhabitants of the apartment we were living in had been killed during the Holocaust, except for one little boy. Which is an unbelievably distressing thought. Two days later, a colleague from the publishing group where I worked at the time sent an email informing us he was about to start a history project for students called *A Letter To The Stars*. At that moment, I knew how we would deal emotionally with the whole situation. If Arthur would bring his past into our apartment and our lives, he would have to agree to work with you on the *Letter To The Stars* project."

* * *

On March 30, 2003, Trudie and Arthur flew to Vienna for the second time, following an invitation from the *Jewish Welcome Service*, a program set up in the 1980s, inviting Austrian men and women, expelled from their country during the war, to visit their old home. The *Jewish Welcome Services* program is financed by the city of Vienna, the Federal Chancellery, as well as by several businesses. Many German cities offer similar programs.

Together with Arthur and Trudie, 80 "former Austrians" came to Vienna, among whom Hollywood legend Leon Askin, and Margaret and Kurt Goldberger, who would throw a Jewish Christmas party for me a few years later. During their one-week visit, the survivors were welcomed by Federal President Thomas Klestil in the rooms for official state visits and Viennese Mayor Michael Häupl invited them to a "*Wiener Jause*" (Viennese snack) at the town hall. The highlight of their visit to Vienna, however, took place on the very first day: after 64 years, Arthur finally set foot into his childhood apartment again.

"It was like I had known Arthur for a very long time," my mother recalled. "He entered the apartment as if he had already come to visit us 30 times before. He went straight to your room and declared: 'This used to be the piano room.'"

Arthur strode through our apartment with shining eyes, down the long corridor along which he used to ride his bike, to the former dining room, now my mother's study, his parents' bedroom, now our living room, up to the tiny room at the far end of the apartment, which he had shared with his brother Fritz. "It was very surprising to see him move through the apartment with such confidence," my mother said later. "He knew his way around the place, he didn't have to stop and think to get his bearings. It was as if he'd never left."

Arthur's face lit up more and more with every step he took. "Here stood my parents' bed, over there was a stove, and here was the piano," he said, becoming at once a tourist guide of our apartment, remembering every door frame and window catch, his descriptions bringing the rooms of his childhood to life. Arthur's unbridled joy was very catching; we had only known him and Trudie for a mere half-hour and had already taken them to our hearts. Of course, none of us knew, back then, how deeply this encounter would affect all of our lives, but we all felt that this moment was very special indeed.

After we had walked through the apartment twice, we sat in the living room and my mother cut large slices of *Marmorkuchen* (chocolate marble cake). Six months had passed since Fritz and Brigitte Kodras had knocked on our door. In the meantime, my mother had talked to Arthur over the phone a few times and told him about *A Letter To The Stars*. Arthur was very happy to know that I, a young girl from his hometown, wanted to research his mother's story. Now, as we sat at the table, eating marble cake, he pulled out a few documents and photographs from his pocket: Frieda Kernberg wearing a dark dress, a broad smile on her face; Frieda with her two sons in a photographer's studio; the whole family by the lake in *Heidenreichstein*. The photographs were copies of the pictures Arthur had stolen from his parents' photo album – in another time, when he was still called by another name. He had been ten years old back then, only a few months younger than I was on that day.

"I was *so* excited, going back to the apartment and meeting you guys," Arthur told me years later. "It was one of the highlights of my life."

* * *

"Today I am living in her former apartment" – this was the title of the text I wrote about Arthur's mother, Frieda, in the following weeks and that would eventually be published in the *A Letter To The Stars*-anthology *Schüler schreiben Geschichte* (*Students write History*).[2] In May 2003, a huge student commemorative action was organized on *Heldenplatz* (Heroes' Square), as part of the project. The fact Arthur and I had lived in the same apartment being a very moving story, the initiators of the project mentioned it during a press conference. "Our phone has been constantly ringing since then," my mother wrote to the Kerns in an email. In the following days, I did a few interviews; the article of a journalist of the *Associated Press*, for instance, was later published in over 50 American newspapers. Yet one article that appeared in the Vienna daily newspaper *Kurier* (Courier), turned out to be much more significant for the rest of our story.[3]

This article appeared in the Austrian newspaper *Kurier* in May 2003.
The headline reads "Letter to the murdered previous resident".

"It is not every day that one writes an article with such an impact," *Kurier* journalist Josef Gebhard declared when I meet him over a coffee in the fall of 2017. Not often does one remember fifteen-year-old articles, yet Gebhard still has the most vivid recollection of that particular article he wrote back then. Even more important than the text, though, was the photograph accompanying the article: it shows me, as an eleven-year-old girl wearing a friendship charm from a children's magazine about horses, holding a sepia-toned photograph of Frieda Kernberg.

The article was published on a Sunday and read by many Viennese over breakfast. One of them was Valerie Bartos. The 83-year-old was shocked when she discovered the photo. She knew the woman in the picture!

The next morning, Valerie Bartos called the *Kurier* and asked for my mother's contact details, which the newspaper refused to disclose. But Mrs. Bartos was quite persistent and did not give up, calling the *Kurier* again and again until Gebhard agreed on a compromise, giving my mother the phone number of that very tenacious reader and asking her to contact the elderly lady. And so it happened that Valerie Bartos entered our lives, bearing a small parcel from the past for Arthur.

In 1941, shortly before his deportation to Poland, Hermann Kernberg had entrusted a friend with safekeeping all important family and business papers, in the hope they would allow his family a new start in Vienna, should they ever be released from the Polish ghetto. "He was certain of his return," Bartos said years later. "And he wanted to make provisions for this eventuality."[4]

Hermann Kernberg had given the envelope with the documents to his friend Otto Kürth, who ran a textile business on *Kalvariengasse*. Being a "half-Jew," as it was then called, Kürth feared being deported himself. Which is why he passed on the precious envelope to his cousin, Valerie Bartos.

Bartos knew the Kernbergs in passing, her father running a restaurant where Frieda and Hermann had had lunch from time to time. "Hermann Kernberg was a real gentleman, his wife a lovely housewife," she recalled. The then twenty-year-old agreed to keep the documents and hid them in her apartment, fastening the envelope to the bottom of a wooden chest of drawers, in the hope it would escape the Gestapo's notice, in case of a house search.

In March 1941, Hermann and Frieda Kernberg sent a postcard to Otto Kürth from Opole to thank him for his support – it was the last time anyone heard from the Kernbergs in Vienna. But there was still Oswald! Valerie Bartos knew the Kernbergs' youngest son had been sent to France. After the war, she tried time and again to find the boy, yet unlike Egon Col – the liquidator of the family business – she did not manage to determine the child's whereabouts. In the end, she gave up looking for him, but she did keep the documents regardless.

Valerie Bartos died in the spring of 2018, at the age of 98. Quite some time before her death, she would no longer agree to receive any visitors; I was thus not able to interview her for this book, but her son Fritz asked her some questions on my behalf.

"Dear Mrs. Lilly!" Fritz Bartos wrote in typical Viennese fashion in November 2017. "My mother was very surprised when she read the article in the *Kurier*. Actually, it was my father who chanced upon the article, my mother usually only read the *Kronen Zeitung*, a tabloid on Sundays. But as my father also knew about the documents, he called out to my mother in the kitchen: 'I think the *Kurier* writes about something you have.' My mother was then very relieved knowing that matter finally came to a happy conclusion, after all these years."

* * *

"When Arthur learned about the existence of the documents, he reacted with caution at first," my mother recalled. After more than sixty years, receiving a parcel from his parents dating back to a past he had believed forever lost, came as a shock for the 75-year-old. We sent the documents to America with a courier service: Frieda's and

Hermann's passports, business papers regarding the "Aryanization" of the factory, insurance policies, letters, a shipping confirmation to England for some furniture, and photographs. The documents were surprisingly well preserved; having been kept for the past sixty years in a lightproof envelope, the paper had barely yellowed or faded. Valerie Bartos had taken her task as keeper of the documents very seriously, food and tobacco stamps resting untouched amongst the documents.

Holding his parents' papers in his hands after such a long time was an incredible feeling for Arthur and for months, this strike of fate became the major topic of conversation among his circle of friends. "We were all delighted that the box of papers his parents had left with a neighbor was finally returned to him," Gerry Watkins told me years later.

"I know it sounds odd, but I always felt as if Frieda had something to do with it," my mother would often say, later. *Kurier* journalist Josef Gebhard confided in me: "It was moving for me too, I have to say. That I should have been able to play a small part in bringing these two together makes me very happy. Even if handing over these documents was nothing more but a symbol – I still think it was very, very important to Mr. Kern and also to Mrs. Bartos."

The emotional value of these messages from Arthur's family is immeasurable. Yet as it turned out, the parcel from the past bore more than a purely symbolic value. "When I got the documents from Mrs. Bartos, there were several insurance policies which I hadn't been aware of," Arthur explained to me years later. "So I applied for that. They paid out two out of the three and I got about thirty thousand dollars." A late inheritance from his parents.

* * *

Within just two months, Arthur had set foot in his childhood apartment for the first time since his escape and had received a parcel from his parents, the existence of which he had not even been aware. From the start, our friendship was placed under good auspices.

From then on, we began to regularly send each other postcards or emails. In the first years, Arthur would write in a slightly bumpy German, but as I grew up, we switched to English. "Arthur always called at the funniest hours of the day," my mother remembered. "He called at times at which we didn't expect a phone call from Los Angeles because of the time difference. Whenever he couldn't sleep, he would call us in Vienna."

It was extremely important to Arthur – for whom friendship meant family – not to lose contact with us. "Please let me hear from you and Lilly," he would often complain, when we had not written in a long time. "It took so long to find you, we don't want to lose you."

In June 2004, Arthur and my mother were interviewed for yet another article about the *A Letter To The Stars* project, published this time in the Israeli newspaper *Haaretz*. "The Kerns and Maiers are becoming world famous!!!" I read in one of Arthur's emails, which he concludes with the following friendly words: "but enough gossip for today."

Eleven-year-old Lilly Maier being interviewed
about the *A Letter To The Stars* project.

Arthur always felt a strong connection with Austria. "It is my homeland after all," he declared when I asked him about it later. "I have always felt Austrian. Back when I was in France, and also in America, I felt Austrian for a very long time. It was only once I graduated from college that I started feeling American. Even today, I still think of my first homeland very often. Because both Trudie and I were eligible for restitution, we're also getting a monthly pension from Austria."

"One of the things that I felt about that is, if I get my Austrian citizenship back, it would be like a boom to the old Austrian government. And I didn't want that," Arthur told me. Trudie agreed with her husband's view. "'Why do they want to take me back after kicking me out?' But that was the only time Artie and I thought that way about Austria."

Being now in possession of a whole series of documents about his family's story – thanks to Mrs. Bartos' parcel – Arthur wanted to share them with his children and grandchildren. Throughout 2005, he and Trudie made copies, translated the documents, and wrote short explanatory texts. In the end, their work was 200 pages thick, which they had professionally bound. Arthur called the result *The Plunder, the Destruction and the Dispersion of the Hermann Kernberg Family during the Holocaust Years*. He also sent a copy to my mother and me: "We made the book for our family, of which you are now a part."

* * *

In the spring of 2006, Trudie and Arthur planned another trip to Vienna. It was their third visit to Austria and the second time I was to meet them. This time, they did not arrive at the airport, but at the port, having taken a river cruise on the Danube from Romania to Vienna via Hungary. When the *M.S. River Odyssey* docked at the port, Arthur and Trudie were greeted by a stranger, with whom they nonetheless shared a lot: Mrs. Bartos.

"I could finally hug Valerie Bartos and thank her in person," Arthur said, smiling. On the same evening, he visited us on *Gussenbauergasse*. Three years had passed since our first meeting, and yet it seemed to me Arthur had just been with us the week before. "You welcomed me like a family member," he liked to recall even years later.

At the end of their visit, Arthur and Trudie invited all their Viennese friends for lunch. We met at *Grünspan's*, a chic beer garden at the foothills of the Viennese Woods. "I finally had all the players together who were instrumental in the return of the documents my parents had entrusted to Otto Kürth," he wrote in the conclusion of *The Plunder.*

After lunch, Arthur asked a waiter to take a picture of us: Trudie sat on the far left, next to her, frail and tiny Valerie Bartos, and her husband Fritz. My mother and I sat next to them and at the far end of the table, Brigitte and Fritz Kodras. Standing behind my mother and me, Arthur placed a hand on each of our shoulders. Turning around to face us all, he declared, a broad smile on his face: "You are all my Viennese family."

Arthur standing behind his "Viennese family," in 2006:
from left to right, Trudie, Valerie and Fritz Bartos, Sabine
and Lilly Maier, Brigitte and Fritz Kodras.

27. A LETTER TO THE STARS

On May 5, 2003, the Austrian Memorial Day against Violence and Racism in Memory of the Victims of National Socialism, I stand amongst a huge crowd on *Heldenplatz* ("Heroes Square") in Vienna, where, in 1938, hundreds of thousands of Austrians acclaimed Adolf Hitler, after he proclaimed the annexation of "his homeland" to Nazi Germany. Today, exactly 65 years later, 15,000 students have gathered here from all over Austria to take part in a very special commemoration ceremony.

In the past weeks, we have researched the life stories of thousands of victims of the Nazi regime, as part of the *A Letter To The Stars* project. Then we wrote letters to these persons and brought them with us to *Heldenplatz*. My letter is written in the words of an eleven-year-old and addressed to Frieda Kernberg:

Dear Frieda, I live in the apartment you lived in at the time. My room is the piano room. I have met your son Oswald Arthur. He has survived and he is a very kind person. He got married and has three children. His wife is also very nice. He met her at college when she helped him with a math assignment. He found that so amazing that he fell in love with her. I hope you like it in Heaven. Your Lilly.

Heldenplatz is the forecourt of the *Hofburg*, the former city palace of the Habsburg monarchy, today the seat of the Federal President of Austria. Looking around me, I might think I am at a festival: teenagers crowd the lawns, a few teachers and adults among them. A young woman waves a large rainbow banner with "Peace" written on it. Today is not supposed to be a mournful event, but a moving and vibrant commemoration. Actor Harald Krassnitzer (best known for his role as an inspector in the legendary German crime-show, *Tatort*) leads the ceremony, the moving violin solo from *Schindler's List* following a performance from participants of the Austrian talent show *Starmania*.

"Dear students from all over Austria," Leon Zelman, the director of the *Jewish Welcome Service* begins. On May 5, 1945, 58 years ago to the day, Zelman was released from Mauthausen concentration camp. He was seventeen years old and weighed only 83 pounds. "Today you have fulfilled my dream," Zelman declares. "The dream of an Austrian youth stepping out of the shadow of the past and standing up for a world and a country where racism and anti-Semitism have no place. The signal you're sending today can't be any clearer! I am proud of you – I am proud of this new Austria!"[1]

After Zelman's speech, a few students, together with Holocaust survivors, lay stones on the balcony of the Hofburg, in memory of the members of the latters' families, murdered during the war – that same balcony on which Hitler once stood. Then Austrian Federal President, Thomas Klestil, steps onto the stage. "You, dear Students," he begins, "you are detectives of humanity and remembrance – you are giving the victims of the Holocaust a living memorial that future generations will remember. And so, in a sense, we are turning the course of history: during the Nazi regime, names were replaced by numbers, written on the prisoners' clothes; today we – you – return their names and thereby their identities to the victims."

It is twelve-thirty. All over Austria – in every city and every village – the church bells have just rung in commemoration of the victims of the Holocaust. One minute later, gathered on *Heldenplatz*, we release 80,000 huge white balloons – one for each Austrian man and woman murdered by the Nazis during the Holocaust.[2] The balloons rise in huge clouds into the sky, drifting in the wind. Some cover hundreds of miles to Lower Austria, the Czech Republic, Slovakia, Hungary, and even Poland. A few days later, one of these balloons lands in Opole, next to the former ghetto where Arthur's family was detained.

80,000 balloons. So many the sky over Vienna turns completely white for a few minutes, and the entire airspace over the city is blocked. Letters are fastened to the balloons, thousands and thousands of hand-written "letters from the present to the past for the future." Among those letters, the one I wrote to Frieda Kernberg – my very own *Letter To The Stars*.

May 5, 2003: 80,000 white balloons rise into the sky above Vienna – one for every Austrian man and woman murdered during the Holocaust.

* * *

A Letter To The Stars was the biggest school project for contemporary history in Austria. Until today, over 50,000 students have taken part in it, researching the lives of Holocaust victims and survivors. Not only was it the biggest, but it was also the first project of its kind in Austria – and that was in 2003, 60 whole years after the end of the Second World War, and much later than comparable projects in Germany.

For decades, Austria considered itself the "first victim" of National Socialism and the Germans. The so-called Austrian victim myth dates back to the Moscow Declaration of 1943, in which the Allies described Austria as "the first free country to fall victim to Hitlerite aggression."[3] Even though the document also states that "Austria is reminded, however, that she has a responsibility which she cannot evade for participation in the war on the side of Hitlerite Germany," that particular sentence was often overlooked and ignored in Austrian public perception and debate.

In dealing with its past, Austria lagged behind Germany for decades. "The Germans might have kept silent, more or less tenaciously, about their personal state of mind, but on a political level, they were forced to take responsibility. The Austrians, on the other hand, managed to break away from the Germans and the Nazi legacy," Austrian historian Helene Maimann writes in her essay *"Über das Beschweigen der Verbrechen"* (On the Silencing of Crimes).[4]

My mother went to school in Upper Austria in the 1970s. "Every time we would have been about to study the Second World War and National Socialism, summer holidays were about to begin – quite coincidentally," she often told me. "We never managed to get past the 1930s." Things first started to change by the end of the 1980s during the Waldheim Affair.[5] After journalists revealed Kurt Waldheim – then a candidate for the office of Federal Presidency and former UN-Secretary General – had hidden his war past and membership of the *Sturmabteilung* (SA), the whole world suddenly discussed Austria's victimhood. Although Waldheim was elected Federal President by a majority of Austrians, he was completely isolated on the international level, the USA even denying him entry.

In the summer of 1991, Federal Chancellor Franz Vranitzky officially admitted Austria's complicity for the first time: "Austria bears a co-responsibility for the suffering of other people and nations, not as a state, but as inflicted by Austrian citizens," he said, addressing the National Council. "We acknowledge all of our history and the deeds of all parts of our people, the good as well as the evil. As we lay claim to the good, so we must apologize to the survivors and the descendants of the dead for the evil."[6]

A year after Vranitzky's speech, the Republic of Austria commissioned the *Dokumentationsarchiv des Österreichischen Widerstands* (Documentation Centre of Austrian Resistance) to establish a list of the names of all Austrian Holocaust victims. Several historians worked on the project for almost ten years, compiling a database with names, addresses, dates of birth, and deportation destinations for 62,000 people (they couldn't find any information about the 18,000 remaining victims).

In 2002, the *Dokumentationsarchiv* sent a CD-ROM with a copy of the database to journalists, among whom Andreas Kuba (then working at the magazine *NEWS*) and Josef Neumayr, editor-in-chief of the trade magazine *Extradienst.* "We looked at the CD the very same day," Josef Neumayr told me during a conversation in his Vienna apartment, in the fall of 2017. "And it was super impressive. It was a never-ending list of names. Over 62,000 names, names, names."

"From Anna Abel to Sender Zysmanowicz, as I recall," Andreas Kuba added. The names haunted the two journalists, who both felt the need to fill this "austere" list with life. "We cannot bring all these people back to life, but we can give them back their names, faces, and dignity," they thought. And what better way to do so than to inspire the youth of a country that had looked away for so long?

Neumayr and Kuba promptly decided to quit their jobs as journalists and developed the *A Letter To The Stars* project within just a few months. They created a homepage linked to the database and invited schools all over Austria to take part in the project. A search engine enabled the students to search for people who might have had the same name as themselves, attended the same school, or – as in my case – lived in the same apartment.

In many respects, *A Letter To The Stars* was the first time the Austrian Nazi past was discussed extensively on such a large scale. Teachers talked about it with their students, who discussed it with their parents, the debate reaching the heart of the Austrian society. Not everyone shared the opinion that the country was ready for it, though. "We had lots of very interesting discussions at the very highest level," Neumayr recalled. "And God knows I do not wish to denigrate the people we talked to, but the message of very important people of this country was quite clear: 'Leave this be, for God's sake. Don't do it. Don't open the lid.' That a young generation should deal with the Holocaust was simply unconceivable for them."

However, the project was supported by the famous journalist and well-connected editor-in-chief of *NEWS*, Alfred Worm, who managed to involve high-profile supporters and funders for *A Letter To The Stars*. Federal President Thomas Klestil took on the patronage of the project, well-known Holocaust survivors, such as Simon Wiesenthal and Leon Zelman, as well as renowned politicians and clerics joined the support committee. Austrian banks and insurance companies donated large sums of money; even companies such as Siemens or the oil company OMV financed the project.

"The fact the companies had just started to come to terms with their past at the time certainly also played a significant part," Andreas Kuba believes. "Somehow it all fit together." The city of Vienna and the German embassy also contributed financially to the project.

A Letter To The Stars generated enormous interest within the schools. Already in the first year, over 400 schools and 550 classes took part in the project. Overwhelmed by such a massive response, Kuba and Neumayr managed to get some of the historians, who had worked on the creation of the database as members of the commission of historians, into their team. "They worked almost 24 hours a day in our office, answering all the requests from the schools," Kuba told me. One of these historians was Markus Priller.

* * *

In the fall of 2017, I meet Markus Priller in his office at the headquarters of the Austrian Red Cross, where he leads *ProjectXchange*, a follow-up project of *A Letter To The Stars*. I have known Priller since April 2007, when we were together in New York. Ten years later, he still looks the same.

Along with Kuba and Neumayr, Priller became the most important team member of *A Letter To The Stars*. In the beginning, though, the historian had to get accustomed to working with journalists. "Andi's and Josef's journalistic approach was quite challenging," Priller confessed to me. "And then the big event with the balloons, during which the *Starmania* stars performed. I did feel a little uncomfortable about that. But then I realized it was all part of the special quality of the project. I realized there were actually two sides to it: the scientific aspect and the journalistic approach. And these wonderful pictures of the balloons, for instance, were also very important for the survivors."

What the historian valued most, however, was the impact the study of the Holocaust had on Austrian students. "Some students, for instance, would research a person born in 1925," he says to me. "That means the person was fourteen in 1940. And that's when one realizes: the murdered person was the same age as I am today. The horror, the inconceivability of the extermination, it all becomes much clearer to students than when one talks about the Nazis in general. I believe such moments enable us to develop an attitude of responsibility, leaving a longer-lasting impression when dealing with that page of history."

* * *

I was eleven when I took part in *A Letter To The Stars* and wrote a short biography of Frieda Kernberg. I was in my first year of high school at the time and did not have history class yet, the subject being only taught the year after. I was only allowed to be part of the project because my parents knew Kuba and Neumayr. A fortunate coincidence as it turned out: had my mother not signed me up for *A Letter To The Stars*, the article in the *Kurier* would never have been written and Mrs. Bartos would never have found Arthur. "Thanks to the work of an eleven-year-old student, the only thing that is left from his family was returned to Arthur Kern. And that means very, very much to him, today," Neumayr and Kuba wrote in the accompanying text of the anthology *Briefe in den Himmel – Schüler schreiben Geschichte (A Letter to the Stars – Students write History).*[7] The text I wrote about Frieda was also published in the book. "I am deeply moved by the whole book," Arthur wrote to me in an email. "I read what all these kids wrote and think how different things would have turned out if the Austrians in 1938 had shared the same beliefs as these students today. Trudie and I are immensely proud of you, Lilly, for how well you have done. Of the 15,000 students who took part in the project, only 100 stories appeared in the book and your work is one of them. I have read many of these stories with tears in my eyes."

* * *

Originally, *A Letter To The Stars* was supposed to be a one-off action. "We did not want to put something admonishing, big, set in stone out there," Josef Neumayr insisted. "On the contrary, we wanted to create something that would move and touch people and we wanted this touching moment to last in people's memory. Let others build stone monuments – not us."

The project was supposed to be a one-off – the fact it was not was due to chance meetings between students and Holocaust survivors. Like the meeting between Arthur and I.

"I never met Arthur personally, but your story was still one of the most beautiful and inspiring for me, in the *Letter To The Stars* time," Markus Priller confesses during our meeting. "And then that next step, that decision to pursue the project, your story played quite a decisive part in it."

From 2004 on, the history project focused on facilitating exchanges and contact between students and survivors. The *Jewish Welcome Service* provided the project initiators with a list of 2,469 "former Austrians," living all over the world and willing to share their stories with the Austrian youth. From now on, school classes could contact survivors, write letters and emails and possibly even meet with them in person.

"A very important reason why this all worked so well was it was children and teenagers who were interested in the survivors," Andi Kuba explained to me. "Perhaps the survivors wouldn't have shared their story with an adult from Austria, but children are innocent. And that set something in motion, where they said: 'By all means! I want to pass on my legacy.'"

I took part in that second project too, this time writing a double biography of Arthur and Trudie. In the spring of 2004, the two of them sent me a thick envelope, crammed with documents, addressed to *"Fräulein* Lilly Maier." Thanks to these documents and email interviews, I wrote the text *"Eine große Liebesgeschichte inmitten der Leidensgeschichte"* (A great love story amid a tale of sorrow), which was also published in a second *A Letter To The Stars* anthology.[8]

That same year, *A Letter To The Stars* organized the official Liberation Ceremony at the former Mauthausen concentration camp. 20,000 people attended the ceremony – among whom many survivors – ending with the release of hundreds of peace doves soaring in the sky above the former concentration camp.

In 2006, I was fourteen years old and a fourth-grade student in high school. For the first time, I was taught about National Socialism at school and took part in an *A Letter To The Stars* project as part of the school curriculum and not by myself: *Blumen der Erinnerung* (Flowers of Remembrance).

"That was the most beautiful project we did together." Kuba, Neumayr, and Priller agree on this point. The University of Applied Arts installed a screen of roses above a carpet of 100,000 white roses, on which the names of the Austrian victims of the Nazis were projected one night long. On the next day, 25,000 people gathered in the city center – many students, but also interested adults – to pick up roses and take them all over the country, to all the houses where Holocaust victims had lived before their deportation. I laid three white roses in front of the "*Judenhaus*" (Jew-house) on *Nußdorfer Straße 60*, Frieda's, Hermann's, and Fritz's last official home address.

"Especially in Vienna, the roses on the front doors made suddenly – and for the first time – visible how many people were concerned. How many had been killed or deported," Andreas Kuba recalled. "We got a lot of feedback afterward, of people living in these houses starting to get interested in the building's history, as a result of the flowers."

Not all reactions were positive, though. Critics blamed the initiators, claiming the project was overwhelming for the students and trivializing the commemoration of the Holocaust. "Some people even reproached us for having used gas-filled balloons during the event on *Heldenplatz*," Kuba said to me. Especially in the countryside, this coming to terms with history met with no little resistance. "There was this one municipality, where an inhabitant had left a white rose," Markus Priller recounted. "A hairdresser. And she was boycotted afterward by a large part of the local population, just because she had revived that page of history." On the whole, however, the positive reactions by far outweighed the negative ones.

A few survivors, who had traveled from America, especially for the occasion, took part in the roses-project. "People were incredibly moved by that symbolic gesture of laying down roses together with students," Priller recalled. "Afterwards a therapist from San

Francisco, who was working with survivors, called me on the phone, asking 'What did you do with them? It is unbelievable; they came back completely changed, filled with an entirely new sense of life. They talked positively about Austria and now have a completely different take on the subject."

The next project *"Botschafter der Erinnerung"* (Ambassadors of Remembrance) was born out of the wish to enable as many survivors and students as possible to meet. In April 2007, I was among the first group of students, which traveled to New York. Over the course of one week, we met more than 100 Holocaust survivors in the city, many of whom we are still in contact with today. Other groups traveled to London and Israel to meet with former Austrians. One year later, many of the survivors – among whom Kurt and Margaret Goldberger, Johanna Trescher, Arthur, and his friend Aaron – flew to Austria themselves.

Arthur and his best friend, Aaron Low, in Vienna, 2008.

* * *

In 2008, *A Letter To The Stars* planned its biggest event yet, on the occasion of the 70th anniversary of Austria's annexation to Nazi Germany. In early May, the organizers invited two hundred former Austrians to Vienna for one week.

I was 16 at the time and had just met Arthur in Los Angeles a few weeks before. His visit to Vienna was supposed to be his last journey to Austria. Trudie found the long flights too exhausting by then and had stayed at home. Aaron Low accompanied his friend Arthur in her stead.

"Their trip to Vienna a few years ago was a wonderful 'bookend' to the time they spent in France during their early years," Aaron's son, Steve, told me later. "I know how special that trip was to my dad."

Arthur, Aaron, the Goldbergers, Johanna Trescher – for the first time, all "my" survivors were in the same place. So my father could get to know them too, he invited all of us for lunch on May 1. The next few days, I was constantly out with Arthur or one of the others, or else helping out at the imperial *Parkhotel Schönbrunn*, where most of the survivors had been accommodated.

"Are you Arthur's Lilly?" – "Oh, you're Kurt's Lilly?" I would hear time and again when giving someone directions or handing out the program flyer for the day. It seemed everyone I met had heard about me, either from Arthur or from Kurt. The two eighty-year-olds were in a joking mood, as always, and coming up with various bets about which of them I would be visiting next.

Arthur spent the beginning of the week showing his friend Aaron around his native city and introducing him to all the members of his "Vienna family": Brigitte and Fritz Kodras, Valerie and Fritz Bartos, my mother – as well as a newcomer, Ernst Lindner.

In 1938, Ernst Lindner had attended fourth grade at the elementary school on *D'Orsaygasse*, together with Arthur. Arthur and Ernst Lindner had had no contact for almost seventy years, until Lindner – just like Valerie Bartos – read an article about Arthur and me in a newspaper.

"As a child, I had been three or four times in the apartment on *Gussenbauergasse*, at Arthur's and Fritz's," 90-year-old Ernst Lindner told me ten years later, when we met in a Vienna *Kaffeehaus*. "His mother was not a great cook, I remember that," he added, laughing. For two years, Arthur and Lindner had exchanged letters and now, for the first time after all these years, they finally met. "I was very excited," Arthur confessed to me later.

As part of the visit, *A Letter To The Stars* had organized for all survivors to speak before school classes. Arthur would have loved to come to my school, but it was closed on that day, and together with Aaron, we went to Innsbruck instead.

"We spoke before two different groups," Aaron told me later. "Once at a school and then, in the evening, in front of a group of adults." Arthur was very touched by the questions the students asked him. "One of the most interesting questions was presented by a young man, who asked, 'Do you feel more like an American or more like an Austrian?' I answered very honestly that after living in the USA for the last 67 years I feel more American, however, there is a saying in German *'Die Heimat zieht noch immer'* (*Home is calling*). And that is also true for me: Home is still calling.'"

Back in Vienna, I accompanied Arthur to a memorial ceremony at the Parliament, where the Holocaust survivors who had been invited to Austria were guests of honor. "Remembering the events of that time and supporting the people who have to live with the memory of their horrible experiences is a matter of justice," said Federal Council president Helmut Kritzinger. At the same time, a commemoration ceremony for students was held at *Heldenplatz* by *A Letter To The Stars*, and at half past twelve, we walked together the half-mile from the Parliament to *Heldenplatz*, through the *Volksgarten* (People's Garden). Upon their arrival, Arthur, Aaron, Kurt, Margarete, Johanna, and the other survivors were greeted with thunderous applause by thousands of students. More than one had to wipe tears from their eyes.

Huge panels with portraits and quotations from the invited survivors had been set up all around *Heldenplatz*. The following sentence was written on Arthur's panel: "If the Austrians in 1939 had been like the Austrians today, in 2008, I would not have been orphaned and I would still be an Austrian today!"

Vienna, May 2008: panels with quotations by Austrian Holocaust survivors commemorate the victims of the Nazis.

* * *

The invitations in 2008 were the last large-scale project organized by *A Letter To The Stars*. Quite unexpectedly and much to the team's surprise, it had come beforehand to very violent public attacks

against the project on the part of institutions who had once supported it, like the *Dokumentationsarchiv* or the *Jewish Welcome Service*.

"The *Jewish Welcome Service* hates us," Joseph Neumayr explained
to me during one of our conversations in 2017. "Leon Zelman always
loved us, but after his death, the *Jewish Welcome Service* had a big
problem with us."

Andi Kuba agreed, saying: "In retrospect, they must have felt
threatened by us. They probably thought we would do something
like this more often – inviting survivors. Which would have deprived
them of their business, so to speak."

Fueled by the *Jewish Welcome Service* and the *Dokumentationsarchiv*, a press campaign was launched for several months against
A Letter To The Stars, psychologists and historians reproaching the
project for inviting the survivors to Austria, thus allegedly trauma-
tizing them anew, and exploiting them for high-media spectacle
purposes.[9] *A Letter To The Stars* was also criticized for accepting
donations from "guilty" companies that had employed concentration
camp prisoners during the Nazi period and would now "exploit" the
project to improve their image.[10] Public outrage was so great a few
companies withdrew their donations to the project.

"Many survivors we had invited stood up for us then," Kuba
described to me. "They explained: 'We're adults, we know what we're
doing. We know we won't be traumatized anew.' And then the mood
slowly began to change again. In the end, it was a very beautiful
event, even though I'm still disappointed to this day by some people's
attitude – people who work in the same field as us."

* * *

Despite all the quarrels, in the end, *A Letter To The Stars* perma-
nently changed the remembrance culture in Austria. "These young
people, along with the project organizers, have achieved something
that had never been achieved before on such a broad scale," Betsy

Anthony from the *United States Holocaust Memorial Museum* in Washington, D.C. declared. "And this commemorative work brings solace and inner peace to the survivors."[11]

Neumayr, Kuba, and Priller also insist on the fact that people's take on history changed within a very short time. "If you're still so stupid today to deny the Holocaust, then you're in the dark corner of society. And I think that's right, that's where these people belong," Josef Neumayr declares. "And that was a very rapid development – we have only launched *A Letter To The Stars* fifteen years ago."

Arthur often told me *A Letter To The Stars* was "a wonderful project." For him, as well as for dozens of other Holocaust survivors I have met over the years, the project was an incredibly moving and reconciliatory experience, having young people from their native country come up to them, wanting to know about their story.

The project had also a lasting impact on us – the now adult youth. Among the thirty students who went to New York with me, three became historians. I for one never really wondered what course of study I would choose, being interested in history since I was eleven years old. The fateful encounter with Arthur awakened my interest in contemporary history, but it was my taking part in *A Letter To The Stars* that showed me what historical work involves. I researched Frieda Kernberg's life story when I was eleven years old, Arthur and Trudie's when I was twelve, and then when I was fifteen, I visited for the first time an archive, ahead of the New York trip. I met many other survivors through the project – incidentally, many of them had also left on a *Kindertransport*. And so it happened that I decided, years later, to write my bachelor thesis on the after-effects of the *Kindertransports*. In my master's thesis, I studied the French *Kindertransport* and wrote a biographical study based on Arthur's example. And now, having almost finished writing this book, I will start working on my doctorate in Jewish history.

Many Austrian and German students complain today, saying National Socialism and the Holocaust are taught far too extensively. Yet at the same time, recent studies have shown that forty percent of German and two-thirds of American teenagers do not know what Auschwitz was.[12] Indeed it is by no means a problem of the Holocaust being taught too extensively at schools rather than the subject not properly reaching the students. This is exactly why projects such as *A Letter To The Stars*, or visits of Holocaust survivors at schools are of such great importance. This is why I completed a training program in 2012 to be a guide at the Dachau Concentration Camp Memorial Site, leading dozens of school classes through the site every year. For many of them, it is the first time they hear about National Socialism outside the classroom.

* * *

In May 2005, an excerpt of the text I wrote about Arthur and Trudie for *A Letter To The Stars* was published in the magazine *NEWS*.[13] A few days later *A Letter To The Stars* received an email from a young woman.

"I have just read the story about Arthur Kern, published in *NEWS*, and I decided to write to you on the spot," the message began. "I come from Bosnia and I am 24 years old. I have experienced war as well, and I know what misery and suffering it causes. I was thus all the more moved when I read the stories of these people. Stories that preserve what many people today may have suppressed or forgotten, or might not even want to admit, believing war can never happen to them. That's what I thought too. And yet today, ten years after the end of the war in my country, I wonder whether my inner war against what I have experienced will ever come to an end… Because anyone who has ever seen the true face of war knows that you carry it within you your whole life. War does not only destroy cities and villages, claiming countless human lives. No, it also takes the dreams, the innocence, and the carefreeness of those who have survived it. Leaving behind scarred human souls… Why am I writing to you? Because I was deeply touched by your action which has given me hope that one day we might live in a world free of hate and destruction. If we all take to heart what the survivors of each war have to say. Your project made this possible. I would like to thank you for this!"

EPILOGUE

"That's it!" I declare around four o'clock in the afternoon. "I have no more questions."

It is the day after Thanksgivukkah in November 2013 and we are still sitting in the festively decorated hotel lobby. Six hours have passed since the beginning of my interview with Arthur, six hours during which we have also sustained ourselves at Katella Deli, a Jewish restaurant famous for its oversized Reuben sandwiches.

"You're kidding! You got it all done?" Trudie asks, astonished.

"Yes!" Just to be on the safe side, I cast a glance at my list of questions one last time, but it is true. "Or is there anything you would like to add, Arthur?"

"Just this one thing," the 85-year-old replies. "It is such a wonderful feeling for Trudie and me, having watched you grow from a child to an impressive young lady." Then he laughs and gets up to hug me.

* * *

In the summer of 2011, three years after Arthur's last visit to Vienna, I move to Munich and begin my history studies. Two years later,

Arthur falls seriously ill. But after several operations, he almost entirely recovers. Even aged 85, he will not be defeated and soon everyone at the hospital is accustomed to his jokes and pranks. In November 2013, I see Arthur at the Kerns' Thanksgivukkah party, and in February 2014 I visit him in his new apartment at the *Senior Living Community*, where he moved to with Trudie a few days before.

Lilly Maier and the extended Kern family during the wedding of Arthur's granddaughter Sami in 2022.

For Arthur, leaving his house in North Hills – where he has spent 55 years – is very painful. "It was very hard on Dad," his son Aaron tells me later. "You can imagine for anyone growing up with that experience, stability and security were paramount." Trudie likes her new home from the start, yet it is a few months before Arthur settles in. But then he livens up and makes a lot of new friends who quickly come to love him and his crazy sense of humor.

In early summer 2015, Arthur once again experiences health issues and at the start of July, the 86-year-old is admitted to a hospital. At the time, I am preparing my move to New York where I will study journalism from August on. "Dad is now in the convalescent hospital and is doing well," Aaron writes to me on July 15. A few days later, though, the doctors diagnose an incurable form of leukemia, giving Arthur only a few weeks to live.

Arthur is well aware of his situation: he draws up a list of those he wants to say goodbye to personally and constantly tries to cheer up the people around him with his jokes. "Dad is ready to go," Aaron writes to me. Dozens of people visit him at the hospital in the following days: Arthur's friends, former colleagues, and of course, his OSE family. In a video that Danny shot at the hospital, Arthur holds Trudie's hand and sings the *Kern Family Song* with a booming voice. Everyone chimes in for the "Boom-Killy-Vitsky" chorus.

On August 3, Arthur is released from the hospital and sent back home with hospice care, so he can be surrounded by his family. Two days later I book a flight to see Arthur one last time. But I am too late. He dies on August 6.

I am at my grandparents' at Lake Attersee when Aaron calls to tell us the sad news. "Lilly?" he asks as I pick up the phone. At first, I think Arthur is on the phone. Aaron's voice sounds just like his father's.

A few days before, my mother and I spoke to Arthur for the last time. Arthur and I have been speaking English together for years, yet this time we do not. Arthur wants to speak German one last time, his childhood language. "You are one of the best things that have happened to me in my life, Lilly," Arthur says. I cry, but he is composed. "If I don't make it till you are here and we don't see each other anymore, I want to say *Servus* to you. I love you more than anything. Bye-bye!"

* * *

Three weeks after Arthur's death, I fly to Los Angeles to be with Trudie, Aaron, David, Danny, and all the others. Just like Arthur would have wanted it, it is not a mournful visit. We sit together and tell each other stories, remembering how Arthur's song sheet caught fire on Hanukkah, because he sat too close to the candle, and laughing a lot as we recall his countless attempts to trick and fool Trudie.

Lilly, with Arthur and Trudie in their new home in the
Senior Community, in Los Angeles, 2014.

I would like to visit Arthur's grave, but there is none. "Both my parents had decided they wanted to be cremated and after both passed, combine the ashes and have them sent out to sea," Aaron tells me. Arthur also did not want a funeral, wishing for his friends and family to hold a party instead. A few months after his death, according to his wish, the Kerns host a big *Celebration of Life* party.

Over 80 people gather on October 25, 2015, in one of the common rooms of the *Senior Living Community*. Aaron and Ellie Low are there, as well as Norbert and Marion Rosenblum, Dale and Dell Carpenter, Morris and Renee Eisenberg, Fred and Ileene Weiss, Susie Katz, and her son. No one wears black on that day, everyone has come dressed in colorful clothes. Pictures of Arthur's long life hang on the walls and as is usual at Jewish festivities, there is plenty to eat. One by one, friends and relatives rise to their feet and tell what influence Arthur has had on them.

"Live, love, laugh – that was our father's code," Danny, the youngest Kern son says. "Helping others and bringing smiles to their faces, that was his gift and his passion. But it was his special love for Mom which gave true meaning to his life. She was his rock, his perfect match – and whatever he accomplished, they accomplished together." Danny glances over to Trudie, who smiles just like the rest of the people gathered in the room.

"And even though we did not have the good fortune of knowing his parents, our grandparents, Hermann and Frieda, and his older brother, our uncle Fritz, we know they are looking proudly upon Pops and his legacy of kindness, generosity, and laughter," Danny continues. "One more thing: as most of you know, Dad, together with Mom, made lots of friends over the course of their lives. I'd like to share a story of such a friendship that has quite a few curious and unexpected twists and turns."

For the next twenty minutes, Danny goes on to describe how Arthur received the envelope containing his parents' documents, thanks to a chain of chance encounters and friendships. "Dad couldn't have been happier than when Lilly wrote a letter to his mother Frieda," Danny says, talking about *A Letter To The Stars*. "That's a truly wonderful story... but it doesn't end there!" As Danny describes how Valerie Bartos recognized the picture in the *Kurier*, a whisper goes through the room. "A chance meeting in Turkey, leading to a chance visit to my father's childhood home in Vienna, which in turn incidentally allows a woman to recognize Frieda's picture and read about my father, who happens to have survived the Holocaust. That's the kind of stuff life is made of! My father's life!" Danny concludes. "A man who reached out to others and made friends everywhere he went."

Arthur's extended family on Thanksgiving 2015, a few months after he passed away. First row from left to right: Leslie, AJ, Trudie, Shira. Second row from left to right: Elise, Danny, Rachel, Alex, Cash, David, Nena, Aaron, Sami.

* * *

It is springtime and the chestnuts are in bloom in *Grünspan*, the beer garden in Vienna to which Arthur once invited his "Vienna family." The *Ottakring* cemetery is just around the corner. In May 2018, as I write the last pages of this book, I want to go there and visit the grave of my Viennese grandparents. But I somehow lose my way inside the hilly cemetery with its many twisting turns and paths and suddenly find myself standing before the grave of a Kern family. The grave looks abandoned; clearly, no one has tended to it for quite some time. On impulse, I decide to lay down my flowers here. My grandparents would certainly understand it, and Arthur having no grave himself, I am finally able to bring "him" flowers for the first time. Squinting at the sun, it seems to me I can hear Arthur chuckle in the distance. From the grave, one enjoys a wonderful view of Vienna. I think he would have liked it here.

Arthur knew I would write this book about him. "Promise me something," he asked me shortly before he died. "Promise me you will translate the book into English." It was important to him that his children and grandchildren would be able to read his story.

I am immensely sad that Arthur himself could not read this book. That he will never learn what I discovered about his time in France. That he will never be able to leaf through his New York foster care record, the existence of which he was not even aware. That he will never read what his friends and life companions had to say about him.

Working on his biography, I felt incredibly close to Arthur, as if he was still alive, in a way. Now that I have completed this book, I hope many other people will read his story – and thus keep it alive.

It would have meant a lot to Arthur to find that not only he but also numerous members of his OSE family appear in the book. And above all Aaron Low, his "brother," who died three years after him. Arthur's story, the story of the French *Kindertransport* children is the story of an extraordinary rescue. It seems almost unbelievable, in retrospect, how many people, organizations, and tireless commitment it actually took to save Arthur and the other Jewish refugee children. As adults, the former OSE protégés became successful Americans, family fathers, and lifelong friends.

After all the terror and the murder of his family, Arthur still grew up to become a happy man, a man full of optimism and the ability to forgive. Because even though he had experienced, in early childhood, how brutal and inhuman people can be, he was also given the opportunity to discover how generous and selfless they can be – in the OSE homes. "In spite of Nazism and cruel dictatorship, we never gave up believing in the humanity of mankind," Ernst Papanek wrote in 1965 in a letter to his former protégés. "You were and you are the proof for this belief."[1]

* * *

On November 25, 2016, Rachel, Shira, and I are comfortably seated in a cozy sofa in their parents' living room, in Seal Beach. It is Black Friday, the day after Thanksgiving and although it is already early afternoon, we are still in our pajamas, sharing two large blankets. We have reached episode two of the *Gilmore Girls* Thanksgiving special, *A Year in the Life*, and argue over our favorite characters. Aaron pops in from time to time and shakes his head, faced with our obsession with the series.

Before episode three begins, I get up to fetch some leftovers from yesterday's feast from the fridge for us. It is my third Thanksgiving at the Kerns – after having been strictly restricted to chopping vegetables the year before, I was entrusted this year with the baking of the quite complex pumpkin pie. "Turkey tastes better cold anyway," Shira mumbles, as I return to the living room, carrying a huge plate. Her mother Leslie joins us and we all start to make woolen holiday ornaments.

On the next day, we drive over to Trudie for brunch, where we also meet the rest of the Kern family. Once again, Trudie has booked the table right in the middle of the *Senior Living Community* restaurant, so everyone can see how big her family is. Before we order our food, Trudie presents every woman with a silk scarf she painted herself, having shortly before begun to follow in *Mutti*'s artistic footsteps.

Shira and I tell about our studies, Rachel talks about her new job in a start-up in San Francisco. Sami shows pictures she has taken six months before when we visited *Universal Studios* together. "Do you remember the crazy stories Grandpa used to come up with about the scar on his leg?" Alex asks and we all start to laugh. The kids fidget on their chairs, but the prospect of hot chocolate is enough to persuade them to remain seated.

"Are you coming for Thanksgiving next year?" little AJ asks me. I will. And the year after. And the year after.

STOLPERSTEINE

On May 11, 2023, a little over 20 years after my first meeting with Arthur, and five years after this book was first published in German, a very special ceremony took place in Vienna. A group of people – among them my mother, Aaron and Leslie Kern, along with friends and volunteers – gathered right in front of our old building in *Gussenbauergasse* 1 to lay four *Stolpersteine*, or stumbling stones, for Arthur's family.

Stolpersteine are brass cubes, or plates, inscribed with the names and years of birth and death of men and women murdered by the Nazis. They are usually put in front of the persons' last dwelling place. These memorial stones were first initiated in 1992. As of today, far over 100,000 stones have been laid in Austria, Germany and 30 other European countries.

At the end of my speech during the inauguration ceremony, I said: "I am so happy that Arthur's oldest son Aaron and his daughter-in-law Leslie are here with us today. It is actually Aaron's 70th birthday today; what a nice way to celebrate it by honouring his late father, his uncle and his grandparents.

Despite everything, Arthur loved Vienna and I am sure he would have appreciated us setting these stones today to show the connection his family had to this house, and to honour their memory. We decided to make a fourth stone for Arthur and to use his birthname on it, so he can be remembered here, together with his parents and brother."

Lilly Maier, Aaron and Leslie Kern attended the inauguration ceremony for the *Stolpersteine* for the family of Arthur Kern. The stones read:

"Here lived: Frida Kernberg (nee Goldfeld), born Dec. 26, 1897. Deported to Opole on February 2, 1941. Murdered in the Holocaust.

Hermann Kernberg, born Oct. 11, 1894. Deported to Opole on February 2, 1941. Murdered in the Holocaust.

Fritz Kernberg, born Dec. 19, 1925. Deported to Opole on February 2, 1941. Murdered in the Holocaust.

Oswald Kernberg, born Oct. 19, 1928. Saved by a *Kindertransport* to France 1939."

REMARKS

Arthur Kern's papers comprise two parts: on the one hand, a book compiled for his family (*The Plunder, the Destruction and the Dispersion of the Hermann Kernberg Family during the Holocaust Years*), which includes a collection of letters and documents he translated himself. (Arthur donated some of these documents to the *Simon Wiesenthal Center* in Los Angeles, where they are available for the public.) The second part of his papers includes unsorted letters, documents, certificates and official documents, photo albums, and autobiographical short stories, all of which are kept by Arthur's widow, Trudie, and their eldest son, Aaron. I consulted and analyzed the entire material in November 2015 and August 2016. The documents from Arthur's papers are not mentioned specifically in the following notes, as they are not publicly accessible. Copies of all documents are in my possession. A few of these documents (mainly photographs and letters) Arthur brought to America himself as a twelve-year-old. The chief part of it, though, he obtained decades later, through his own research, from various organizations among which OSE, IKG, the Quakers, and the Vienna City Administration. Arthur also received letters his parents sent to relatives who had already managed to emigrate and who gave them to him years later.

Between the fall of 2013 and the spring of 2018, I conducted dozens of interviews with Arthur's family members and friends, as well as with historians and archivists. Unless otherwise stated, the quotations in this book are taken from these interviews. Copies and transcripts of the interviews are in my private possession.

I was able to consult files on OSE, on the *Israelitische Kultusgemeinde Wien* (IKG), and on the Quakers at the *United States Holocaust Memorial Museum* (USHMM), the originals of which are kept in the archives of the organizations themselves. The *Wiener Gewerbeamt* (Magistratsabteilung 63) provided information about the Kernbergs' factory. Ernst Papanek's papers are kept at the *New York Public Library*, available in their local archive system under the following denomination: *Ernst Papanek Papers. Manuscripts and Archives. The New York Public Library. Astor, Lenox and Tilden Foundations* (hereinafter referred to as EPP). The files of OSE's American branch (AMEROSE), as well as the files of the *German Jewish Children's Aid* (GJCA) are kept at the *YIVO Institute for Jewish Research* in New York. Arthur's 130-page foster care record is not publicly available; a copy of it is in my private possession. In the following notes, I use abbreviations of the archives, as well as their own classification system. Much of the quoted literature is German, and while the quotes have been translated, the notes refer to the original titles and page numbers.

NOTES

PART 1 – VIENNA

"WE HAD A GREAT LIFE!"

1 Statistik Austria: Average annual population 1870-2016, http://www. statistik.at/web_de/statistiken/ menschen_und_gesellschaft/ bevoelkerung/bevoelkerungsstand_ und_veraenderung/bevoelkerung_ im_jahresdurchschnitt/022311.html (consulted on May 23, 2017).

2 Vocelka, Karl: Geschichte Österreichs. Graz, 2000, p. 279-285.

3 Zweig, Stefan: Die Welt von Gestern. Erinnerungen eines Europaers. Frankfurt/Main, 1985, p. 58.

4 Habres, Christof: Jüdisches Wien. Entdeckungsreisen. Vienna, 2011, p. 35.

5 Malleier, Elisabeth: Jüdische Frauen in Wien, 1816-1938. Vienna, 2003, p. 15. Orthodox Judaism was more strongly represented in Austria than

it was in Germany. Between 1900 and 1934, 20 to 30% of all Viennese Jews were orthodox.

6 General Cadaster File Samuel Hersch Kernberg.Vienna 1928-1961. MA 63, GISA Service Center Archive.

7 Schubert, Kurt: Die Geschichte des österreichischen Judentums. Vienna, 2008, p. 118.

8 Botz, Gerhard: Nationalsozialismus in Wien: Machtübernahme, Herrschaftssicherung, Radikalisierung. 1938/39. Vienna, 2008, p. 58 and p. 99-105.

9 The "Decree on the Swearing-in of Austrian Civil Servants" ("Erlass über die Vereidigung der Beamten des Landes Österreichs") of March 15, 1938, matched the

German "Law for the Restoration of the Professional Civil Service" ("Gesetz zur Wiederherstellung des Berufsbeamtentums") of April 7, 1933. Likewise, the so-called Nuremberg Race Laws applied in Austria from May on; an "office for genealogical research" ("Gauamt für Sippenforschung") was created in Vienna for purposes of verification. See: Schubert: Die Geschichte, p. 118.

10 Ibid., p. 115-117; Botz: Nationalsozialismus in Wien, p. 126-136. The prevalence of violence and so-called "wild," namely unauthorized, aryanizations on the part of "normal citizens" got so much out of control that on March 14, 1938, the Nazi leadership in Vienna ordered the SS to take action against it.

11 Habres: Jüdisches Wien, p. 35.

12 Botz: Nationalsozialismus in Wien, p. 502-523.

GETTING THE CHILDREN OUT

1 The emigration questionnaires are preserved at the archive of IKG in Vienna, a digital copy is kept at the USHMM. There are two forms concerning the Kernberg family, bearing the identification numbers 27361 and 28670.

2 Cadaster File Kernberg, MA 63.

3 Law on the appointment of administrative commissioners and supervisors ("Gesetz über die Bestellung von kommissarischen Veraltern und kommissarischen Überwachungspersonen"). In: Gesetzblatt für das Land Österreich (Ostmark), April 13, 1938. Historical law and legislation texts online, Österreichische Nationalbibliothek.

4 Protective custody or preventive detention were euphemistic terms used by the Nazis to refer to people who had been arrested by them without a court order.

5 Samuel Kernberg's proxy to the Comité Israélite pour les Enfants, Feb. 22, 1939. RG-43.113M, 28, USHMM.

6 IKG: List of the urgent cases to France, 1939. A/W 1986, RG-17.017M, USHMM.

7 Unless otherwise specified, all of the following information in this chapter is taken from the correspondence of the Viennese IKG, record A/W 1986, RG-17.017M, USHMM.

8 Schmid, Claudio: Certificat Médical March 1, 1939. RG-43.113M, Reel 28, USHMM.

9 Interview Arthur Kern, July 12, 1995, Los Angeles, USC Shoah Foundation.

10 Maier, Lilly: Frieda Kernberg – "Ich wohne heute in ihrer damaligen Wohnung," in: A Letter To The Stars (ed.): Briefe in den Himmel – Schüler schreiben Geschichte. Vienna, 2003, p. 122-124, here p. 123.

LEAVING VIENNA

1 Lindenbaum, Walter: Von Sehnsucht wird man hier nicht fett. Texte aus einem jüdischen Leben, ed. by Herbert Exenberger. Vienna, 1998, p. 78-80.

2 Unless otherwise specified, all of the information in this chapter is taken from the correspondence of the Viennese IKG, record A/W 1959 and A/W 1986, RG-17.017M, USHMM.

3 Göpfert, Rebekka: Der jüdische Kindertransport von Deutschland nach England 1938/39. Geschichte und Erinnerung. Frankfurt/Main, 1999, p. 76-77.

4 Becker, Hanna: Martha Wertheimer und ihr Wirken nach der "Kristallnacht," in: Kingreen, Monica (ed.): "Nach der Kristallnacht": Jüdisches Leben und antijüdische Politik in Frankfurt am Main 1938-1945. Frankfurt on the Main, 1999, p.87-211, here p. 199.

PART 2 – FRANCE

THE *KINDERTRANSPORT*

1 Baumel-Schwartz, Judith Tydor: Never Look Back: The Jewish Refugee Children in Great Britain, 1938-1945. West Lafayette, 2012, p. 5; Id.: Unfulfilled Promise. Rescue & Resettlement of Jewish Refugee Children in the United States 1934-1945, Alaska, 1990, p. 15; Göpfert: Kindertransport nach England, p. 60-61.

2 Heinrich Himmler Circular, Dec. 31, 1938. BArch R 58/276 Bl. 289. Quoted from: Göpfert: Kindertransport, p. 66.

3 Concerning foster families, see: Ibid., p. 114-123; Concerning exile schools: Feidel-Mertz, Hildegard: Identitätsbildung und Integration. Exilschulen in Großbritannien, in: Benz, Wolfgang (ed.): Die Kindertransporte 1938/39, p. 102-119.

4 Curio, Claudia: „Unsichtbare" Kinder. Auswahl- und Eingliederungsstrategien der Hilfsorganisationen, in: Benz, Wolfgang and Andrea Hammel (eds.): Die Kindertransporte 1938/39. Rettung und Integration, p. 60-81, here p. 63; Göpfert: Kindertransport nach England, p. 91-92.

5 Baumel-Schwartz: Never Look Back, p. 4.

6 List of all the *Kindertransports* organized by the IKG from Dec 10, 1938 to August 22, 1939. A/W 1964-1, Reel 878. RG-17.017M, USHMM.

7 IKG: Die Frage der jüdischen Kinder und Jugendlichen in Wien. [Spring 1939]. 100044, Reel 252, RG-17.007M. USHMM, p. 4; Society of Friends: Report of the Children's Department of the

Friends Centre, Vienna. Nov. 38 – Sept. 39. RG-59.027M, USHMM, p. 1; Hofreiter, Gerda: Allein in die Fremde: Kindertransporte von Österreich nach Frankreich, Großbritannien und in die USA 1939-1941. Innsbruck, 2010, p. 40-44.

8 Curio: "Unsichtbare" Kinder, p. 65.

9 Schwarz, Rosa Rachel: Aus der Sozialarbeit der Gemeinde Wien unter Hitler 1940. 0.1/73, Bad-Kaduri-Collection, Yad Vashem, p. 6.

10 Interview with Franzi Danneberg-Löw, interview collection of the Dokumentationsarchiv des Österreichischen Widerstands. See also: DÖW (ed.): Erzählte Geschichte. Volume 3: Jüdische Schicksale. Vienna, 1993.

11 Hofreiter: Allein in Fremde, p. 108.

12 Curio: "Unsichtbare" Kinder, p. 72.

13 Ibid., p. 78.

14 Decker, Kerstin: Heinrich Heine: Narr des Glücks. Berlin, 2005, p. 291.

15 Unless otherwise specified, all of the information in this chapter is taken from the correspondence of the Viennese IKG, record A/W 1985 und A/W 1986, RG-17.017M, USMM.

16 Hofreiter: Allein in Fremde, p. 82.

17 Ibid., p. 83.

18 The transport was initially meant to take place on the 21st and that date is erroneously stated on many IKG documents.

19 The play is also available in book form: Mona Golabek: The Children of Willesden Lane. Beyond the Kindertransport: A Memoir of Music, Love and Survival. New York, 2002.

ARRIVAL IN PARIS

1 IKG Youth Welfare Office, Paris, March 6, 1939, Comité, A/W 1986, USHMM.

2 Most of the books on OSE were written by OSE itself, which might make it more complicated to objectively verify statements. It is therefore advisable to consult biographies of individual OSE members, written by independent historians. For example: Göbetzberger, Claudia: Dr. Ernst Papanek – Widerstand im Dritten Reich. Leben, Werk und Exil eines österreichischen Sozialdemokraten, Vienna University, 2005.

3 Hazan, Katy: Rire le jour, pleurer la nuit. Les enfants juifs cachés dans la Creuse pendant la guerre, 1939 – 1944. Paris, 2014, p. 11-13.

4 There is a certain measure of confusion in literature, as to what exactly the abbreviation OSE stands for in France. Alternatively, the name "Union des Sociétés pour la protection de la santé des populations juives" is sometimes indicated, but that is the French name of the Union OSE and not the name of the French branch of OSE. Regarding OSE's work in France, see: Hazan, Katy and Klarsfeld, Serge: Le sauvetage des enfants juifs pendant l'Occupation, dans les maisons de l'OSE, 1938-1945 / Rescuing Jewish children during

the Nazi occupation: OSE children's homes, 1938-1945. Paris, 2009.

5 Hazan: Rire le jour, p. 11-14.

6 Hazan/Klarsfeld: Le sauvetage 1938-1945, p. 13 and 71.

7 Göbetzberger: Dr. Papanek, p. 113.

8 Pogranova, Slavka: Ernst Papanek und die Kinder von Montmorency, Sorbonne Paris, 2002, p. 21.

9 Papanek, Ernst: with Edward Linn: Out of the Fire. New York, 1975, p. 45-46.

10 Id.: Die Kinder von Montmorency. Frankfurt/Main, 1983, p. 49.

11 Comité: Institutions welcoming children coming from Vienna, March 22, 1939. A/W 1986, RG-17.017M, USHMM.

12 OPEJ, http://www.opej.org/fr/Pages/histoire-et-Mémoire.aspx (consulted on 08.07.2017).

13 All quotes of Erich Grünebaum/Eric Greene in the entire book are taken from: The Loneliest Boy. Durango, 2000. The book is unpublished and does not have any page numbers.

VILLA HELVETIA

1 Comité to IKG Welfare Office, Paris, April 6, 1939, A/W 1985, USHMM.

2 Trude Frankl Report, April 1939. A/W 1985, RG-17.017M, USHMM, p. 3-4.

3 Göbetzberger: Dr. Papanek, p. 110f.

4 Interview Arthur Kern, 1995, USC.

5 Papanek, Ernst: One Year Children's Houses of the OSÉ. Montmorency 1940. The report is written in English. It is a photo album and therefore there are no page numbers. EPP, Box 41.

6 Ibid.

7 Things seen in Paris. How Hope and Encouragement are brought to the Refugees. In: The World's Children. The Official Organ of the Save the Children Fund and of the declaration of Geneva. Vol. 19. London, June 1939.

8 Frankl report, USHMM, p. 3f.

ERNST PAPANEK: MORE THAN JUST A TEACHER

1 Göbetzberger: Dr. Papanek, p. 8 and 20.

2 Hansen-Schaberg, Inge und Papanek, Hanna (ed.): Ernst Papanek. Pädagogische und therapeutische Arbeit. Kinder mit Verfolgungs-, Fucht und Exilerfahrungen während der NS-Zeit. Vienna, 2015, p. 7.

3 Hanna Papanek: Als Jugendliche in den OSE Heimen: Geschichte und Geschichten zu Ernst Papanek, in: Hansen-Schaberg, Inge (ed.): Ernst Papanek. Vienna, 2015, p. 173-270, here p. 234 and 242.

4 Göbetzberger: Dr. Papanek, p. 83-85.

5 Hazan: Rire le jour, p. 100-101.

6 Papanek: Out of the Fire, p. 42.

7 Hazan/Klarsfeld: Le sauvetage 1938-1945, p. 74.

8 Ibid., p. 71.

9 Hammel, Andrea: Familienbilder im Spannungsfeld. Autobiographische

Texte ehemaliger Kindertransport-Teilnehmer, in: Benz, Wolfgang and Curio, Claudia (ed.): Die Kindertransporte 1938/39. Rettung und Integration. Frankfurt /Main, 2003, p. 168-200, here p. 191; Feidel-Mertz: Identitätsbildung und Integration. Exilschulen in Großbritannien, p. 104; Wexberg-Kubesch: Vergiss nie, p. 59.

10 Hazan: Rire le jour, p. 100-101.And: Papanek: Kinder von Montmorency, p. 98.

11 Göbetzberger: Dr. Papanek, p. 126.

12 Pogranova: Papanek und die Kinder, p. 57. And: Papanek, Ernst: Jüdische Jugend in einer Welt des Krieges und der Verfolgung (Juni 1944), in: Hansen-Schaberg, Inge (ed.): Ernst Papanek. Vienna, 2015, p. 61-79.

13 Göbetzberger: Dr. Papanek, p. 20-21; Hansen-Schaberg, Inge: „Sie waren unentbehrlich" – Ernst Papanek und die Rettung traumatisierter Kinder, in: Bildung und Erziehung 62 (2009), p. 105-122, here p. 111-116.

14 Papanek: Fire, p. 48. *Out of the Fire* was completed after Papanek's death by ghostwriter Edward Linn and Papanek's family, unfortunately resulting in the distortion of some of the sources. Direct quotes from Ernst Valfer or Hanna Papanek, for example, were wrongly attributed to various persons. Pseudonyms were also used sometimes, without referring to them as such. Regardless, *Out of the Fire* is a major source, as it presents in great detail Papanek's views and opinions, and in particular his educational methods.

15 Göbetzberger: Dr. Papanek, p. 146; Pogranova: Papanek und die Kinder, p. 58.

16 Rühl-Nawabi, Gabriele: Pädagogische und therapeutische Grundlagen: Die Rezeption des individualpsychologischen Ansatzes Alfred Adlers durch Ernst Papanek, in: Hansen-Schaberg, Inge (ed.): Ernst Papanek. Vienna, 2015, p. 34-39, here p. 38.

17 Papanek, Ernst: Die Kinderfürsorge der OSE. 500 Refugeekinder aus Frankreich nach den Vereinigten Staaten. New York, 1940, p. 3.

18 Hanna Papanek: Als Jugendliche, p. 213.

19 Rühl-Nawabi: Papaneks Adler Rezeption, p. 36.

20 Papanek: Fire, p.126-28.

21 Ibid., p. 64.

22 Hazan/Klarsfeld: Le sauvetage 1938-1945, p. 74. And: Pogranova: Papanek und die Kinder, p. 54-55.

23 Ivanov, Alexander: ORT, in: Diner, Dan (ed.): Enzyklopädie jüdischer Geschichte und Kultur 4 (Ly-Po). Darmstadt, 2013, p. 444-449. OSE and ORT have been closely linked since their creation in Russia, both moving their offices to Berlin after the Russian Revolution.

24 One Year OSÉ, EPP, Box 41.

25 Göbetzberger: Dr. Papanek, p. 136.

26 The papers of Ernst Papanek were divided in two parts and entrusted to two different archives: one part is kept at the *New York Public Library*, and another part at the International Institute for Social History, in Amsterdam. In the field of the Papanek and OSE research, I am the only researcher who has analyzed the New York papers, every other work

referring only to the Amsterdam documents.

27 Papanek: Fire, p. 107-108.
28 Göbetzberger: Dr. Papanek, p. 196.
29 Frankl Report, USHMM, p. 4.
30 Papanek: Kinder von Montmorency, p. 105.
31 For an edited and published version of the house rules, see: Hansen-Schaberg/Papanek (ed.): Ernst Papanek, p. 50-52.
32 One Year OSÉ, EPP, Box 41.
33 Hanna Papanek: Als Jugendliche, p. 180; Papanek: Fire, p. 140.
34 Papanek: Fire, p. 116-117. And : Göbetzberger: Dr. Papanek, p. 134-135.
35 Pogranova: Papanek und die Kinder, p. 3.

VILLA LA CHESNAIE IN EAUBONNE

1 Comité to IKG, Paris, March 13, 1939, Comité, A/W 1986, USHMM.
2 Krohn, Helga: „Holt sie raus, bevor es zu spät ist! " Hilfsaktionen zur Rettung jüdischer Kinder zwischen 1938 und 1940, in: Kingreen, Monica (ed.): „Nach der Kristallnacht." Jüdisches Leben und antijüdische Politik in Frankfurt am Main 1938 – 1945. Frankfurt/Main, 1999, p. 91-118.
3 Frankl Report, USHMM, p. 3.
4 Kanner, Mia Amalia. With: Kugler, Eve Rosenzweig: Shattered Crystals. Lakewood, 2009, p. 103
5 Interview Arthur Kern, 1995, USC.
6 Papanek: Fire, p. 54-56.
7 Göbetzberger: Dr. Papanek, p. 128-129; Hanna Papanek: Als Jugendliche, p. 257.
8 Papanek: Fire, p. 63.
9 Regarding Anna Feigenbaum Krakowski, see: Hanna Papanek: Als Jugendliche, p. 254-60.
10 Papanek: Fire, p. 58.
11 Ibid., p. 59-61.
12 Hanna Papanek: Als Jugendliche, p. 251.

THE SUMMER OF 1939

1 Herlin, Hans: Die Tragödie der St. Louis. Munich, 2001; Mautner Markhof, Georg J. E.: Das St. Louis-Drama. Graz/Stuttgart, 2001.
2 Schröder, Gustav: Heimatlos auf hoher See. Berlin, 1949.
3 Papanek: Fire, p. 64.
4 Mautner Markhof: St. Louis, p. 128; and: Die Passagiere der „Saint-Louis" erzählen..., In: Pariser Tageszeitung, June 23, 1939.
5 Papanek: Fire, p. 79.
6 Transcripts of letters from children in the homes, France, 1939-1940. EPP, Box 5.
7 All following descriptions are based on photographs of the OSE children's homes photographs, Montmorency. EPP, Box 41.
8 Papanek: Fire, p. 86.
9 Ibid.
10 Aus der Pariser Emigrantenkolonie. In: Pariser Tageszeitung. Paris, June 15, 1939.

11 Letter from an anonymous thirteen-year-old girl in Eaubonne, EPP, Box 5.

12 W., E.: Montmorency-Poem 1939, EPP, Box 8.

THE BEGINNING OF THE WAR

1 Friedemann, Bedürftig: Chronik des Zweiten Weltkriegs. Gütesloh/Munich, 2009, p. 14-17.

2 Papanek: Kinder von Montmorency, p. 25.

3 Papanek: Fire, p. 15-17.

4 Interview Arthur Kern, 1995, USC.

5 Corazza, Stephanie: The Routine of Rescue: Child Welfare Workers and the Holocaust in France. Phil. Diss. University of Toronto, 2017, p. 2.

6 Papanek, Hanna: Elly und Alexander: Revolution, Rotes Berlin, Flucht, Exil – eine sozialistische Familiengeschichte. Berlin, 2006, p. 119.

7 Hazan/Klarsfeld: Le sauvetage 1938-1945, p. 73.

8 Papanek: Fire, p. 28.

9 See: Heimsoeth, Hans-Jürgen: Der Zusammenbruch der Dritten Französischen Republik: Frankreich während der „Drôle de Guerre" 1939/1940. Bonn, 1990.

10 One Year OSÉ, EPP, Box 41.

11 Vormeier, Barbara: Frankreich, in: Krohn, Claus-Dieter (ed.): Handbuch der deutschsprachigen Emigration 1933-1945. Darmstadt, 1998, p. 213-250, here p. 232-233.

12 See: Maierhof, Gudrun (ed.): Aus Kindern wurden Briefe – Die Rettung jüdischer Kinder aus Nazi-Deutschland. Berlin, 2004.

13 Papanek: Fire, p. 14.

14 Interview Arthur Kern, 1995, USC.

15 Bourrel: Eaubonne : Les enfants juifs de la Chesnaie, April 23, 2010, p. 10.

16 Friedemann: Chronik des Zweiten Weltkriegs, p. 50-62.

17 Göbetzberger: Dr. Papanek, p. 147-149.

18 Papanek: Fire, p. 169.

FLIGHT TO THE SOUTH

1 As of January 2017: Names of Righteous by Country, in: Yad Vashem, www.yadvashem.org/righteous/statistics.html (consulted on May 6, 2018).

2 Corazza: Routine of Rescue, p. 23.

3 Papanek: Fire, p. 170.

4 Ibid., p. 173.

5 Göbetzberger: Dr. Papanek, p. 151.

6 Kanner: Shattered Crystals, p. 104.

7 Papanek: Fire, p. 178-179.

8 Ibid., p. 182-185. Not much is known about Jean-Louis de Neuville. He is described as a patriot and an observant Catholic. In 1944, he fell as a common soldier during the combats for the liberation of France. See: Kiener, Michael C. and Plas, Pascal (ed.): Enfances Juives: Limousin-Dordogne-Berry. Terres de refuge 1939-1945. Saint-Paul, 2006, p. 373-374.

9 Interview Arthur Kern, 1995, USC.

10 Göbetzberger: Dr. Papanek, p. 153.

11 Kanner: Shattered Crystals, p. 105.

12 Gurvic to Papanek, Vichy, June 14, 1940. EPP, Box 5.

CHÂTEAU DE MONTINTIN

1 Papanek: Kinder von Montmorency, p. 132.
2 Documents about the ceasefire with France, in: Max-Planck-Institut für Ausländisches Öffentliches Recht und Völkerrecht (ed.): Zeitschrift für ausländisches öffentliches Recht und Völkerrecht. Vol. 10. Berlin/Leipzig, 1940, p. 851-856, here p. 855-856; Wetzel, Juliane: Frankreich, in: Benz, Wolfgang (ed.): Lexikon des Holocaust. Munich, 2002, p. 75-76, here p. 75-76.
3 Papanek: Fire, p. 138-139 and 196-197.
4 Krohn, Claus-Dieter: Vereinigte Staaten von Amerika., in: Krohn (ed.): Handbuch der deutschsprachigen Emigration 1933-1945. Darmstadt, 1998, p. 446-466, here p. 454.
5 Regarding the description of the flight, see: Papanek: Fire, p. 204-211.
6 Regarding the famous escape route, see: Lackner, Herbert: Die Flucht der Dichter und Denker. Wie Europas Künstler und Wissenschaftler den Nazis entkamen. Vienna, 2017, p. 119-127.
7 For a list of all 320 children who lived at some point in the *Montintin* OSE home, see: Kiener/Plas (ed.): Enfances Juives, p. 430-441.
8 Ibid., p. 351.
9 Kanner: Shattered Crystals, p. 288.
10 Kiener/Plas (ed.): Enfances Juives, p. 404.
11 Papanek: Fire, p. 198-199. Just like he did for many of the adults, Papanek gave Asta a pseudonym, referring to her as "Lucia" in his book.
12 Wetzel, Juliane: Gurs, in: Benz, Wolfgang (ed.): Lexikon des Holocaust. Munich, 2002, p. 94, here p. 94.
13 All the letters of the children in this chapter: EPP, Box 5.
14 Hazan/Klarsfeld: Le sauvetage 1938-1945, p. 103.
15 Hazan, Katy and Allali, Michèle: Une mémoire pour le futur – 90 ans de l'OSE. A Legacy for the Future – 90 Years of OSE. Paris, 2003, p. 33; Hansen-Schaberg, Inge: Kindheit und Jugend, in: Krohn, Claus-Dieter (ed.): Handbuch der deutschsprachigen Emigration 1933-1945. Darmstadt, 1998, p. 81-94, here p. 84.

"IT *VRAIMENT* SUCKS!"

1 Kiener, Michael C. and Plas, Pascal (ed.): Enfances Juives: Limousin-Dordogne-Berry. Terres de refuge 1939-1945. Saint-Paul, 2006.
2 Kanner: Shattered Crystals, p. 128.
3 Hazan/Klarsfeld: Le sauvetage 1938-1945, p. 104.
4 All letters to and from Papanek quoted in this chapter: EPP, Box 5.
5 Hanna Papanek: Als Jugendliche, p. 257.
6 Papanek: Fire, p. 189.
7 Hazan/Klarsfeld: Le sauvetage 1938-1945, p. 20.

8 Kiener/Plas (ed.): Enfances Juives, p. 356.

9 Hazan/Klarsfeld: Le sauvetage 1938-1945, p. 24.

10 Kanner: Shattered Crystals, p. 119.

11 Miki: Im Montintiner Heime (New Year 1941). Acc. 2000.187, USHHM.

12 Sigmund Freud Museum: Freuds verschwundene Nachbarn. Vienna, 2003, p. 15.

13 DÖW: Opole, http://ausstellung. de.doew.at/b207.html (consulted on April 4, 2018).

14 Wetzel: Frankreich, p. 75; and: Marrus, Michael Robert Paxton:

Vichy France & The Jews. New York, 1981.

15 Corazza: Routine of Rescue, p. 24.

16 Wetzel: Gurs, p. 94.

17 Hazan, Katy: Le sauvetage des enfants juifs de France vers les Amériques, 1933-1947, in: Harter, Hélène (ed.): Terres promises: mélanges offerts à André Kaspi 2008, p. 481-493, here p. 19.

18 See her captivating biography: Samuel, Vivette: Rescuing the Children. A Holocaust Memoir. Madison, 2002.

19 Hazan/Allali: 90 Years OSE, p. 35.

AMERICA AS A LAST HOPE

1 Rotholz, Horst: Purimgedicht. Acc. 2000.187, USHMM.

2 Göbetzberger: Dr. Papanek, p. 159.

3 AMEROSE founding notification, Dec. 31, 1940. GJCA, RG 249, MKM 8.11/187, YIVO. AMEROSE sent out a founding document for their taking over hiring of OSE's worldwide agenda. The date of 1940 is therefore often erroneously mentioned in the literature, as the foundation date of the American branch of OSE, instead of 1929.

4 See: Graham, Otis: Unguarded Gates: A History of America's Immigration Crisis, Lanham, 2003.

5 Baumel: Unfulfilled Promise, p. 27-31.

6 Zucker, Bat-Ami: Frances Perkins und die amerikanische Flüchtlingspolitik 1933 bis 1940, in: Maierhof, Gudrun, (ed.): Aus Kindern wurden Briefe – Die Rettung jüdischer Kinder aus Nazi-

Deutschland. Berlin, 2004, p. 165-185, here p. 172-173.

7 Regarding GJCA, see: Hartig, Christine: Zwischen Emigrationshilfe und Amerikanisierungserwartung – Die Arbeit der German Jewish Children's Aid, in: Feustel, Adriane and Hansen-Schaberg (ed.): Die Vertreibung des Sozialen. Munich, 2009, p. 130-151; and: Ostrovsky, Michal: "Children Knocking at Our Gates": "German Jewish Children's Aid" and the Rescue Activity of the American Jewish Community during World War Two. Phil. Diss. Bar Illan, Israel, 2012; From 1942 on, renamed to European Jewish Children's Aid.

8 Number of Admitted Children per Year, January 1, 1942. GJCA, RG 249, MKM 8.1/10,YIVO.

9 Ostrovsky, Michal: "We Are Standing By": Rescue Operations of the United States Committee for

the Care of European Children, in: Holocaust and Genocide Studies 29 (2015), p. 230-250, here p. 232.

10 There is no standardized abbreviation for USCOM. The organization often referred to itself as "US Committee," while the Quakers used USCOM. Tydor Baumel-Schwartz shortens the name to USC, which is confusing, as this is the official abbreviation used for the Unitarian Service Committee. I follow Ron Coleman's example and use USCOM.

11 Ostrovsky: Standing By, p. 237-238.

12 Allen Bonnel to James G. Vail, Marseille, June 18, 1941. ASFC, USHMM.

13 Baumel: Unfulfilled Promise, p. 59; Corazza: Routine of Rescue, p. 51; Hobson Faure, Laura: Attentes européennes, réalités américaines: L'émigration des enfants de l'OEuvre de Secours aux Enfants de la France occupée vers les États-Unis, 1941-1942, in: Hazan, Katy (ed.): L'Oeuvre de Secours. Paris, 2014, p. 166-183, here p. 170.

14 Baumel: Unfulfilled Promise, p. 51; Hartig: Arbeit GJCA, p. 134-135.

15 Memo about arrival of SS Mouzinho children, August 2, 1941. GJCA, RG 249, MKM 8.27/481, YIVO.

16 Ostrovsky: Standing By, p. 239.

17 Zeitoun, Sabine: L'Oeuvre de Secours aux Enfants (O.S.E.) sous l'occupation en France – Du légalisme à la résistance, 1940-1944. Paris 1990, p. 139; Hansen-Schaberg, Inge: Lebensgeschichtliche Hintergründe zur pädagogisch-politischen Arbeit Ernst Papaneks und Anmerkungen zu seinem Werk, in: Papanek,

Hanna (ed.): Ernst Papanek. Vienna, 2015, p. 11-31, here p. 15; Baumel: Unfulfilled Promise, p. 83-84.

18 Papanek to AFSC, New York, January 15, 1941. AMEROSE, RG 494, 549.2/62, YIVO.

19 Bussang, Marion: Papa Papanek's 500 Children. They Suffer in Europe but He Hopes to Save Them. In: New York Post, Dec. 26, 1940.

20 This list was not available in the files, but a later list, established for the second transport, referred to the numbers given to the children on the 500 names list, thus enabling me to ascertain that Oswald bore the number 35. Compare: List of children, candidates for emigration to the United States. 2nd Transport, July 10, 1941. AMEROSE, RG 494, 549.2/27, YIVO, p. 4.

21 Unless otherwise specified, all of the information in this chapter is taken from correspondence of Papanek, OSE, AMEROSE and GJCA. See: EPP, Box 5 and 6, as well as AMEROSE, RG 494, 549. 1/1 and 8/104 and 2/27, YIVO and GJCA, RG 249, MKM 8.1/12 and 8.16/290, YIVO.

22 OSE was not the only organization that sought to send its protégés to America. The children also came from the homes run by the Rothschilds, the Unitarians and the Secours Suisse, some even directly from French internment camps.

23 Hazan/Klarsfeld: Le sauvetage 1938-1945, p. 26.

24 Corazza: Routine of Rescue, p. 55.

25 Ibid., p. 78; Hazan, Katy and Weill, Georges: The OSE and the Rescue of Jewish Children, from the Postwar to the Prewar Period, In: Jacques

Semelin (ed.): Resisting Genocide. The Multiple Forms of Rescue. New York [u.a.], 2011, p. 245-263, here p. 255.

26 Interview with Anna Fiedler, June 19, 1984, DÖW Interview collection.

27 Göbetzberger: Dr. Papanek, p. 161-163.

28 All information concerning Oswald is hereafter taken from the Oswald Kernberg file, kept at the OSE archive or at the USHMM (RG-43.113M, Reel 28).

JOURNEY TO FREEDOM

1 List of the 100 children sent to the USA, June 1941; and Union OSE to AMEROSE, Montpellier, [1941]. Both: AMEROSE, RG 494, 549.2/27, YIVO.

2 Hans Singer and others to Oswald Kernberg, Marseille, May 25, 1941. Postmark dated from June 26, 1941. Arthur Kern Collection, Simon Wiesenthal Center, 90-123A/18.

3 Allen Bonnel to James G. Vail, Marseille, June 18, 1941. ASFC, USHMM.

4 Hazan: Rire le jour, p. 72.

5 Letters to Papanek, EPP, Box 5 and 6.

6 Kanner: Shattered Crystals, p. 128.

7 Ibid., and p. 237.

8 Ibid., p. 133

9 Ireny Lowy to Lotte Marcuse, August 15, 1941. GJCA, RG 249, MKM 8.27/481, YIVO.

10 Chomski, Isaac: Memoirs. RG-10.206.01.12, USHMM.

11 Gumpert, Laura: Humble Heroes: How the American Friends Service Committee struggled to save Oswald Kernberg and three hundred other Jewish children from Nazi Europe. Senior Thesis, Haverford College, 2002, p. 22-23.

12 Kanner: Shattered Crystals, p. 135.

S.S. MOUZINHO

1 Quoted from Lackner: Flucht der Dichter und Denker, p. 129.

2 Chomski, RG-10.206.01.12, USHMM.

3 Unless otherwise specified, all information in this chapter is taken from the letters of the Quakers. See: Acc. 1995.A.0368.1, USHMM. And: AMEROSE RG 494, 549.1/1, YIVO.

4 A camino da Colonia, June 1941. In: O Século. Acc. 2015.365.1, USHMM.

5 Gumpert: Humble Heroes, p. 22.

6 Kanner: Shattered Crystals, p. 135; Baumel-Schwartz, Judith Tydor: Jewish Refugee Children in the USA (1934-1945): Flight, Resettlement, Absorption, in: Gigliotti, Simone and Tempian, Monica (ed.): Young Victims of the Nazi Regime; Migration, the Holocaust, and Postwar Displacement. London, New York, 2016, p. 12-37, here p. 26.

7 Morris Troper to Eleanor Roosevelt, Lisbon, June 7, 1941. RG 249, MKM 8.27/482. GJCA, YIYO.

8 Affidavit in Lieu of passport for Oswald Kernberg, 1941. GJCA, RG 249, MKM 8.28/498, YIVO. And: New York Passenger Lists, 1820-1957, Records of the U.S. Customs Service, Record Group 36. National Archives at Washington, D.C. Microfilm 6574, p. 125. Consulted via Ancestry.com.

9 Lillian Traugott to Lindsley Noble, Philadelphia, August 20, 1941; Quoted from Gumpert: Humble Heroes, p. 12.

10 Cahier de Dessin (drawing book). Arthur Kern Collection, Simon Wiesenthal Center, 90-123 A/12.

PART 3 – NEW YORK

ARRIVAL IN NEW YORK

1 Unless otherwise specified, the following information in this chapter is taken from the correspondence between OSE and GJCA. See: EPP, Box 5 and 6. Also: AMEROSE, RG 494, 549.1/4, YIVO. Also: GJCA, RG 249, MKM 8.5/85 and 8.27/481, YIVO.

2 45 Exiled Children Arrive on Liner. In: New York Times, September 3, 1941.

3 Hansen-Schaberg: Hintergründe Papanek, p. 16.

4 Hobson Faure: Attentes européennes, p. 178-179.

5 Wexberg-Kubesch: Vergiss nie, p. 13.

6 Hansen-Schaberg: Sie waren unentbehrlich, p. 106.

7 Papanek: Fire, p. 241.

8 Baumel-Schwartz: Unfulfilled Promise, p. 64

9 Baumel-Schwartz: Jewish refugee children USA, p. 29.

10 All following information on GJCA and Oswald is taken from Oswald Kernberg's classified foster care file. GJCA, RG 249, YIVO.

THE FATE OF FRIEDA, HERMANN, AND FRITZ KERNBERG

1 DÖW: Deportationen Wien-Opole, Februar 1941: „...in diesem elenden Nest," https://www.doew.at/erinnern/fotos-und-dokumente/1938-1945/deportationen-wien-opole-februar-1941-in-diesem-elenden-nest (consulted on April 4, 2018).

2 DÖW: Opole. And: Götz, Aly: Die Verfolgung und Ermordung der europäischen Juden durch das nationalsozialistische Deutschland 1933-1945. Vol. 9: Polen. Generalgouvernement August 1941-1945. Munich/Oldenburg, 2014, p. 15.

3 Spector, Shmuel (ed.): The Encyclopedia of Jewish Life Before and During the Holocaust: K-Sered. New York, 2001, p. 939.

4 Moser, Jonny: Die Judenverfolgung in Österreich 1938-1945. Vienna, 1966 (DÖW publication), p. 23.

5 Götz: Polen 1941-1945, p. 17.

6 DÖW: Opole.

A YOUTH IN NEW YORK

1 Unless otherwise specified, all information about Oswald in this chapter is taken from the classified Oswald Kernberg foster care file. GJCA, RG 249, YIVO. General information on OSE and GJCA is taken from the correspondence: AMEROSE, RG 494, 549.5/65, YIVO and GJCA, RG 249, MKM 8.27/480, YIVO. Also: EPP, Box 5 and 6.

2 US Bureau of the Census: Sixteenth Census of the United States, 1940, T627, Page 8A; Enumeration District: 3-1446. National Archives and Records Administration, Washington, D.C.

3 Hazan/Weill: OSE Rescue, p. 245-263.

4 Hobson Faure: Attentes européennes, p. 174.

5 Hazan/Weill: OSE Rescue, p. 255

6 Hazan/Klarsfeld: Le sauvetage 1938-1945, p. 32-36; Hazan/Weill: OSE Rescue, p. 256.

7 See the list established by Hanna Papanek: Als Jugendliche, p. 267-69.

8 Papanek: Fire, p. 31.

OSWALD BECOMES ARTHUR

1 Unless otherwise specified, all information about Oswald Kernberg in this chapter is taken from the classified Oswald Kernberg foster care file. GJCA, RG 249, YIVO.

2 Indicator 1947. Yearbook Stuyvesant High School, p. 14.

3 AFSC: Refugee Case File 20274, Oswald Kernberg. Acc. 2002.296, USHMM.

4 Service Européen des Recherches to OSE, Paris, Feb. 20, 1948; Wulman to J. Eisenstaedt, New York, March 24, 1948. RG-43.113M, 28, USHMM.

5 Cadaster document Kernberg, Vienna City Office MA 63.

6 Certificate of naturalization of Oswald Arthur Kern, Dec. 18, 1950. Soundex Index to Petitions for Naturalization filed in Federal, State, and Local Courts located in New York City, 1792-1989. The National Archives at New York City.

PART 4 – LOS ANGELES

THE KERN FAMILY

1 109 Consecutive Engine Tests Run at Santa Susana. In: Valley Skywriter Nr. 13, April 3, 1959.
2 NASA Langley Research Center's Contributions to the Apollo Program, https://www.nasa.gov/centers/langley/news/factsheets/Apollo.html (consulted on April 28, 2018).

THE GREAT REUNION

1 All information in the following chapter is taken from a video recording and two memory books about the "50th OSE-St. Louis Reunion" sent to all participants after the event.
2 Henry Schuster's quotes are taken from: Kaplan, Gabriella: Children of Special Blessing. 200 youngsters were taken from Nazi Germany and reunited 50 years later. In: The Jewish Journal, May 12, 1989, p. 31-32, here p. 32.
3 Kanner: Shattered Crystals, p. 238.
4 OSE exists until today and is mainly active in France. In 2017, the Jewish social organization was awarded the *Grand Prix Humanitaire* from the renowned *Institut de France*.

LIFE AFTER THE *KINDERTRANSPORT*

1 Hansen-Schaberg: Kindheit und Jugend, p. 82.
2 Göpfert: Kindertransport nach England, p. 13.
3 Letter from Eric Green, March 1981. Quoted from: Baumel-Schwartz: Unfulfilled Promise, p. 140.
4 Sonnert and Holton present their very exciting results in the book: What Happened to the Children Who Fled Nazi Persecution. New York, 2006. The book focuses on the children who were able to flee Nazi Germany and Austria in the 1930s and 1940s and emigrate to the United States, many among them with the help of the *Kindertransports*. For the information described hereafter, see the chapter "Socioeconomic Achievements," p. 65-92.
5 Barnett, Ruth: Familiengedächtnis. Erste und zweite Generation in der therapeutischen Praxis, in: Benz, Wolfgang (ed.): Die Kindertransporte 1938/39. Rettung und Integration. Frankfurt/Main, 2003, p. 156-170, here p. 165.
6 Sonnert/Holton: What Happened, p. 187-193; Also: Barnett, Ruth: Therapeutic Aspects of Working Through the Trauma of the Kindertransport Experience, in: Hammel, Andrea (ed.): The

Kindertransport to Britain 1938/39. New Perspectives. Amsterdam, New York, 2012, p. 157-171, here p. 157.

7   An analysis of the memory book is also available online: OSE Children In Foster Homes: Statistical Survey, in: Shattered Crystals, http://www.shatteredcrystals.net/sc_ose4.htm (consulted on May 6, 2018).

8   Whiteman, Dorit Bader: The Uprooted: A Hitler Legacy: Voices of Those Who Escaped Before the "Final Solution." Cambridge, 2001, p. 406; Barnett: Therapeutic Aspects, p. 163; Moskovitz, Sarah: Making Sense of Survival: A Journey with Child Survivors of the Holocaust, in: Krell, Robert (ed.): Messages and Memories. Reflections on Child Survivors of the Holocaust. Vancouver, 1999, p. 11-21, here p. 16.

9   Kröger, Marianne: Kindheit im Exil. Ein Forschungsdesiderat, in: Benz, Wolfgang (ed.): Die Kindertransporte 1938/39. Rettung und Integration. Frankfurt/Main, 2003, p. 17-33, here p. 18; Wexberg-Kubesch: Vergiss nie, p. 13.

10 How do you define a Shoah survivor?, in: Yad Vashem, http://www.yadvashem.org/yv/en/resources/names/faq.asp. And: Survivors and Victims, in: USHMM, https://www.ushmm.org/remember/the-holocaust-survivors-and-victims-resource-center/survivors-and-victims (both consulted on May 6, 2018).

11 Wexberg-Kubesch: Vergiss nie, p. 14.

12 Curio: „Unsichtbare" Kinder, p. 60.

ARTHUR AND HIS FAMILY

1   54 percent according to Shepard, Helga: The Kindertransport Survey. The Results of the Survey. New York, 2000. See also: Fast, Vera: Children's Exodus. A History of the Kindertransport. London, New York, 2011, p. 170.

2   Moskovitz: Making Sense, p. 16.

3   84 percent according to: AJR Kindertransport Survey, https://ajr.org.uk/kindertransport-survey/ (consulted on May 9, 2018); 87 percent according to: Shepard: Kindertransport Survey; 92 percent according to: Sonnert/Holton: What Happened; and 93 according to the participants in the OSE-Reunion: OSE Children In Foster Homes: Statistical Survey.

4   Drucker, Olga: Kindertransport Association Conference 2010 – Enduring Impact. In: Kinder-Link, Volume 21, Winter 2011, p. 1-8, here p. 8.

5   Barnett: Familiengedächtnis, p. 168.

6   Ibid.

7   Sonnert/Holton: What Happened, p. 162.

8   Into the Arms of Strangers: Stories of the Kindertransport. Directed by Mark Jonathan Harris. USA, 2000. And: My Knees Were Jumping. Remembering the Kindertransports. Directed by Melissa Hacker. USA, 1996.

A PARCEL FROM THE PAST

1 Mozes Kor, Eva: The Power of Forgiveness. Las Vegas, 2021. The first two quotes are taken from the German edition: Die Macht des Vergebens. Salzburg, 2016, p. 82, 113 and 116.

2 Maier, Lilly: Frieda Kernberg – „Ich wohne heute in ihrer damaligen Wohnung," in: A Letter To The Stars (ed.): Briefe in den Himmel – Schüler schreiben Geschichte. Vienna, 2003, p. 122-124.

3 Gebhard, Josef: Brief an die ermordete Vorbewohnerin. In: Kurier, May 3, 2003.

4 Id.: „Er war von seiner Rückkehr fest überzeugt". In: Kurier, May 12, 2003.

A LETTER TO THE STARS

1 For transcripts of all the speeches, see: A Letter To The Stars (ed.): Briefe in den Himmel – Schüler schreiben Geschichte. Vienna, 2003.

2 Many books mention 65,000 Austrian Holocaust victims, as 65,000 Austrian Jews have been killed during the Holocaust. *A Letter To The Stars* talks about 80,000 people, adding to the number of victims other groups of persecuted and murdered people (such as Sinti and Roma, homosexuals, disabled persons, political opponents etc.).

3 Karner, Stefan and Tschubarjan, Alexander: Die Moskauer Deklaration 1943: „Österreich wieder herstellen". Vienna, 2015, p. 162.

4 Maimann, Helene: Über das Beschweigen der Verbrechen, in: A Letter To The Stars (ed.): Holocaust – Die Überlebenden. Schüler schreiben Geschichte. Vienna, 2005, p. 211-214, here p. 212.

5 Concerning Waldheim, see: Lehnguth, Cornelius: Waldheim und die Folgen. Der parteipolitische Umgang mit dem Nationalsozialismus in Österreich. Frankfurt/Main, 2013.

6 Kriechbaumer, Robert (ed.): Österreichische Nationalgeschichte nach 1945: Die Spiegel der Erinnerung, die Sicht von innen. Vienna, 1998, p. 97-98.

7 A Letter To The Stars (ed.): Briefe in den Himmel, p. 263.

8 Maier, Lilly: Eine große Liebesgeschichte inmitten der Leidensgeschichte, in: A Letter To The Stars (ed.): Holocaust – Die Überlebenden. Schüler schreiben Geschichte. Vienna, 2005, p. 126-131.

9 Event mit „Kirtagscharakter". In: Standard, Dec. 20, 2007.

10 A Letter To The Stars – Eine Kritik der Lagergemeinschaft Ravensbrück & FreundInnen, https://www.ravensbrueck.at/wp-content/uploads/2015/06/OeLGRF_Kritik-Lettertothestars2006.pdf (consulted on May 10, 2018).5,10]]}}}],"schema":"https://github.com/citation-style-language/schema/raw/master/csl-citation.json"}

11 Anthony, Betsy: Sie bringen den Überlebenden Frieden, in: A Letter To The Stars (ed.): Holocaust – Die Überlebenden, p. 246-247, here p. 247.
12 Vier von zehn Schülern wissen nicht, was Auschwitz ist. In: Welt, Sept. 28, 2017. And: Zauzmer, Julie: Holocaust study: Two-thirds of millennials don't know what Auschwitz is, In: Washington Post, April 12, 2018.
13 Maier, Lilly: Den Hass im Herzen besiegen, in: NEWS Nr. 18 (2005), p. 68-69.

EPILOGUE

1 : Papanek to former OSE children, New York, Dec. 15, 1965. EPP, Box 5.

ACKNOWLEDGEMENTS

My special thanks go to Arthur's family, who is looking forward to this book at least as much as I do and who has supported me for years. Trudie, Aaron, David, Danny, Leslie, Nena, Elise, Alex, Sami, Rachel, and Shira – *I love you guys*!

My wonderful agent, Christine Proske from *Ariadne-Buch*, managed to find a home for *Arthur and Lilly* within a few weeks after we first met and has since then tirelessly supported and accompanied me. My thanks also go to the entire *Heyne* team who made that original book possible and to Tracy Ertl and Lori Preuss of TitleTown Publishing for helping me fulfill Arthur's dying wish in making this English version reality, so his family will finally be able to read it. Thank you to Dominique Rotermund, who did a wonderful job translating this book. I could not have had more luck in finding a person so talented with words and who at the same time shares such a deep understanding of the rescue operations that saved Arthur and all the other children. This is to endless rounds of emails and discussing the best possible ways to translate children's poems without losing their little peculiarities. Maybe we will do it again sometime!

A few aspects of *Arthur and Lilly* are based on my research at the *Ludwig-Maximilians University* in Munich, under the supervision of Dr. Mirjam Zadoff and Prof. Michael Brenner. Thanks to Betsy Anthony, Vincent Slatt, Ron Coleman, and Megan Lewis from the *United States Holocaust Memorial Museum*; Katy Hazan and Dominique Rotermund from OSE; Jessica Pigza and Katie O'Connell from the *New York Public Library*; Susanne Uslu-Pauer from the Archive of the Jewish Community in Vienna; Susie Mamzhi from the *Simon Wiesenthal Center*; Gunnar Berg from YIVO, and Christine Vecchio from the *Staten Island Museum*.

My thanks also go to Christine and Isabelle Allertshammer, who transcribed my numerous interviews, and to Levi Ufferfilge for his tireless explanations of Judaism.

My mother Sabine invited Arthur into our home – and into our lives – and signed me up for *A Letter To The Stars*. Without her, Arthur and I would not have become friends and I would never have written about our story. Thank you for that and so much more!

My wonderful test readers have accompanied me for months in the writing of this book. Huge thanks to Roxy, Karen, and Tine from my writing group – Sophia, who read my first text about Arthur, and above all, Katrin, for identifying all my Anglicisms, Austrianisms, and otherwise twisted thoughts. Thanks to my father Wolfgang, without whom I would never have made it through the final correction phase.

It has been a special experience for me to visit the places in which Arthur used to live. Thanks to David de Lassagne and Jean-Claude, who enabled me to visit *Montintin*; Marie-Caroline and Liv Soavina, for their tour of *Villa La Chesnaie*, and Julien Trotet, as well as the entire police station of Montmorency, for the nice hours I have spent there.

I have interviewed dozens of people for this book – adult OSE children, friends of Arthur's, as well as historians: thanks to Ernst Valfer, Otto Kernberg, Lisl Terner, Eric Greene, Norbert and Marion Rosenblum, Gus and Hanna Papanek, Suzie Katz, Dale and Dell

Carpenter, Siegfried Knop, Elfriede Schloss, Fred and Ileene Weiss, Ernst Lindner, Esther Starobin, Friedrich Bartos, Fritz Kodras, Carol Low, Gerry Watkins, Janet Taylor, Andrea Low, Don Davis, Laura Hobson Faure, Gerda Hofreiter, Marsha Rozenblit, Ellen Levitt, Gerhard Sonnert, Ruth Koob, Peter Halban, Katrin Sippel, Josef Gebhard, Josef Neumayr, Markus Priller, and Andi Kuba.

I would like to draw special attention to Arthur's best friend, Aaron Low, who helped me along the way, but who, sadly, did not witness the publication of this book. I feel certain Arthur and he are sitting somewhere on a cloud, playing tricks on each other. As always.

PHOTO CREDITS

p. 8: Sabine Maier

p. 348: Kurier/Gerhard Deutsch

pp. 2, 301: Lilly Maier

pp. 357, 368: Verein Lernen aus der Zeitgeschichte

pp. 16, 17, 19, 24, 30, 46, 153, 195, 226, 231, 233, 255, 261, 266, 273, 277, 287, 290, 292, 311, 354, 365: Private Archive of Arthur Kern

pp. 5, 139: OSE/ Mémorial de la Shoah, fonds privé Oswald Kernberg

pp. 75, 78, 79, 94, 121: Ernst Papanek Papers, The New York Public Library. Courtesy of the United States Holocaust Memorial Museum Photo Archives.

pp. 77, 86, 90, 95, 149: OSE/ Mémorial de la Shoah

p. 124: OSE/ Mémorial de la Shoah, fonds privé José Ainouz

pp. 211, 216: Simon Wiesenthal Center Archives Los Angeles, California

pp. 38, 180, 188: OSE/dossier personnel Kernberg

pp. 199, 205: Collection of the newspaper O Século, Álbuns Gerais n. 81, Dok. 1807P (p. 199) and Dok. 1836P (p. 205), both: PT / TT / EPJS / SF / 001-001- / 0081 / 1807P. Courtesy of ANTT

pp. 334, 336: Rachel Kern

pp. 52, 219, 376, 333, 382: Private Archive of Lilly Maier

pp. 16, 268, 378: Private Archive of Trudie Kern

p. 207: United States Holocaust Memorial Museum, 59625, courtesy of Milton Koch

ABOUT THE AUTHOR & TRANSLATOR

Photo by Sophia Lindsey

Lilly Maier was born in Munich, Germany, in 1992 as the daughter of Austrian journalists. She holds an MA in Jewish History from the Ludwig-Maximilians University in Munich and a second MA in Magazine journalism from New York University, where she studied as a Fulbright scholar. Since 2012, she has been working as a museum guide for the Dachau Concentration Camp Memorial Site. She regularly gives lectures about her Kindertransport research at places like the Jewish Heritage Museum or the Leo Baeck Institute in New York or at the "Kindertransport Association" conference in Detroit.

This book was translated from German to English by Dominique Rotermund. Dominique works as an archivist at the OSE Archive and History Department in Paris. She is also a freelance translator, mainly translating general literature, historical texts, and testimonies.